About This Book

Why is this topic important?

Facilitation skills are by far the most valuable skills for leading any kind of group communication, problem solving, or decision making. Facilitation has become a critical and powerful method of leadership, especially in organizations that rely on input and commitment from all employees. Leaders, team leaders, managers, trainers, counselors, human resource professionals, salespeople, mentors, and, of course, facilitators, will benefit from the concepts, tools, methods, and information provided in this book. In one-on-one communication, facilitation skills help people reach verbal agreements that are supported with action and follow-through. Whether working in cross-organizational settings or cross-functional teams, negotiating sales contracts, designing and leading meetings, resolving conflict, or collaborating one-on-one, professionals benefit greatly when they are skilled in facilitation.

What can you achieve with this book?

This book is a resource to both new and experienced facilitators and can serve as a textbook for anyone who teaches facilitation. The reader will find this book a handy reference as well as a comprehensive coverage of facilitation. It helps readers understand the facilitator's role and a full range of skills, processes, and knowledge needed to become an effective facilitator. Recognizing the many types of situations facilitators may face, this book presents basic skills and also addresses a variety of facilitation opportunities, challenges, and problems.

How is this book organized?

The reader will find a discussion of the role of the facilitator in Part 1, a comprehensive description of many verbal and nonverbal techniques in Part 2, and step-by-step processes and tools in Part 3. Part 3 also contains chapters on how to facilitate conflict resolution in groups and how to facilitate difficult situations. Instruction in designing and leading group work is featured in Part 4, and Part 5 illustrates how various levels of facilitator competency are called for in different types of group and organization work. Part 5 also discusses facilitating meetings, teams, virtual teams, and organization-wide projects. Finally, Part 6 discusses the art of facilitating and what makes a great facilitator. A CD-ROM is also included that contains a Facilitator Skills Profile as a PDF. The Profile can be printed, distributed, and completed. The reader receives scores in eleven competency areas with suggestions for further reading in the book.

WORD(S) OF THE DAY

GROUP   TEAM

SYNERGY

GOALS   RESULTS

PROCESS   STRUCTURE

CONCENSUS
     Problems
     Causes
      Approaches

GOAL SETTING

DECISION MAKING

PROBLEM SOLVING

BRAINSTORMING

AFFINITY DIAGRAM

FISHBONE DIAGRAM

PARETO CHART

T-Chart

About Pfeiffer

Pfeiffer serves the professional development and hands-on resource needs of training and human resource practitioners and gives them products to do their jobs better. We deliver proven ideas and solutions from experts in HR development and HR management, and we offer effective and customizable tools to improve workplace performance. From novice to seasoned professional, Pfeiffer is the source you can trust to make yourself and your organization more successful.

Essential Knowledge Pfeiffer produces insightful, practical, and comprehensive materials on topics that matter the most to training and HR professionals. Our Essential Knowledge resources translate the expertise of seasoned professionals into practical, how-to guidance on critical workplace issues and problems. These resources are supported by case studies, worksheets, and job aids and are frequently supplemented with CD-ROMs, websites, and other means of making the content easier to read, understand, and use.

Essential Tools Pfeiffer's Essential Tools resources save time and expense by offering proven, ready-to-use materials—including exercises, activities, games, instruments, and assessments—for use during a training or team-learning event. These resources are frequently offered in looseleaf or CD-ROM format to facilitate copying and customization of the material.

Pfeiffer also recognizes the remarkable power of new technologies in expanding the reach and effectiveness of training. While e-hype has often created whizbang solutions in search of a problem, we are dedicated to bringing convenience and enhancements to proven training solutions. All our e-tools comply with rigorous functionality standards. The most appropriate technology wrapped around essential content yields the perfect solution for today's on-the-go trainers and human resource professionals.

www.pfeiffer.com *Essential resources for training and HR professionals*

The Facilitator Excellence Handbook

Second Edition

FRAN REES

Pfeiffer

A Wiley Imprint
www.pfeiffer.com

Library of Congress Cataloging-in-Publication Data

Rees, Fran.
    The facilitator excellence handbook / Fran Rees.—2nd ed.
      p. cm.
    Includes bibliographical references and index.
    ISBN 0-7879-7070-0 (alk. paper)
    1. Teams in the workplace. 2. Group facilitation. 3. Group relations training. 4. Group problem solving.
  5. Consensus (Social sciences) I. Title.
    HD66.R3938   2005
    658.4′022—dc22
                                                  2005009861

Acquiring Editor: Martin Delahoussaye
Director of Development: Kathleen Dolan Davies
Developmental Editor: Susan Rachmeler
Production Editor: Nina Kreiden
Editor: Suzanne Copenhagen
Manufacturing Supervisor: Becky Carreño

Printed in the United States of America
SECOND EDITION
Printing 10 9 8 7 6 5 4 3 2

CONTENTS

PART 2
Basic Facilitation Skills 31

PART 6
Facilitator Excellence **359**

Getting the Most from This Resource

Facilitators are entrusted with an exciting role: to create an atmosphere of trust and synergy from which come results. In a world of experts, specialization, and ever-changing methods and technology, there is a critical need for facilitators to help people collaborate, innovate, and collectively meet the challenges of today's world. The purpose of this book is to develop and foster excellence in facilitators—and in so doing increase the ability of people to work creatively and productively together.

Bringing people together to solve problems, plan, make decisions, and obtain resources requires both the science and art of facilitation—a powerful and essential form of leadership. Collaboration among diverse professionals and workers does not happen automatically when people come together, even when people sincerely desire to cooperate. When people must work in groups to plan, decide, innovate, implement, and share responsibility, they need facilitators who inspire them to put forth extraordinary efforts to accomplish what cannot be achieved by individuals alone.

What's New in the Second Edition

This second edition contains four new chapters: Facilitating Difficult Situations, Facilitating Conflict Resolution, Facilitating Virtual Teams, and What Makes a Great Facilitator? These chapters round out the first edition's focus on skills and basic techniques by addressing some of the more difficult aspects of facilitating. The chapter on virtual teams explores dilemmas facilitators face when the teams and groups they work with are scattered geographically. Suggestions are presented to help facilitators deal with the very real challenges of today's global workplace. The chapters on difficult situations and conflict resolution give facilitators ideas and processes for guiding groups through some of the typical problems groups face when working together. The chapter addressing the question of what makes a great facilitator promotes the concept that facilitation is more than skills and techniques and gives facilitators direction in developing a "core purpose" for facilitating.

Also included in this second edition is a CD-ROM of the Facilitator Skills Profile (formerly sold separately as a booklet). This questionnaire allows the reader to evaluate his or her level of facilitator skill, identify strengths and areas needing improvement, and find quick references to sections in the book that relate to specific skills.

Definitions

The terms *facilitate, facilitator, facilitation, group,* and *team* are used frequently throughout this book. Definitions of these terms as they are used here are given below:

- *Facilitate:* To make easier or less difficult.

- *Facilitator:* A person who makes a group's work easier by structuring and guiding the participation of group members. Facilitators generally work in a meeting setting, but can also work with a group outside of meetings. A facilitator may also take a neutral (questioning and listening) role when helping others.

- *Facilitation:* Any meeting of a group of people at which a facilitator structures and manages group process to help the group meet its goal. A facilitation may also be a meeting between two people: a facilitator and an individual who accepts process help and guidance.

- *Group:* A collection of individuals with a reason for being together. Membership in the group may be voluntary or imposed. The life of a group may be short or long and its formation either extemporaneous or planned.

- *Team:* A type of group whose members and leader work closely together to achieve mutually agreed-on goals. The word "team" implies interdependence and synergy; a team can be thought of as a closely knit, well-functioning group. In addition to accomplishing goals and tasks as a group, a team strives to become a cohesive unit and to improve the teamwork skills of its members.

Facilitation as Science and Art

Facilitation is both a science and an art. A facilitator applies a specific set of skills and methods, "group technologies," along with a sharp attention and sensitivity to people, to lead a group to peak performance.

Facilitators skillfully blend group technologies with personal style to create the art of facilitation. A truly skilled facilitator makes this form of leadership appear effortless by artfully combining structure with freedom so that the group can operate with maximum flexibility and creativity within realistic boundaries.

Facilitation skills are becoming as essential to professionals as presentation and traditional communication skills, if not more so. Facilitation has become a vital communication skill, particularly effective in group and team settings, in which everyone's input, support, creativity, and collaboration are needed. Professionals in many walks of life are being called on to work effectively in group settings in dynamic and challenged organizations. Presentation and traditional communication skills are not adequate to meet the demands of fast-paced, changing, or technically driven companies. As companies and organizations rely more and more on individual employees to contribute to process improvement, quality control, innovation, planning, decision making, and cost management, facilitation becomes a critical skill for many professionals. In business, community, educational, and religious organizations, the demand for people who can facilitate groups and meetings is increasing. In today's organizations, facilitators add an essential ingredient to discussions, meetings, teamwork, and overall organizational effectiveness.

Facilitation skills are also important in one-on-one communication situations, which call for clear communication, planning, commitment, or resolution of previous misunderstandings.

Levels of Facilitation

This book addresses three levels of facilitator skill development:

    I. The Meeting Facilitator

    II. The Team Facilitator

    III. The Organization Facilitator

The facilitator role becomes more complex at each level. Basic facilitation skills are beneficial when one is leading a discussion or a meeting; managers, leaders, and most professionals frequently find themselves needing to facilitate meetings and could benefit from having Level I skills.

Team facilitators (Level II) are needed to work with ongoing work teams, self-directed teams, or cross-functional project teams. Teams need facilitation for their ongoing meetings, as well as coaching and training in working together as a team. Facilitating a team requires knowledge of how a team develops over time and the ability to teach and demonstrate group processes and methods to the team. In many organizations, the team leader must function as the team facilitator at least some of the time. Organizations that rely heavily on work teams and project teams will be more likely to succeed if they have trained team facilitators to support team efforts.

Organization facilitators (Level III) are highly skilled, experienced facilitators who also understand the overall business and cultural issues facing an organization. They are often essential to major change efforts. Although few organizations have designated "organization facilitators," there are usually a few professionals and leaders within any organization who evolve into this role because of their skill at facilitating and working cross-organizational issues. These facilitators may be supervisors, managers, human resource professionals, senior trainers, or experienced team or project leaders. They may have had little formal training in facilitation, but have naturally developed and acquired the art, skills, and methods needed to facilitate higher-level meetings, projects, and change efforts.

Many organizations have positions that by their nature require a high level of facilitation skill. Jobs in the areas of internal consulting, organization development, organizational effectiveness, human resource management, and training require people who can work across the organization in a facilitation and leadership role. These people need Level III facilitation skills to do their jobs.

Traditionally, management and leadership training does not address facilitation skills. However, many principles of effective facilitation (working with clear goals and objectives, listening to people, motivating others to participate and become involved, obtaining support and buy-in, collaborating, capitalizing on the creativity and synergy of subordinates, helping people work cooperatively together) are important competencies for managers and leaders as well. Facilitation is truly a leadership skill, essential when leaders want the groups they lead to share in goal setting, decision making, and problem solving. Facilitation is also an essential skill in teamwork, community and volunteer work, and in fast-changing, technical companies that rely on cooperation from several functions to make and implement decisions.

In recent years, companies have downsized to cut costs and have frequently eliminated one or more layers of management. Teams have been put in place and given much of the decision power formerly reserved for middle management. In these downsized companies, facilitation is a skill they cannot afford to do without.

To compete effectively, organizations must collaborate with and listen more to customers, suppliers, and others who have an impact on their success in the marketplace. This requires face-to-face meetings, teamwork, and ongoing cooperation with people from different functions, levels, and organizations. In these diverse group settings, a facilitator is needed: someone who can organize a meeting, lead a discussion, and move people from discussion to consensus. Whoever facilitates such meetings must remain neutral, not be threatened by diversity of opinions, and have methods to manage discussions to a fruitful outcome. Whether this person is a manager, a team leader, a team member, a person from another function in the organization, or an outside facilitator—he or she needs facilitation skills.

It is increasingly common for organizations to operate in more than one country, as well as to serve customers in many countries and from quite diverse cultures. Facilitators and organization leaders are faced not only with the challenge to foster collaboration throughout a geographically close community but also to ensure open channels of communication among teams, customers, and vendors from different parts of the globe. Problems must be solved not only cross functionally but also cross culturally, with distance being a key factor in getting people to work productively together. Facilitators today must coach and influence teams to develop rapport and cooperation with people whom they may never meet face to face but who even so may provide critical support and input to their jobs as team members. Facilitation skills must be adapted and applied to electronic communication and geographically distant teams and groups.

How This Book Is Organized

Part 1 of this book gives an overview of facilitation and the role of the facilitator. Part 2 describes in detail the verbal, nonverbal, and recording skills required of facilitators. In Part 3, various facilitation methods and tools are described that help groups be productive. Instructions are given for how to use each tool. Part 4 focuses on designing an effective facilitation after assessing the group and situation. Several examples of how to organize and enhance group work are included, along with detail on how to open and close a facilitation. Part 5 focuses on the facilitator in action and looks at several types of assignments: the meeting facilitator, the team facilitator (both face-to-face and virtual), and the organization facilitator. A Facilitator Competency Matrix outlines required skills for the three types of facilitation assignments. Part 6 concludes the book with chapters on managing oneself as a facilitator, the art of facilitating, and what makes a great facilitator.

The CD-ROM in the back of the book contains the Facilitator Skills Profile, a fifty-five-item questionnaire to help readers assess their level of skill as a facilitator. Those who print out and complete the questionnaire can determine their score to indicate the overall level of skill they have achieved: beginning, improving, basic, skilled, or mastery. In addition, a Facilitator Competence Profile Graph can be used to determine levels of competence in eleven areas: attitudes, role understanding, participation, group memory, consensus, designing meetings, managing meetings, tools and methods, feedback, listening, and group dynamics. The reader is guided to identify areas of strength and areas needing improvement, along with suggestions for how to improve as a facilitator.

Overview of Facilitation

Facilitation is a form of leadership. Facilitators, like leaders, have the opportunity to play a special role: to inspire, direct, and structure participation among people so that creativity, ownership, and productivity result. Because of this, facilitation skills are a critical factor in an organization's success. The first two chapters of the book explore Facilitation in Organizations Today and the Role of the Facilitator.

CHAPTER 1

Facilitation in Organizations Today

A fact of organization life is that groups are needed to do what cannot be done by individuals alone. However, groups are not always effective. Most of us have experienced a lack of progress in groups made up of capable and talented individuals. When left alone, without training or methods, groups can bog down in a variety of ways. Some typical things that impede progress in group settings are:

- Poor attendance by members;

- Too few meetings;

- Too many meetings;

- Long-winded discussions without resolution;

- Lack of clear group goals;

- Lack of agreement about goals;

- Change in group goals or focus;

- Lack of resources;

- Dominant group members (or leader);

- Unresolved disagreements;

- Personality differences and clashes;

- Lack of buy-in to group goals or decisions;

- Absence of a group leader;

- Lack of leadership ability;

- Members interrupting one another;

- Long-standing differences causing lack of cooperation;

- Problems resolved too quickly and ineffectively;

- Opposing factions, departments, or organizations;

- Personal agendas affecting member behavior and opinions;

- Members giving in to decisions without really supporting them;

- Decisions and actions not written down, so members "forget" or are not clear about what was said from meeting to meeting;

- Breakdowns in communication due to geographically separated group members; and

- Misunderstandings and other problems due to cultural differences or lack of cross-cultural understanding or both.

The list could go on and on. A group is as complex and difficult as the sum total of the problems and people that comprise it. Without skilled leadership and proven methods, groups will be minimally effective. Over recent years, organizations have increasingly drawn on those with facilitation skills to help groups be more productive.

Organizations use facilitators in a variety of ways. Some identify and develop facilitators whose main job is to facilitate. Others use a core of facilitators who spend a percentage of their work time facilitating. Still others train team leaders, managers, and human resource professionals in facilitation skills and rely on these professionals to facilitate as an important part of their jobs. From time to time, organizations also use outside consultants or trainers to facilitate special meetings or team efforts. Of course, some organizations use a combination of all these approaches to fill their facilitation needs.

In many organizations, those with human resource responsibility are seen as a natural pool of facilitator talent. Although human resource professionals may be the most trained and experienced in facilitation, relying on them to facilitate may be self-defeating. First, it overloads the already busy human resource person. Second, it assumes that facilitation is only for special occasions and that someone outside the immediate group must be called in—thus limiting the development of facilitation skills by others. Third, it severely limits the pool of facilitators available to an organization. A better strategy is to target people within each major department or group to be trained in facilitation skills.

Although most organizations recognize the benefits of having a facilitator at meetings and of having leaders who can facilitate groups, few actually assess their need for facilitation skills or for strategically developing the facilitation skills of their employees. Few management or leadership training programs include facilitation skills, although increasingly leaders are seeking out resources and training in facilitation and team leadership.

Benefits of Facilitation

Facilitation improves group effectiveness by overcoming some of the inherent difficulties of working in groups. Most organizations cannot produce or operate efficiently unless people work together and cooperate. Indeed, facilitation skills are critical at all levels in the organization. Employees must be taught the basics of clear and productive one-on-one and group communication. Many of the basic facilitation skills—asking questions, listening, paraphrasing, clarifying, and summarizing—are useful, even critical, in most organizational settings.

Time and again, the following three topics are cited as the top concerns in today's organizations: *communication, teamwork,* and *conflict resolution.* Each of these concerns is related to how people work together and relate to one another, which is the overall focus of good facilitation. In fact, *good facilitation is at the heart of all three of these endeavors.* One of the key benefits of facilitation is that it has the potential to successfully address these concerns. Throughout this book, we will be highlighting skills, methods, techniques, and processes that *foster productive communication, improve teamwork,* and *resolve the natural conflicts* that arise in organizations and groups.

Managers and team leaders need facilitation skills to capitalize on the synergy of their groups, gain full support and buy-in for important efforts, manage differences and diversity, and successfully work through the inevitable factions and conflicts that arise. Organizations that rely heavily on self-sufficient and self-directed teams are increasingly discovering that something important is missing: facilitators or those with facilitation skills. In some organizations, those with good facilitation skills are in great demand, not only to lead meetings but to take on more and more leadership and management responsibilities.

Some of the most common and important benefits of facilitation are:

* Group members are more motivated to support the decisions made;

* The best efforts of groups usually yield better results than individual efforts;

* Maximum participation and involvement increase productivity;

* Managers and leaders are better able to draw on those they lead as resources, an ability that is critical to organizational success;

* Everyone has a chance to be influential and useful, and people sense that they are an integral part of a team effort;

- Organizations can be flexible and produce results more quickly because people are committed to the decisions made;

- Decisions are made where the work must be done;

- People realize that responsibility for implementing decisions lies with everyone;

- Innovation, problem-solving, and implementation skills are built;

- People are encouraged to think and act for the overall good of the organization;

- Higher-quality decisions can be made;

- A forum is provided for constructive conflict resolution and clarifying misunderstandings; and

- Negative effects such as low morale, low involvement, and withholding information from others, as well as attitudes such as "It's not my job" and "Just tell me what to do" are less likely.

Goals of an Effective Facilitation

An effective facilitation makes the work of a group easier. However, one should also aspire to achieve the best possible results. Obviously, the group should do what it set out to do in the first place; however, altering the original goals is sometimes for the best. A facilitator must not only help the group discuss issues, but should also guide the group to set and achieve identifiable results. Group members should be able to tell someone else what was accomplished at the meeting. They should feel that they were thoroughly involved and useful at the meeting—not that it was a waste of their time.

An effective facilitation is one in which group members are actively involved and feel useful; facilitation methods are applied appropriately; and tangible results are achieved that contribute to the progress of the group.

The test of an effective facilitation is what happens *after* the meeting. After this type of meeting, decisions will be supported 100 percent by all group members, actions will be completed, handoffs made, and communication channels kept open.

For a facilitation to be productive, it is very important to set goals up front and to be realistic about what can be accomplished. One of the biggest problems is that when a group is fortunate enough to have a skilled facilitator, people expect miracles! An overly ambitious agenda is tackled, but not finished.

Sometimes facilitations simply do not go well, for a number of reasons: poor facilitation methods or skills, poor group member conduct and attitudes, lack of readiness or understanding on the part of group members, other stresses that affect the meeting, a poorly planned meeting—or all of these. Facilitators, especially as they gain experience and become more skilled, are able to recognize what factors contributed to failure. Even "failed" meetings are useful by pointing out what needs to be done next time.

A group sometimes fails to make progress because it has decided not to take the advice of the facilitator. Because facilitators do not *force* groups to act or decide, failure in this case is probably not the facilitator's responsibility, although it is not always clear whose responsibility it is. Ideally, the facilitator, the group, and the group leader have participated in the meeting to the extent that success or failure can be attributed to everyone present.

Facilitators must be careful not to simply blame themselves for failure or judge their work too harshly. The point is not to place blame, but to understand what factors contributed to a poor meeting. Many things must come together for a meeting to be productive. The facilitator's responsibility is to present the group with quality methods, processes, and suggestions, leaving the group free to use them or not. If the group chooses to take a different approach, the facilitator may or may not be able to help it. However, it is important for him or her to remain respectful of the group's freedom to choose, while pointing out the advantages and disadvantages of certain decisions to the group. In some cases, the facilitator may elect not to continue working with a group, if it is not ready or willing to try facilitation methods.

Good facilitations often include developmental goals. When a group is taking part in a productive meeting, this can be an ideal time to help it develop further as a team. Team-appreciation, team-building, and team-strengthening activities can be included. The most effective facilitations help the group do its task and achieve results, while also building trust and cohesiveness in the team.

Given the global nature of many organizations, an effective facilitation takes advantage of the opportunity to foster cross-cultural understanding and awareness. An effective facilitation allows time to address how group issues, problems, and goals are affected by differences in culture or geography. Cross-cultural groups, or teams separated geographically, can learn to view their concerns from different perspectives with the goal in mind to continually clarify goals, resolve issues, and solve problems as a group.

Facilitation Applied

Facilitation is a form of leading and communicating with the intent of achieving maximum creativity, involvement, and commitment to the task at hand. Facilitation skills and methods have been designed and have evolved over time to help groups overcome the inevitable problems associated with group work, but facilitation is also valuable for communicating one-on-one.

A skilled facilitator must determine what specific facilitator role is needed for each situation. Table 1.1 illustrates how the facilitator role and facilitation outcome may vary from situation to situation.

Facilitation and Leadership

Facilitators lead groups by giving groups tools and methods to help group members work productively together. A facilitator, however, does not determine a group's vision and purpose. That is the leader's role. Leaders seek

Table 1.1. Facilitation Situations, Roles, and Outcomes

Facilitation Situation	Facilitator's Role	Optimal Outcome
One-on-One	Use facilitation skills and methods to achieve productive face-to-face communication.	Both parties leave with clear understanding of what was said and what steps to take next. Respectful working relationship is begun or continued.
Discussion	Use facilitation skills to help a group have a productive discussion, clarify a discussion goal, and decide next steps.	The group has a productive discussion, with a record of ideas, actions to take, or decisions made. If the group cannot reach a conclusion or consensus, there is at least agreement as to the issues that must be addressed.
Facilitating Meetings	Use facilitation skills to help plan, facilitate, and evaluate a meeting. Involve all group members and leader.	A successful meeting is planned, conducted, and evaluated. People leave with clear action items, decisions made, or issues identified. Group members take ownership for meeting follow-up.
Team or Ongoing Group	Act as ongoing facilitator and coach. Facilitate meetings and coach the team in how to be effective. Over time, may train the team or group to facilitate itself.	Team or group achieves its goals and tasks successfully, due to skillful facilitation and increased effectiveness in working together.
Facilitating Across the Organization	Contribute to organization's overall effectiveness by facilitating cross-functional, inter-team, and organization-wide meetings. Apply facilitation skills in a broad variety of organizational situations; train others in facilitation skills; act as a consultant to help the organization become more effective at making decisions, solving problems, and meeting goals.	Increased organizational effectiveness due to the application of facilitation skills and methods throughout the organization.

to inspire action and commitment in their followers so that a vision will be realized, or at least progress will be made toward it.

Facilitators are operationally neutral to the vision and purpose of the groups they serve, although most facilitators probably identify with the vision and purpose in some fashion. By using group process and providing the structure the group needs to formulate, assess, and carry out its goals, a facilitator does provide a form of leadership.

Facilitators are willing for the group not to need them at some point—to teach the group to carry on by itself. Facilitators let go of the need to influence decisions and be looked up to as an "expert." They build decision-making and problem-solving skills in the group. They influence group success, but not the content of the group's work. They take charge by giving process guidance, group skills, and structure. Facilitators take risks, as leaders do, but these are always in the arena of group process.

The question arises: Should leaders be facilitators? At times leaders can benefit greatly by stepping aside from the content of people's work to facilitate the process. Effective leaders have to lead through persuasion, through collaboration, as well as through facilitation. Leaders can be seen operating on a continuum between a highly persuasive and directive style on one end and a highly facilitative style on the other (see Figure 1.1). Different situations demand different approaches.

In today's world of fast-paced change, the importance and impact of decisions, technological demands, and competition, leaders rely heavily on information gleaned from sources both within and outside their organizations. They do not naively expect others to follow just because they say so. Leaders must seek and maintain followers' involvement and buy-in to make things happen. They must be comfortable operating at any point along the continuum.

The leader who can take the role of a facilitator blends his or her role of visionary, decisive leader with that of listening and empowering leader. As a facilitative leader he or she involves followers as much as possible in creating the group's vision and purpose, carrying out the vision and purpose, and building a productive and cohesive team. Facilitation can be seen in this light as a leadership *approach*.

Figure 1.1. Leadership Continuum

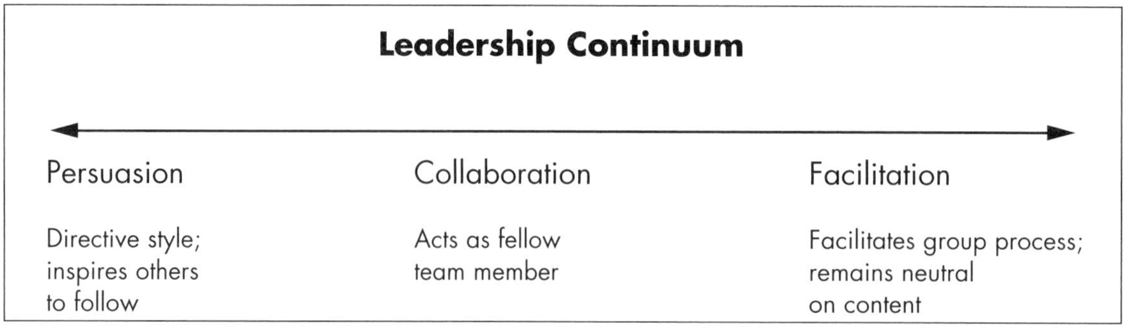

Leadership Continuum

Persuasion	Collaboration	Facilitation
Directive style; inspires others to follow	Acts as fellow team member	Facilitates group process; remains neutral on content

A Vision for the Future

As organizations come to realize the importance of group productivity and effectiveness at all levels, the role of the facilitator will become increasingly important. The more change in an organization, the more need for group communication, group involvement, and group decision making. The more complex a project is, the more that close cooperation and teamwork are needed for success. The faster the pace of change, the less time organizations have to build and train hierarchies and the more they must rely on project groups. In many companies today, much of the work actually is accomplished through project teams that are assembled for the duration of a project and then disbanded. Such project teams are more effective with skilled facilitation.

In the future, perhaps organizations will realize that facilitation is as critical a skill for everyone as making a presentation or using computers. Organizations that want to increase their overall effectiveness might consider developing and/or providing the following:

• Basic facilitator training for all supervisors and professionals who lead groups and/or meetings;

• Basic and advanced facilitator training for all project leaders;

- A core of trained and experienced facilitators, available to design and facilitate important meetings, while also having other responsibilities;

- A core of trained and experienced team facilitators, available to coach teams, especially in the start-up stage of a project, who would develop facilitation skills in the team;

- A few facilitators with Level III facilitation skills, available full time to facilitate organization-wide, complex projects. In some cases, a facilitator may be assigned to only one project at a time;

- Training in cross-cultural understanding and communication for leaders and facilitators; and

- State-of-the-art skills and techniques to help facilitators increase collaboration, trust, and productivity among people who work from multiple locations around the world.

In summary, facilitation helps organizations meet a number of needs: employee involvement and productivity, team leadership, informed decision making, flexibility, responsiveness, and innovation—to name a few. It is not likely that organizations will be slowing down in the near future or that they will cease to face challenges that require teamwork. Facilitators and those with facilitation skills have much to contribute.

Role of the Facilitator

The word "facilitator" comes from the verb "facilitate," which means "to make easier or less difficult." The role of a facilitator is to make group success easier by using effective group processes. The facilitator ensures that group members use the most effective methods to accomplish tasks efficiently and beneficially, with adequate time to consider ideas and alternatives. The facilitator provides method and structure so a group can focus its energy and creativity on a particular task, topic, or project. A facilitator serves as a guide, a servant, and a catalyst to help the group do its work.

Manager of Group Process

The facilitator's role is to manage the *process* and to remain neutral about the *content* of the discussion. The process is how the group members work together, how members interact with one another, how decisions are made, and whether all group members are present. Content refers to the subject at hand or what decision the group faces, including what ideas are put forth, what arguments are proposed, what decisions are made, and what actions are planned.

Both process and content are present at all times in group work, and the facilitator must guide and manage the process so that the group can focus its energy and creativity on the content. To guide the process, the facilitator suggests methods to help the group both clarify and achieve its goals. Although the facilitator may take the content into account when determining which process to use, he or she does not voice opinions on it.

A facilitator must be able to distinguish between process and content and to determine how the group should proceed. He or she takes an active role describing, suggesting, leading, and intervening to make it easier for the group to complete its tasks successfully. A skilled facilitator continually observes the process of the group's work: Are the objectives clear? Are they being adhered to? Is the meeting on schedule? Are the group methods working? Are people listening to one another? Who talks with whom? Is everyone contributing? Is the energy level of the group high or low?

A facilitator leads by influencing how a group works together, by using proven processes and structure, and by challenging and coaching the group to grow more adept at working together over time.

Responsibilities of a Facilitator

An effective facilitator has the following responsibilities:

- Remain neutral on content;

- Draw out participation;

- Ensure balanced participation;

- Encourage dialogue among participants;

- Provide structure and processes for group work;

- Listen actively and ask others to do the same;

- Encourage different points of view;

- Record, organize, and summarize input from group members;

- Move group through stages of group decision making and consensus;

- Use effective facilitation processes to help the group resolve conflict in a positive and productive way;

- Encourage the group to evaluate its own progress and development;

- Capitalize on differences among group members for the common good;

- Protect group members and their ideas from attack or from being ignored;

- Emphasize that the group is a reservoir of knowledge, experience, and creativity and use facilitation skills to tap this resource; and

- Guide the group to identify cross-cultural or geographical differences that might affect productivity or teamwork, and facilitate the group to discover ways to deal effectively with these challenges.

The Evolving Role of the Facilitator

Because of the ever-changing nature of organizations, the role of the facilitator is evolving as well as expanding. Traditionally a facilitator worked with a group of people in a face-to-face setting, usually in the format of a group meeting. As teams became more predominant in organizations, facilitators were useful, and often essential, to the effectiveness of the team. Team meetings were the key format for team decision making and planning, and a skilled facilitator could guide the process so that all team members could participate and the team could be productive as a whole.

As teamwork became more crucial in organizations, leaders realized the importance of increasing teamwork across geographic boundaries. Team members were expected to work with other team members who may or may not be in the same geographic location. Computer and Internet technology, in addition to videoconferencing and the telephone, made it possible to communicate from virtually anywhere. The concept of *team* expanded to include *virtual teams* whose members may be separated even by great distances.

As the world and organizations became more global, communication, coordination, and teamwork continued to be critical to success. More and more, people had shared responsibilities across geographic and organization boundaries. People were called upon to work as a team within their organizations, as well as to "team" with representatives, vendors, and customers from other organizations around the world. As the global networks became tighter, organizations had to adapt the way they distribute and organize work.

Facilitators in the global environment of today's organizations also must adapt. The process of getting people to communicate, collaborate, resolve conflict, and build trust as a team and as an organization has become much more complex. Skilled facilitators may be comfortable working in face-to-face, group settings while lacking knowledge and skill in guiding the process of teamwork across geographic distances. They may be experienced in working with diverse backgrounds and cultures in a location where people can frequently come face to face to meet, discuss, and resolve issues. However, they may lack confidence and experience working with teams and organizations that must rely on electronic communication across numerous cultures, time zone differences, and language barriers.

Today's facilitators must work closely with organization leaders, teams, and individuals to create open channels of communication and cooperation so that they can facilitate the process of global communication, decision making, and problem solving. Although the basic concepts of good facilitation remain the same, the environment in which the facilitator provides guidance is vastly different from what it was in the past. Facilitators can do well to form liaisons so they can share with one another and continually update their role and their skills.

Humanizing the Workplace

Facilitators and facilitative leaders play a role in building a stronger sense of humanity and spirit in organizations. By improving communication and teamwork, facilitators and the groups with which they work have the opportunity to make organizational environments more humane.

In workplaces today, an ongoing tension exists between two extremes. At one extreme are conditions that dehumanize or starve the human spirit, and at the other extreme are conditions that humanize or feed the human spirit (see Exhibit 2.1). We constantly work with the tension between these two extremes in our lives, at home, at work, and in our relationships. As facilitators and leaders we work with methods and approaches that draw organizations and the people who work for them toward the humanizing side of these two extremes, and understand that moving toward the dehumanizing side causes harm to settings where people must work together toward a common goal.

Today's workplaces have the potential of being either humanizing or dehumanizing places to work. Depending on an individual's assignment and situation, the workplace may create hardship and stress or opportunity for growth and contribution.

There are many reasons that today's workplaces are stressful. Time pressure, pressure to do quality work with inadequate resources, lack of competent leadership, expectations for performance without sufficient training, requirement to do more with less and to handle what reasonably may be more than one person's job, noisy and unattractive surroundings in which to work, rapidly changing technology, lack of opportunity for promotion, grueling travel, fewer benefits, too much change, and even boring work—these and many other factors lessen one's job satisfaction and make the workplace less humane.

Increasingly, machines and technology have taken over many workplaces, and people are expected to function both as "part of the machine" and be

Exhibit 2.1. Workplace Continuum

Dehumanizing	**Humanizing**
Isolation	Belonging
Loss	Gain and abundance
Loneliness	Connection, interaction
Futility	Meaning
Rejection	Recognition and acceptance
Being devalued, not needed	Being valued, useful
Stress	Positive action with purpose
Fear and anxiety	Courage and empowerment
Threat	Goals to stretch for
Chaos	Systems and structure balanced with freedom
Technology dominates	Technology serves human endeavors
Incompetence	Competence
Overly competitive environments	Productive collaboration with subsequent rewards
Harsh environments (pollution, noise, etc.)	Safe, humane workplaces
Boring work	Interesting, compelling work
Work overload	Realistic workload

"super human." Market downturns have left many people willing to work longer hours for less money. Having seen their colleagues, family members, and friends lose jobs, people feel they should be happy to have a job at all! In some environments, people are afraid to speak up about what they see or know to be a problem, whether it is poor quality, inadequate resources, or inequitable treatment. Managers are pressed to "make the numbers" with fewer people. Individuals are pressed to meet high levels of productivity for longer and longer periods of time. Those with high-level, demanding, professional jobs are expected to work long hours and be available on an on-call basis. It is more and more customary to expect people to work from home as well as at the office.

Instead of feeling pride in their jobs, many people feel tired and exploited, their livelihoods threatened. Burnout has become the norm in many workplaces, and even basic human needs are not being met in some instances. Common civilities, a sense of future and opportunity, and a sense of fulfillment or accomplishment are outcomes people would prefer from working hard, but unfortunately these "luxuries" are less and less available to many people.

How can facilitators make a difference? Is it possible to relieve the tension of less humane workplaces and move organizations toward the humanizing end of the continuum? The art and practice of facilitation provides opportunities to alleviate some of the workplace stress. When groups and teams are facilitated on a regular basis, some of the above problems are alleviated. An atmosphere of facilitation and collaboration increases the chance that people will be able to contribute meaningfully at work, as well as solve some of the nagging problems they face. When leadership cares enough to listen and encourage people to speak up to improve the status quo, as well as the bottom line, there is a greater chance that an atmosphere of trust will develop and that humanizing systems will be put in place.

Facilitators provide a model for skilled listening, feedback, communication, and collaborative problem solving. Since the workplace is in a constant state of flux, facilitators can open the way to teams and individuals to improve on the situations mentioned above. It is unrealistic to expect that all things mentioned above will improve; however, when facilitation is prevalent in an organization (among team leaders, managers, and individuals), people are more apt to feel engaged in the process of making a positive difference.

As facilitators we work primarily with people and communication. We work at that point at which human beings interact with other human beings in the complex settings of work and organizations. Some of our tools and methods have technical aspects to them, but our primary concern is getting people to work and communicate effectively together. At the core value of why we facilitate is the need for the human element, the human factor, in organizations to operate more effectively. A great facilitator understands the critical importance of the human factor in our world today.

In summary, the role of a facilitator is to ensure that a group has the processes and structure it needs to accomplish its best work. A good facilitator needs to be adept at helping organizations, teams, and individuals share responsibility across organizations, cultures, and vast geographic distances. Facilitators also have the role and opportunity to influence organization leaders to find ways to make workplaces humane and people-friendly places to work.

PART 2

Basic Facilitation Skills

One of the facilitator's main responsibilities is to create an atmosphere of openness and trust in order to help people feel free to contribute and work creatively together. The basic techniques a facilitator uses can either encourage or discourage participation; successful facilitators learn and apply appropriate techniques to obtain the most balanced, productive participation from group members.

Facilitators must be keenly aware of basic techniques and practice applying them until they become second nature. These techniques are covered in the next five chapters. They include Verbal Techniques: What to Say, Nonverbal Techniques: What to Do, Recording Techniques, Reading the Group, and Facilitating Consensus. Facilitating even the most basic group discussion requires the use of these fundamental skills.

Verbal Techniques: What to Say

What a facilitator says can be thought of as verbal techniques or verbal skills—one of the most basic and simplest sets of skills facilitators use. Skilled facilitators apply a variety of verbal techniques to facilitate discussions, bring groups to consensus, and help groups manage through confusion and conflict. What a facilitator says influences the group in many ways. The skilled facilitator's comments, questions, summaries, feedback to the group, explanations, directions, and suggestions blend together to guide and help a group be productive.

Verbal skills range from asking questions to encourage group participation to summarizing to help a group understand its own complex inputs. As a facilitator, you must be keenly aware of a variety of verbal techniques and use them appropriately to achieve a balance of participation and to steer a group toward productive solutions and decisions. With practice, these techniques become easier and more natural, but as a new facilitator you may have to plan consciously to put techniques into action.

The verbal techniques listed here are some of the most important. They will be described in detail later in this chapter.

- Asking questions

- Probing

- Paraphrasing

- Redirecting questions and comments

- Referencing back

- Giving positive reinforcement

- Including quieter members

- Encouraging divergent views

- Shifting perspective

- Summarizing

- Bridging

Asking Questions

Perhaps the most basic facilitator skill is asking well-timed, appropriate questions to focus and steer a group through a particular process, such as brainstorming, prioritizing, evaluating, or coming to a decision. A skilled facilitator uses two basic types of questions when working with a group: open-ended and closed-ended.

Open-ended questions cannot be answered with a simple "yes" or "no," nor can they be answered by supplying a fact. Open-ended questions encourage participants to supply ideas, opinions, reactions, or information. Use open-ended questions when you want people to think and participate, especially to generate a lot of ideas or data. An open-ended question can be very effective to explore a subject more deeply or to help group members be more honest with one another.

Open-ended questions usually begin with "What," "How," "Who," or "Why." Some examples are:

- "What is your reaction to that?"

- "How can this process be improved?"

- "What alternatives do we have?"

- "What suggestions do you have for . . . ?"

- "Why do you think there has been such a downturn in sales?"

- "How does that relate to our goal of . . . ?"

- "What do others in the group think?"

Open-ended questions start a group thinking, but closed-ended questions are used to find facts or guide the group toward closure. A closed-ended question is directive, calling for a "yes," a "no," or a fact. Closed or fact-finding questions are used to move on to the next step in the process, to wrap up a discussion, to obtain more specific information, or to direct group members to reach consensus. Here are some examples of closed questions:

- "Do you all agree, then, that this is the best choice?"

- "Have we covered everything?"

- "Are you ready to move on?"

- "Is everyone willing to support this decision 100 percent?"

- "Is this a realistic objective for today's meeting?"

- "Do we need Tom to be here for this decision?"

- "Can everyone stay another half hour to finish this discussion?"

Use caution when using closed-ended questions for several reasons: (1) Too many closed-ended questions may stifle or frustrate the group; (2) closed-ended questions, if not worded carefully, can put the group on the defensive, or create a negative atmosphere; and (3) a facilitator who uses too many closed-ended questions may actually steer the group in the direction he or she wants it to go (or so it may appear to group members).

Use closed-ended questions selectively. See Figure 3.1 for a summary of their use.

When working with a group to come to consensus, use a combination of open-ended and closed-ended questions. Open-ended questions are needed to start the group thinking and generate a quantity of ideas. Closed

Figure 3.1. When to Use Closed-Ended Questions

When to Use	**When to Avoid**
To check for understanding: "Does everyone understand the process we will be using?"	To encourage brainstorming and creativity: "Do you have any ideas for alleviating this problem?" (Ask an open-ended question instead: "What ideas can you think of to alleviate this problem?")
To find out specific process information: "How much time do you think you will need to complete this step?"	To draw everyone out: "Does anyone have anything to add to that?" (Ask an open-ended question instead: "What do others think about that?")
To check for agreement: "Does everyone agree that these are the top three priorities?"	To intervene in a closed group: "Is everyone being open about this issue?" (Ask an open-ended question instead: "What thoughts and opinions are people holding back?")
To encourage expression of different viewpoints: "Does anyone have a different opinion?"	To foster openness and trust: "Is everyone willing to keep this confidential?" (Ask an open-ended question instead: "How do you suggest we deal with the issue of confidentiality?")
To check out the group's needs: "People seem a little tired. Do we need to take a break now?"	To encourage quieter or reluctant members: "Ellen, do you have something to say to that?" (Ask an open-ended question instead: "Ellen, how do you feel about that?")
To obtain buy-in on meeting objectives: "Are these realistic objectives for today's meeting?"	To probe for more information: "Is more detail needed?" (Ask an open-ended question instead: "What more can you tell us about that?")

questions are needed to evaluate and narrow down the ideas to a workable number. Here are some examples of how to use open and closed questions in a discussion to reach consensus:

To Generate Ideas

"What goals are we trying to accomplish?" (open-ended)

(List goals the group comes up with.)

To Narrow Down a List

"Which goal should we try to accomplish at this meeting?" (closed-ended)

"Does everyone agree that this is the right goal for today's meeting?" (closed-ended)

To Move to the Next Step

"Your goal, then, is to identify the top two problems you wish to focus on over the next few months. What problems are you facing?" (open-ended)

(List problems the group comes up with.)

To Evaluate a List of Items

"We've listed fourteen problems. Let's take some time to look at them. What do you notice about these problems?" (open-ended)

(Record input as the group discusses characteristics of the problems. Summarize the input and steer the group to the next task.)

"Are you ready, then, to try to narrow down these problems to the top two?" (closed-ended)

Continue this process, using group prioritization methods (discussed in Chapter 9, Ranking and Evaluating Material), to help the group reach its goal for the meeting. Each step of the way, use open-ended and closed-ended questions to navigate the group through its dilemmas to a consensus decision. Generally speaking, skilled facilitators use more open than closed questions, probing the group so that it delves to the heart of issues and problems. However, one of the most important questions to ask is a closed question, when you think the group is reaching consensus: "Is everyone in agreement, then, that this is the best decision?" Another important closed question checks out the commitment of the group to the decision: "Will everyone agree, then, to support this decision 100 percent?"

People in today's fast-paced, results-oriented organizations are generally pressed for time and become adept at using closed questions to obtain information and data quickly. Unfortunately, many people lack the skill of knowing when and how to use open-ended questions and frequently run into trouble by asking only closed questions. Often, only the open questions lead to valuable information. Open questions allow more time for subpoints and auxiliary issues to surface that affect the quality of the data or information received. For example, in a one-on-one discussion, the speaker may ask a closed question such as, "Will that shipment for customer WBBT be ready on time?" A "yes" answer will satisfy the speaker, but important information may not have been shared. Had the speaker asked a more open question such as, "How is the shipment for customer WBBT coming along?" he or she might have heard more information such as, "It's going to be ready on time, but the shipping department is really short-handed this week and is running behind. I doubt that customer WBBT will receive the shipment on time." Frequently, in their hurry to receive data, people will ask not only a closed question, but the *wrong* closed question. In the example above, the speaker really needed to ask the closed question, "Will customer WBBT receive the shipment on time?" Even if you pose the right closed question, it is often better to ask an open question as well to gain information that might alert you to a potential problem.

When facilitating one-on-one or group discussions, be aware that questions can be revised as needed. If you realize that a question is not going to give the response you need, revise it. Sometimes closed questions obtain the same results as open questions, depending on the mood of the group, tone of voice, and the topic. However, when dealing with a difficult issue or a silent, closed group, an open question usually leads to the most complete, forthright responses.

Probing

Probing is a technique facilitators use to find out more information and to keep someone talking. Knowing when to probe is an important skill, as probing can make a positive difference in the quality and depth of the discussion and can unblock a group that is stuck. For example, when a group is making generalizations that do not further people's understanding of the topic, move the discussion along by probing for more details or examples.

Probing may help a group in one or more of the following ways:

- To find the root of an issue or problem;

- To enlighten other group members;

- To explore a concern or idea that may otherwise be overlooked;

- To encourage group members to explore issues in greater depth and to value their own thinking process;

- To open up the group to more honest sharing of information and concerns;

- To increase the trust level in the group;

- To uncover key facts that have not been brought out; and

- To increase creativity and open-mindedness.

Some of the most effective ways to probe are nonverbal: nodding the head, keeping direct eye contact, and remaining silent. These will often encourage a group member to explore his or her own thinking further as you listen. Verbal techniques for probing range from a simple "Oh?" or "Hmmm" to more direct questions or requests, such as:

- "Why is that?"

- "What makes you think so?"

- "Tell me more about . . . ."

- "Does this relate to what Juan said earlier about . . . ?"

- "Explain what you mean by . . . ."

- "Could you be more specific?"

- "Can you go further into that?"

- "Can you give us an example?"

- "What else happened?"

Used selectively and in a caring, open way, probing is a useful and essential technique. However, do not overdo probing, as it may result in one or more of the following:

- Group members may feel interrogated;

- Other group members may feel left out while a dialogue goes on between you and one person;

- You may lose, or appear to lose, neutrality;

- It may appear that you have a hidden agenda; or

- Probing may lead the group down a path that goes nowhere.

Paraphrasing

Paraphrasing is the act of *restating*, in your own words, what a person has said. This is a useful technique to check understanding with the speaker.

This gives the rest of the group a chance to check out their understanding as well. If you did not hear the message correctly, the speaker can correct the misunderstanding. For example, paraphrase by saying: "Let's see, Erica. If I understand correctly, you are saying. . . ." Use this technique primarily to increase understanding in a group and be careful not to use paraphrasing as an excuse to "sneak in" an opinion. Also, avoid giving the impression that you paraphrase to try to improve on, or add to, what was said. Whenever possible, the words of the group member should be honored and heard as coming from that person. Paraphrasing is highly useful, however, when a group member is struggling with expressing a difficult concept or idea or has expressed several ideas at once. Paraphrase to help the person clarify the idea or to focus on each idea that was presented so that it can be noted. Here are examples of how to paraphrase in some typical situations:

- (Group member not clear): "Let me see, Marina, if I understand what you are saying. . . ."

- (Group member presents several ideas or makes several points): "I think I hear several ideas we may want to capture. First, I think I heard you say. . . . Is that right?" (After capturing this idea): "Next, I heard you say. . . . Shall we capture that idea as well?" (etc.)

In most cases, no paraphrasing will be necessary, especially when you are recording each member's input on a flip chart or white board. Avoid paraphrasing every person's input. The best technique is to listen actively and record the speaker's key words. Here are some tips on how to use the paraphrasing technique:

- Paraphrase only to check for understanding;

- Do not paraphrase to improve upon the speaker's wording;

- Avoid adding to or changing what the speaker said;

- Try to use the speaker's exact wording when possible;

- Paraphrase when a group member is having difficulty expressing ideas more clearly; and

- Paraphrase, or simply restate what was said, when you think other members did not hear the speaker.

Redirecting Questions and Comments

Redirecting invites group members to respond to questions or comments that were directed to the facilitator. This technique encourages dialogue among participants and draws attention away from you. For example, when asked a question by one of the participants, say, "What do the rest of you think about that?" or "Someone else must have a response to that." The purpose of redirecting is to encourage group members to come up with their own solutions and thoughts as much as possible. This honors the group's own abilities and opinions and creates more buy-in. Redirecting puts the responsibility for the discussion on the group's shoulders, not on the facilitator's, and knits the participants together as a team. After a group is accustomed to you not offering opinions on the topic at hand, most group members will avoid asking for your opinion.

If a group member asks you to state an opinion on an issue, respond by redirecting. Here are a few examples:

- "Because the group will have to live by this decision, what I think is less valuable than what group members think. I'd like to toss that question back to the whole group."

- "As a facilitator, my role is to help you with the process; the content is something you will need to work out together. What do others think about that question?"

- "Good question! Let's toss that out to the whole group. What do group members think?"

If asked to share an opinion on the process the group is using, decide whether it is better to answer the question directly or to throw it open to the group. For example, if someone asks, "Do you really think we need the whole day to deal with this issue?" you may choose to respond in one of several ways, depending on the situation:

- "This is a substantive issue, and I'd like to have the whole day to deal with it if needed."

- "Perhaps that's a question we should throw out to the group. Let's go quickly around the room and hear what everyone thinks. Do we really need the whole day for this issue?"

- "I would like to spend the whole day on this issue. However, I am open to hearing others' thoughts. What do others think?"

Redirecting maintains a balance of participation and helps group members respect and build on one another's ideas. Over time, group members become used to this approach and respond to one another more frequently; eventually, they direct their comments to one another.

Referencing Back

Referencing back is the technique of referring back to something one of the group members said earlier for the purposes of enhancing the discussion and tying group members' ideas to one another. When a participant says something similar to comments made earlier, you may want to point this out: "That may relate to what Jim said earlier. Jim, what is your response?" or "That sounds like the idea put forth by Pat and Amelia earlier today. How do the two ideas tie?" This encourages members to acknowledge and build on one another's ideas. This also gives the opportunity to disagree and to point out the differences between the ideas. This technique also encourages participants to listen better to one another. Sometimes, participants repeat what has already been said because they did not hear what was said before or wanted to say it their own way. Point out that a similar comment was made earlier, which encourages people to listen carefully and to relate their comments to what others have already said.

Another powerful benefit to the technique of referencing back is that it demonstrates that you are listening to everyone and giving credit to people for their comments. It is a sad fact in meetings that people often ignore others' comments and proceed as if certain things had not even been said. Referencing back teaches participants to listen to, acknowledge, and build on one another's ideas. Over time, group members will start pointing out that their comments relate to what someone said earlier. For example, a participant may say, "I'd like to reinforce what Tom said earlier about . . . . I've had the same experience. . . ."

This is also a good technique to balance participation. You may choose to refer back to an idea expressed by a quieter group member or one who is not in a position of power in the organization, to make sure this person is given credit and respect for sharing an idea.

Giving Positive Reinforcement

Positively responding to efforts made by group members to speak out is one way to encourage people to take risks in group work. For some people, it is intimidating to come up with a new idea or to point out some difficulty the group is having. For others, it is difficult to interrupt and interject their opinions. Still others fear recrimination. A sensitive facilitator uses positive reinforcement to encourage group members to break out of their comfort zones and participate. Positive comments can stimulate creativity, risk taking, and mutual respect.

A little positive reinforcement goes a long way, so do not overdo it. The trick is to be genuine without being repetitious, distracting, or manipulative. A simple "Thank you" or "Good! Let's write that idea down" can create an atmosphere of enthusiasm and trust. Personalize the meeting by using participants' names: "Thank you, Alanna, for pointing that out." The whole group needs positive reinforcement, too. "That's a tremendous list of ideas! You have all worked very hard" or "Thank you for putting forth such effort on this difficult activity. Let's take a well-deserved break!"

Do not comment after every input or continually thank the group. It is best to strike a balance between being unresponsive and being overly responsive. Use this technique to show support, encouragement, and appreciation for participants and to keep the energy level of the group high.

Including Quieter Members

In most groups and most discussions, there are those who are quieter than others and those who seldom contribute to the conversation. People may hesitate to speak up for a variety of reasons: (1) they may believe they have nothing to add to the discussion; (2) they may be shy about speaking in front of others; (3) they may feel it is impolite to jump in without being asked; (4) they may simply have nothing to say at that time; (5) they may resist being part of the group; or (6) they may wait for an accepting atmosphere before they risk making comments because they may have been in groups in which people were put down or attacked.

The facilitator plays a key role in encouraging all members to participate. First, be aware of who is participating and who is not. Second, use a few basic techniques to manage and try to balance participation at all times. Keep in mind that it is rare for a meeting to have completely equal or balanced participation; however, you are responsible for creating opportunities for everyone to contribute. Here are a few techniques to draw out quieter group members:

- Use a direct, but gentle approach: Call on the person by name and ask for his or her input. "Robin, what is your reaction to this?" or "Jesse, we haven't heard from you yet today; what do you think?"

- Ask everyone in the group to respond to the same question. Go around the group asking each person to respond.

- Refer back to comments made earlier by quieter participants. This continues to draw them into the group.

- Break the group into pairs or subgroups of three or four members each. Ask each small group to come up with responses and then report back to the entire group. This will give quieter participants more opportunity to speak.

- If there are several quieter members, or if one area of the room seems to be quiet, invite those people to contribute. "We haven't heard from some of you yet. What do the rest of you think?" or "Let's hear some comments from this side of the room."

New facilitators often fear that no one will speak up. Occasionally, everyone is silent. Learn to be comfortable with silence, especially after a question has been posed; people need time to think and formulate a response. New facilitators often are nervous with silence and jump in before people have time to contemplate a response. (See the section on silence in Chapter 4, Nonverbal Techniques.) If a group is truly silent and no one speaks up, here are a few techniques to help:

- Open with a nonthreatening, light-spirited icebreaker that requires people to introduce themselves. (See Chapter 14, Opening and Closing Activities.)

- Introduce the session in a way that will stimulate people's desire to speak out. For example, explain how a successful session will benefit each person.

- Use well-focused, open questions to kick off a discussion.

- Do not interrupt, judge, or respond negatively to anyone's input.

- Do not talk too much. Let the participants know from the beginning that you are there to listen and help them have a successful meeting.

- Do your homework before the session. Find out how people may react to the topic of the meeting and design your facilitation to compensate for any possibility. (See Chapter 12, How to Design a Facilitation.)

- If the group seems shy and unused to participating, give them an example of the type of response you are looking for. When someone speaks up, thank him or her for the contribution. Use praise to build people's confidence.

- Avoid rescuing the group and filling in the silence. Let them know you understand that it may be difficult for them to speak up for one reason or another, but also let them know that their comments are valuable and why.

Sometimes groups are accustomed to meeting leaders who act as authority figures, presenting, but not inviting participation. Overcome this mind-set by demonstrating willingness and skill in listening to and recording people's ideas. After the group sees that it indeed can be productive, it will generally loosen up, and discussion will flow more freely.

If the group is particularly closed, and various techniques fail, do not blame yourself. Occasionally a group will not respond to facilitation or to a particular facilitator. Most of the time, you will face the opposite challenge: to manage groups with unwieldy amounts of data to generate, discuss, and prioritize.

Encouraging Divergent Views

Because both groups and facilitators prefer meetings to go smoothly, there is sometimes an effort to stick together, harmonize, and come up with the same views. People are not always comfortable "rocking the boat" or speaking up with a divergent opinion. Groups will often wait for the leader to voice an opinion and then chime in with supporting ideas or data.

Skilled facilitators notice when everyone seems to be agreeing early in the discussion and ask if there are any different or opposing views: "Everyone seems to be in agreement on this issue. Is there a different view or idea that we are overlooking?" or "Does someone have a different opinion on that?" or "This is a difficult and highly important topic. I sense that there may be different ideas and opinions. Does someone have a different viewpoint?"

There are, of course, groups that become firmly caught up in disagreement early on and this, too, blocks productivity. In these cases, after noting the various opinions, try to help the group see the views that are held in common. For example, say:

- "Clearly there is disagreement on this issue. On what can we all agree?" (Then make a list on a flip chart.)

- "There is a lot of disagreement on how we should solve this problem. Can we all agree, however, that the goal is . . . ? If this is our goal, what can we do first to make progress toward it?"

Shifting Perspective

Sometimes you must help a group shift perspective so it sees things from another vantage point. For example, when a group is caught up in detail, intervene by asking the group to look at the big picture. In the opposite situation, when a group is overly focused on the big picture, intervene by suggesting that the group cite details to support big-picture statements. Frequently, when a group is asked to list both the advantages and disadvantages of a particular situation or decision, members will come up with many more disadvantages than advantages, or vice versa. Steer the group toward a more balanced assessment by saying something like, "There are a lot of disadvantages listed here. What are some more advantages?" or "Everyone seems to see a lot of advantages to this idea. What are some of the disadvantages?"

This simple technique encourages openness and creativity, and may be just what is needed to increase the synergy of the group or cause someone to state a major point.

Summarizing

Summarizing is an important technique to keep a group focused. From time to time, generally after a lot of points have been made, data generated, or activities completed, briefly summarize what has been said or done before moving on. The tricky part of summarizing is to *summarize*— be brief and to the point. A tendency of new facilitators is to summarize by going into too much detail. With practice, the skill of being clear and concise can be developed.

Another approach to summarizing is to ask someone in the group to summarize what has been said so far. Be patient with group members, because they may not know how to summarize. Nevertheless, it is a good way to build this skill in the group and to keep everyone alert to what is going on. The best way is to ask, "Would someone like to summarize what has been said so far?" It is not a good time to call on a particular person. Someone might be caught off guard, or time could be wasted if the person is not ready to summarize. After asking if someone will summarize, give people time to think. If no one volunteers, go ahead, saying something like, "Well, let me try to summarize this time." Occasionally ask group members to summarize, as this increases group ownership for the process, teaches group members a valuable skill, and empowers the group to work with its own data.

When summarizing, do not insert your own opinions or weight the summary toward your own views. With practice, you can make a brief, neutral summary without changing the meaning of the discussion so far.

When there have been a lot of disagreements or data is diverse, it may be difficult to summarize the content of what has been said. In this case, simply summarize what has occurred and then make a suggestion, for example, "As you can see, there is disagreement over the best method to . . . . Three methods have been discussed. First . . . , second . . . , and third. . . . The next step will be to evaluate each method and try to reach consensus on which will best achieve your goals."

Sometimes you must summarize what has been going on (the process) and not the content: "A lot of material has been presented on Method A, but no one has presented material on Methods B or C. How can we bring out more information on Methods B and C?"

Bridging

To stop one activity and move on to the next, facilitators use a technique called bridging. Make a "bridge" by saying a few words about what has just happened and what the group will be doing next. Summarizing is simply the first step in making an effective bridge to the next activity. If you are going to give the group a break between activities, summarize, give the group a break, and bridge over to the next activity when the group returns from break. This gives a chance to review the next planned activity to see whether it is appropriate based on what the group has done so far. If the group's energy is depleted, give the group a break before summarizing and then summarize and bridge after the break.

For example, after an active brainstorming session, summarize by saying, "You have come up with a long list of ideas to improve customer service. Our next step will be to make sure everyone understands all of the ideas before we discuss their merits or problems. Are there any items that need further clarification?"

Use all of these verbal techniques to help the group achieve its purpose. Some nonverbal techniques are explored in the next chapter.

CHAPTER 4

Nonverbal Techniques: What to Do

hat a facilitator *does* can be referred to as *nonverbal techniques* or *nonverbal skills.* These skills are just as important as verbal skills. Sometimes they are more important! The way something is said is the real message that comes across, not just the words. People naturally "hear" with all their senses and respond not only to a speaker's words but to gestures, facial expression, posture, and voice inflection.

Group members are affected not only by the words they hear but also by the way you speak, your actions, voice, pace, and so on. You give off signs of the way you are feeling by the words chosen, actions, tone of voice, body language, attitude, and even position in the room. Successful facilitators know that their own nonverbal messages come across, and they learn to observe the nonverbal messages of people in the group.

Some nonverbal messages can hinder a group's productivity, while others create an open, trusting, and engaged atmosphere. Send nonverbal cues to help a group with a discussion or a task. Learn to identify appropriate and helpful nonverbal messages and to avoid nonverbal messages that hinder group work.

Before going further, let's define a "nonverbal message." It is *a fact, an emotion, or an attitude communicated without the use of words or in addition to the words used.* For example, when you say "Hello" to someone, the word only says so much. Most of the message is communicated by your tone of voice, your facial expressions, and your physical movements. If you say "Hello" in a flat voice, look away, and keep walking, you have communicated one message. If you say "Hello" in an enthusiastic voice, look the other person in the eye, reach out your hand to shake hands, and smile broadly, you have communicated an entirely different message.

If you say to a group, "Are there other opinions?" and you scowl a bit, turn your back on the group, and look for something in your briefcase, you really communicated very well that you do not want other opinions. This is called a "mixed message." What you say is not supported by what you do. On the other hand, if you say to a group, "Are there other opinions?" and you look around the room from face to face, take a marking pen in hand, listen intently, and move toward the flip chart, you have probably convinced group members that you really want to hear more opinions. You have delivered a congruent message, a message in which what you say is supported by what you do.

One of your key responsibilities is to build trust in the group. Trust is greatly enhanced by consistently using congruent messages. When working with a group, each of us needs to learn how our nonverbal messages come across and whether they are congruent with our verbal messages. Working with a group may require some adaptation on your part. Over the years of working with facilitators, I have found that some students of facilitation quite naturally use nonverbal messages that support their true message. However, others must learn new ways to communicate nonverbally. Poor nonverbal skills are typically due to lack of experience being in front of a group, to one or two bad habits, or simply to nervousness. With practice and feedback, most people can learn effective nonverbal skills.

Several nonverbal skill areas deserve attention, although this is by no means an exhaustive list. This chapter covers the following:

- Active listening

- Voice

- Eye contact

- Attentiveness

- Facial expressions

- Silence

- Body language

- Position and movement in the room

- Distracting habits

- Enthusiasm

- Dress

Active Listening

Active listening is at the head of the list—the most important and most basic of nonverbal skills. A facilitator who listens actively will overcome many of his or her shortcomings as a facilitator. In fact, you cannot use most of the other facilitation skills without really hearing what has been said. You must really listen in order to record people's ideas, refer back to what was said earlier, paraphrase, and summarize.

Actively listening to another person is a powerful technique for building trust, increasing openness, fostering collaboration, encouraging creativity, and demonstrating respect. Many of the decisions you must make as a facilitator depend on your ability to listen actively to the person speaking. This also encourages group members to listen better to one another.

Active listening can be defined *as the act of listening to another person with the intent to fully understand what he or she is saying.* The listener must focus on the verbal and nonverbal messages coming from the speaker. The active listener clears his or her mind of other thoughts or distractions to fully concentrate on both the words and the other messages conveyed by the speaker. Most important, the listener must try to understand the intent of the speaker, even when the speaker may not be very skilled at conveying the point. When necessary, a good listener must be able to check for understanding by repeating back what was heard. Active listening requires the listener to be fully engaged in the moment, the speaker, and the message. The listener's mind must be open, alert, and focused, without being sidetracked into deciding how to respond. Active listening is indeed "active" work and over time can be quite exhausting. If you are tired when you have been really listening for a while, you may have simply been fully and actively engaged in what you were hearing.

Good listening skills are learned and developed over a lifetime, and many excellent books, training programs, and self-scoring instruments have been created to help people learn to listen. In organizations and cultures where actions, speed, quick thinking, and directness are valued and often demanded—where everyone is in a hurry to hear the facts and get to the bottom line—people often develop good speaking skills without developing the corresponding listening skills. In these settings, people learn to listen selectively for what they need or want to hear, sometimes missing part or all of the speaker's message.

Several skills and techniques will help you become an active listener.

Learn to Listen on Two Levels

Try to understand both the content and what is behind it (feelings, needs, point of view, attitude). Whenever someone speaks, listen for the verbal as well as the nonverbal message. Some of the nonverbals you will *see* are the speaker's facial expression, gestures, and eye contact. Some of the nonverbals you will *hear* are the speaker's tone of voice, pace of speaking, emotional quality of the voice, use of words, and language difficulties.

Try to Understand Without Judging

As you listen, remember not to judge the speaker. Simply listen for the whole message, both verbal and nonverbal. Weigh the facts presented, consider the points made carefully, listen for understanding, but do not judge the speaker to be right, wrong, on target, off base, and so on. Your role as a facilitator is to increase understanding so everyone is heard correctly by the group. By not judging, you are demonstrating to the group that everyone's ideas are to be considered on their own merit, and that the people who pose the ideas are not to be judged. This is a cornerstone in the effectiveness of groups. People should be able to throw out an idea, a concern, or a potential solution and expect that it will at least be given a chance for objective consideration.

Remain Fully Attentive

Engage your whole body in truly listening to the other person. An effective listener shows attentiveness through:

- Good eye contact;

- Occasional head nodding;

- An occasional encouragement to continue ("Go on." "Oh?" "Uh huh.");

- Not interrupting (silence);

- Taking notes;

- Avoiding distracting movements; and

- Facial expressions (open, interested look).

Focus on the Message

As listeners we think much faster than we talk. Listening requires that we slow our thinking and keep our brains from wandering during the time between the speaker's words. There are several ways to focus on the message being sent so your brain does not wander off and lose the speaker's thoughts. Some useful techniques are given below; obviously you will not use all of them at once, but they will keep you focused on the speaker's message:

- Think about what the speaker is saying, not what you are going to say next.

- Periodically review and mentally summarize the points the speaker is making. Imagine that you will have to repeat to someone else what the speaker has said.

- Repeat to yourself the words the speaker is saying. This will keep you focused and reinforce the speaker's message in your memory.

- Listen between the lines for additional meaning. What feelings (enthusiasm, weariness, anger, frustration) are behind the speaker's words?

- Listen for clues to what the speaker may be thinking or feeling but not saying. These clues can be tone of voice, choice of words, facial expressions, body movements, and carefulness with words.

- As the person is talking, use facts you hear to organize what is being said. Group ideas for later summarization.

- Do not become caught up in facts. Use them only to understand the bigger message or ideas behind them.

- Consider what the speaker is *not* saying that may give you an idea of how to probe for further information.

Focus on the Person Talking

In addition to understanding the message, try to understand the person. What do the person's words convey about him or her? Can you find a connection to that person that will increase your understanding and sensitivity to him or her? Try to empathize with the person. Try to project yourself into the situation the other person is describing and to experience similar feelings or sensations. Even if you have never experienced the same event or problem, think of similar feelings you may have had. Even if you cannot relate to the idea being presented, you can relate to the enthusiasm and the hopes behind it. By listening to both the message (the content) and the person (the feelings, the experience, the attitudes, the motivations), you are listening on two levels and are receiving the whole message.

Because facilitators use many skills at once while listening, it helps new facilitators, or those who wish to improve listening skills, to focus on developing one or two listening skills at a time. For example, during your next facilitation, you may decide to focus on the speaker's message by not letting yourself think ahead to what you are going to say. Practice repeating the speaker's words with the intent of hearing every word. Another time, you can choose a different listening skill to focus on.

The Listening Habits Questionnaire that follows will help you assess your listening skills or obtain feedback from group members, supervisors, or colleagues about your listening skills. Although the questionnaire focuses on conversational listening, the skills are essential for facilitation situations as well.

Fill out the Listening Habits Questionnaire and ask a few other people to complete it to assess your listening habits (your boss, colleagues, subordinates, a friend, a spouse). Allow them to remain anonymous. After you have the results, compute an average score for each item based on all the responses you received. Do not include your own responses in the average. For each item, show your response, the average response of others who completed the questionnaire, and the range of responses. (See the example on page 61 following the questionnaire.) The results will tell you several things:

- Those items on which you scored the lowest average are those you may need to improve.

- Items on which you had a broad range of responses (2 to 5, for example) may mean that you listen differently to different people or you may not listen as attentively in some situations as you do in others.

- If you rated yourself considerably higher or lower than others did on certain items, consider that their perception of you may be more accurate. If there is a diversity of responses, then you may be listening differently in different situations. Decide if there are areas you need to improve or in which you need to be more consistent.

After you have identified areas for improvement, write them out like the example below:

- Item 1: I will use more open questions to initiate and expand discussions.

- Item 3: I will avoid interrupting with my own opinions and interrupt only to clarify and encourage more information.

- Item 13: I will make an effort to listen and really hear others, regardless of my personal feelings toward them.

Write "I will. . . ." statements such as these for each of the areas in which you want to improve. Read your list frequently, preferably at the beginning of the day, and select one or two areas to work on that day. You will have many opportunities to practice good listening skills: at work, at lunch with friends and associates, at check-out counters, when solving problems, making phone calls, talking with your children, meeting new people or making business contacts, in meetings, or while managing others.

Listening Habits Questionnaire

Directions: Circle the response that most accurately describes your listening habits.

In conversations with others, to what extent do you:	Very Little	Little	Some	Great	Very Great
1. Use open-ended questions to initiate and expand the discussion?	1	2	3	4	5
2. Use closed-ended questions to find out specifics?	1	2	3	4	5
3. Avoid interrupting, except to clarify and encourage more sharing of information?	1	2	3	4	5
4. Maintain eye contact while the other person is speaking?	1	2	3	4	5
5. Encourage dialogue by sending signals that show you are genuinely interested in what the other person is saying?	1	2	3	4	5
6. Avoid turning the conversation away from the speaker onto yourself?	1	2	3	4	5
7. Mentally review what the speaker is saying as he or she talks?	1	2	3	4	5
8. Keep the discussion focused on the speaker until he or she is finished speaking?	1	2	3	4	5
9. Encourage and listen to suggestions, even when you do not agree with the speaker?	1	2	3	4	5
10. Avoid being distracted while someone is talking?	1	2	3	4	5

Item	Very Little	Little	Some	Great	Very Great
11. Probe for a deeper understanding of the person's comments?	1	2	3	4	5
12. Listen for the underlying tone or feeling as well as the facts?	1	2	3	4	5
13. Listen, regardless of your personal feelings about the person or topic?	1	2	3	4	5
14. Periodically check your understanding by restating in your own words what was said?	1	2	3	4	5
15. Continue checking your understanding until the speaker agrees that your summary of what he or she said is correct?	1	2	3	4	5
16. Summarize and close the conversation so the other person feels that you have appreciated and understood his or her comments?	1	2	3	4	5

Response Sheet for Listening Habits Questionnaire

Item	My Response	Average of Others' Responses	Range of Responses
Example	*3*	*4.2*	*2 to 4*

1. Use open-ended questions to initiate and expand the discussion?

2. Use closed-ended questions to find out specifics?

3. Avoid interrupting, except to clarify and encourage more sharing of information?

4. Maintain eye contact while the other person is speaking?

5. Encourage dialogue by sending signals that show you are genuinely interested in what the other person is saying?

6. Avoid turning the conversation away from the speaker onto yourself?

7. Mentally review what the speaker is saying as he or she talks?

8. Keep the discussion focused on the speaker until he or she is finished speaking?

9. Encourage and listen to suggestions, even when you do not agree with the speaker?

10. Avoid being distracted while someone is talking?

Item	My Response	Average of Others' Responses	Range of Responses
11. Probe for a deeper understanding of the person's comments?			
12. Listen for the underlying tone or feeling as well as the facts?			
13. Listen, regardless of your personal feelings about the person or topic?			
14. Periodically check your understanding by restating in your own words what was said?			
15. Continue checking your understanding until the speaker agrees that your summary of what he or she said is correct?			
16. Summarize and close the conversation so the other person feels that you have appreciated and understood his or her comments?			

Voice

A person's voice has a recognizable and unique quality to it. A voiceprint (like a fingerprint) is a product of the *tone* and pitch of the voice and the *inflection* a person uses. Along with voice tone, accents, *pace* of speaking, and ways of forming words, each person has a unique voice. When you speak, a mood or feeling, sometimes called the "tone," is set. This tone is greatly influenced by not only the words you have chosen, but also the sound and pace of your voice. Become aware of the impact your voice has on a group. The tone you use affects the atmosphere of the room. Without going to the trouble of taking voice and speaking lessons, you can set the tone for a group session by paying attention to the following aspects of your voice.

Tone

Tone of voice involves the pitch of the voice (high or low) and the emotional overtones (enthusiastic, sad, bored, anticipatory, fearful). A higher-pitched voice usually elicits excitement or tension in listeners. A lower-pitched voice is generally calming and helps people slow down or relax. Use the pitch of your voice to set a certain mood in the group—within reason, of course. Too much variation in pitch of voice may cause people to feel manipulated or make you seem foolish or theatrical. Simply vary vocal pitch when necessary to help the group along. To generate some enthusiasm in the group, stand up and raise the pitch of your voice a bit.

Inflection

Inflection is the way a person varies the tone of voice when speaking. In any sentence, a person will raise and lower his or her voice to convey meaning. A person who uses little or no inflection speaks in a monotone. As a facilitator, be aware that the inflection of your voice is a part of your message. Tone and inflection are particularly important when you ask questions. The wrong tone or inflection may threaten people or discourage them from responding.

Pace

The pace with which you speak affects the group as well. Too fast a pace may make the group hyperactive or tire them out. Too slow a pace may put them to sleep. Vary the pace of your speaking to fit the task. A skillful facilitator does not do much of the talking anyway, but when you do speak, use an appropriate pace. For example, if you want people to stand up and go into a small-group activity, speed up your voice, raise the pitch, and put some enthusiasm into the way you speak. If you are asking the group a difficult question, one that requires some quiet thought before responding, slow down your speech, lower your voice, and add a more serious inflection. Again, you are not on stage or manipulating people's emotions. These are just simple techniques to be aware of. They work!

Eye Contact

Another important nonverbal skill is eye contact. Facilitators must maintain eye contact with the group member who is speaking, which shows that one is actively listening. If the listener looks away, the speaker loses a sense of focus as well. Eye contact shows that the listener is really paying attention; the speaker, in turn, can put his or her thoughts into words more easily.

Eye contact does not mean staring into a person's eyes without ever looking away. Eye contact is simply looking at the speaker's eyes and face in a relaxed manner. Allow your eyes to blink occasionally and move to different areas on the person's face, while keeping generally focused on the person's head. Your eyes should occasionally make "contact" with the other person's, but do not stare fixedly. If you are not used to holding this kind of attention on another person when he or she is speaking, it is easy to practice whenever you are listening to anyone speak. You will find that it will become easier over time, although at first it may seem to take a lot of energy and focus on your part. You will probably find that as you learn better eye contact, your listening will greatly improve; you will hear more, understand more, and remember more. Eye contact is a powerful way to focus attention on a speaker.

In some cultures direct or intense eye contact is considered rude, and you must be sensitive to how those from other cultures respond to eye contact. Those for whom eye contact is uncomfortable will give off signals that let you know this. They will look away and will not return eye contact with you. In these cases, be sensitive to others' feelings and cultural norms and adapt your approach. For example, you may look in the general direction of the person, stand still and attentive, but not seek eye contact.

New facilitators often express frustration with the fact that it is difficult to record ideas and maintain eye contact as well. This is truly one of the main difficulties of facilitation. Here are several ways to alleviate this problem:

- Use eye contact frequently as the person speaks, but feel free to record ideas as well. Recording the speaker's ideas is just as powerful as eye contact. It proves that you are listening and validates the person's contribution. Turn back to the speaker when you are finished recording and, if he or she is still speaking, continue to listen actively.

- When possible, maintain eye contact until the speaker makes a main point, then turn to record the idea. You might even say, "Let me interrupt you for a moment to write down that idea." Then turn to the flip chart to write down a brief phrase that captures the idea. When finished writing, turn back to the speaker, resume eye contact, and encourage him or her to continue. A brief phrase or nod of the head will suffice: "Go on, please" or "What else were you saying?" Be careful not to stop the speaker too frequently, as you will interrupt his or her train of thought and make it difficult for the speaker to stay on track.

- Simply tell the group that you will be dividing your attention between looking at group members while they speak and jotting down ideas on the flip chart. Encourage members to talk as you write, if this is what you prefer. Letting them know ahead of time that you will sometimes be turned away from them will help balance out the fact that you are not maintaining eye contact.

Although eye contact is important, it is not the only way to demonstrate good listening as a facilitator. Recording ideas, checking to see if you have captured a person's point accurately, summarizing, and other techniques will prove you have listened well. However, whenever you have the chance, use eye contact to draw in the speaker. Avoid looking at other things in the room while a person is talking, unless you are recording his or her comments on the flip chart. This is part of the art of facilitation—knowing how to keep eye contact and to record ideas as well.

Another helpful technique is to ask someone else to record while you facilitate the discussion. (This will be covered more thoroughly in the next chapter.) Even when using a recorder, you will have to turn to the flip chart occasionally, losing eye contact, and check to see what comments or ideas have been recorded. Still, with a recorder, you will have an easier time maintaining eye contact with group members.

Attentiveness

When facilitators listen actively and maintain eye contact, they are being attentive. Attentiveness is a key facilitation skill. Not only does it involve all aspects of active listening and maintaining eye contact, but it also means listening with all of the senses. Be attentive to what the speaker is saying, how he or she is saying it, what the underlying mood of the message is, what is not being said, the atmosphere in the room, the reaction of others in the room, and so on.

Being attentive means that you cannot be too concerned with the next step in the group process or with the fact that your supervisor just stepped into the room. Attentiveness means listening, observing, and being aware of the subtle, as well as the more overt, things going on around you. This is an art that new facilitators may have difficulty with as they deal with what to write on the flip chart, how to balance participation, and how to monitor the group process. But attentiveness is a goal that all facilitators should strive for. The more attentive you can be, the more apt you are to choose the appropriate intervention, say the right words, or change the next activity for the sake of group progress.

Facial Expressions

Facilitators do not always realize what an impact their facial expressions have on a group. They are busy watching the expressions of group members, but may not be aware that they are frowning, scowling, smiling, or even appear expressionless or "deadpan." Your facial expressions do affect the group. Try to match your facial expressions to the mood you wish to set. When you want the group to relax, open up, and be attentive to one another, try to have a relaxed, attentive look on your own face. Although smiling too much can be distracting and appear insincere, a smile now and then goes a long way to show appreciation, enthusiasm, or encouragement. Imagine how it would be to have a facilitator who never smiled. Learn not to wrinkle your brow, as participants may read this as disapproval or some kind of negative judgment on what is being said. Try to keep a smooth, open look on your face while participants speak, nodding your head now and then to show understanding.

Silence

A skilled facilitator must know how and when to be silent. New facilitators sometimes fall into the trap of continuing to talk when they should stop, be silent, and let the group think. A good example of this is just after posing an open-ended question. This is a time to be silent and let group members think through their responses. You may be tempted to fill a silence in the room and jump in too soon to explain the question, justify it, or even change it—which confuses the group and inadvertently tells group members, "I didn't really mean for you to respond now, because I am going to keep talking." Learn to ask a clear, open-ended question, write it on the flip chart, and then wait for at least ten seconds (count slowly to ten) before saying anything. These ten seconds will creep by at a slow pace for you, but they will speed by for participants. Also, the ten seconds of silence will signal to the group that you are serious about listening and are waiting for the group members to begin their work. Usually, someone will speak up in five to eight seconds. If not, do one of the following to encourage someone to speak up:

- Explain what you meant by the question and then ask it again;

- Give an example of the type of response you are looking for; or

- Reword the question.

After two or more tries with no response, ask the group to tell you why no one has responded and give some choices: (1) They simply have no opinions or data; (2) the subject is ticklish and they would rather not discuss it; (3) something more important is on their minds; (4) the question is too difficult to respond to at this time; or (5) it may not be of interest to the group.

Both new and experienced facilitators fear silence. If the group is silent, they somehow think they have failed or fear that the entire facilitation is a flop. Sometimes you will know ahead of time that the group is going to "go cold" on a topic. If so, the design of the session must compensate for this possibility. Generally speaking, silence on your part is a healthy sign. It usually means that the group is either thinking or responding.

Learn to use silence. When a speaker is finished with a thought, do not jump in with another question. Be silent. Look around the room. Wait for someone else to begin speaking. Do not try to fill every gap with words, questions, summaries, or comments. Sometimes silence is needed, or at the most a gentle nudge ("Anything else . . . ?") and then silence.

Body Language

Body language is the message the body tells. When facilitators speak or listen, stand, sit, move, and make gestures, these actions (or non-actions) have an effect on what they want to accomplish. At times it may be best to have a relaxed posture or to sit down while people are participating. At other times it may be best to move and use arm and head movements to support the message. It is generally a good idea not to make a habit of standing with arms crossed. This can send a message that you are closed or defensive. The most relaxed and open posture is arms to the sides.

Facilitators have an easier time dealing with body language than presenters. Facilitators spend a lot of time recording people's ideas on flip charts, hanging charts, and moving around the room to work with small groups. Body language is typically not much of an issue for them, unless they have bad habits that distract or annoy group members.

Be aware that your body language affects the work of the group. Observing the body language of others and its impact will help you learn how to minimize distracting body language and to develop an open and confident stance that shows genuine interest and concern for group members and the progress of the group.

Position and Movement in the Room

Related to body language is a facilitator's position and movement in the room. The way you handle being in the room can affect the process. Your presence in the room must be supportive, not dominating. When possible, place yourself so that the group is central and you are not in the limelight. It is also a good idea not to remain fixed in one spot (especially the front of the room, the position of power), but to move about the room in an informal manner, being where you are most needed. This might be in the back of the room listening, in the front making notes on a flip chart, sitting down with the group, or working with one of the subgroups.

Much of the time you will find yourself in front of the room next to the flip chart. During this time, stand to the side of the chart as much as possible so that people can read what is written. The chart (which is really the group's work) becomes the central focus.

During a discussion, when you are not recording, stand to the side or back of the room so group members can carry on by themselves. An occasional prompt may be enough to keep a productive discussion going. You may need to take a few notes and summarize when the discussion comes to a breaking point. Such notes can be made on a notepad or on a flip chart at the side of the room where people cannot see them. Later, you can reveal the chart and review the main points of the discussion.

Also, during a discussion, when you are recording, it is a good idea to occasionally move into the room, closer to the participants. This creates a more informal atmosphere (as opposed to being "glued" to the flip chart) and has a tendency to draw people into the discussion. If the room is set up in a U shape, move into the U and draw in those members farthest from the front of the room. No matter how the room is set up, it helps to move around occasionally and to draw people into the discussion by your presence.

When facilitating subgroup work, your most important role is to make sure that each subgroup understands its task. After giving instructions, roam from group to group to be sure that each understands the task and to see if there are any questions. It is not a good idea to interfere, as you may be seen as a power figure, which can limit the involvement of subgroup members. After a subgroup is clear about its task, it will do the best job if you stay away. While subgroups are working, you are free to review what has transpired so far or to prepare for the next activity. Toward the end of the subgroups' task, make a quick round to see if they are ready to return to the large group or if they need more time. Adjust the timing accordingly.

Distracting Habits

Another aspect of body language is unconscious nervous habits. Such habits can be distracting when someone is presenting or facilitating in front of a group. Some common distracting habits are rattling coins or keys in pockets; fiddling with clothes, jewelry, or hair; clicking the top of a marking pen on and off; scratching an arm, ear, or nose; pacing nervously; moving papers, charts, or other material around without purpose; and squinting or frowning.

Because habits become part of facilitators' demeanor unconsciously, they are sometimes hard for facilitators to realize. The best way to discover your own distracting habits is to have someone observe you and point them out or to watch a video of one of your facilitations. Those who attend facilitator training programs may receive useful feedback on distracting mannerisms.

Many distracting mannerisms are the result of not knowing what to do with your hands while other people are talking. Writing on the flip chart helps, but inevitably there will be "dead" time when other people are talking and times when you are speaking. Practice a relaxed stance, arms to your sides or holding a marking pen. Sitting down or moving behind the group—anything that takes attention away from you—will keep distractions to a minimum.

Enthusiasm

At times it is important for the facilitator to convey enthusiasm and other positive feelings, such as anticipation, confidence, and assurance that the group is doing well. Not showing confidence and enthusiasm can dampen the group's spirit and hinder progress. Sometimes the group is doing difficult work that is time-consuming and not immediately rewarding. Reassure the group that it is headed in the right direction, that any problems it is experiencing are natural, and that it is making progress. If this is not the case, intervene. But when starting a group on a task, or to keep its momentum going, be enthusiastic and encouraging.

Enthusiasm must be in harmony with your own style. If you are generally calm and quiet-mannered, do not demonstrate enthusiasm by jumping up and waving your arms. This would be out of character and appear strange to the group. Simply say quietly, "I think you have made especially good progress this afternoon. You are coming up with workable solutions. Let's take a brief break." Say this with genuine enthusiasm and feeling, not in a dull monotone, and the group's spirits are likely to be lifted. On the contrary, if you are normally a high-energy, more demonstrative person, show enthusiasm in a way that is harmonious with your style. Stop the group, wave a hand toward the flip charts and say, "Look at this! I am really pleased by the great work you have been doing today! This calls for a break."

Dress

There are few hard-and-fast rules about appropriate dress in the workplace today, although every company has its unwritten "dress code." However, participants frequently ask if there is a guideline for how to dress when facilitating. Many people have attended presentation-skills workshops where they have been encouraged to dress in a professional manner—usually business suits or comparable clothing.

It is difficult to compile any one set of rules for appropriate dress for facilitators or presenters. It simply depends on the situation. I have seen team presentations made by various teams, all of whom were dressed casually in everyday work clothes. The presentations were excellent and the dress seemed appropriate for the situation. Anything more formal might have appeared out of place. I have been in other situations in which the content of the presentation was diluted due to the sloppy and too casual attire worn by the presenter.

Facilitations are usually more casual by nature. People are expected to "roll up their sleeves" and work, to be physically comfortable, and to focus energy and efforts on working, not on how people look. Over the years, the norms of dressing inside companies has changed so that there are few rules that can apply to all companies. There are, however, a few general guidelines that are helpful, even in today's casual environments:

- Always dress in clean, comfortable, and attractive clothes. Avoid wearing clothes that are dirty, torn, sloppy, or poorly matched.

- Dress to harmonize with the group with which you will be working. If everyone will be in jeans and T-shirts, wear a nice pair of jeans or slacks and a shirt.

- If the group is likely to be dressed in a variety of ways, wear what is most comfortable, clean, and attractive to harmonize with some people and offend no one.

- Because you will be seen as a professional and a leader, dress in a manner that makes you feel confident. If you always wear suits and people are used to seeing you that way, there is no need to change. Be at ease.

- Facilitating can be hard work, with long hours of standing, paying attention, writing, moving around, and organizing materials and activities. Avoid clothes that are tight, pull, or will bother you after a few hours. (High-heeled shoes can be very uncomfortable during a long facilitation; so can a tie or a tight jacket.)

- Avoid wearing your best clothes when facilitating. They can be stained from marking pens (use water-based pens), torn, or stretched as you move flip charts around, hang paper, or transport materials to and from the meeting location.

My personal preference when facilitating is a loose-fitting jacket, a blouse, and slacks, maybe a belt, a little jewelry, and low-heeled shoes. I try to find things that look relaxed and do not draw too much attention to the "outfit." However, a scarf or piece of jewelry can be a nice touch and add some pizzazz. Men do well with slacks and a long-sleeved shirt or sweater, or even a dressy pullover shirt. Ties are fine too, if participants will be wearing them and you are comfortable in them. If you know everyone will be wearing suits and ties, it is probably a safe bet that you will feel best "following suit." Skilled and sought-after facilitators can afford to be more avant-garde in their dress and may even want to do so to make a statement. However, when in doubt, dress in harmony with your group.

All of these techniques—both verbal and nonverbal—must be used with consideration for their appropriateness. Be natural and not mechanical, helping the group along rather than pushing it. Let the group build up momentum of its own and intervene (by calling on someone, for example) once in a while to keep balance. Use techniques only when you believe they will help the group. Sometimes groups do better without a lot of intervention by the facilitator.

CHAPTER **5**

Recording Techniques

A common set of notes everyone can see as the meeting progresses is an essential tool for facilitators. Much of what was said will be lost if it is not written down. People do not always hear what someone else has said, as they are formulating the comments (or counterarguments) they are going to make. So much is said that no one can remember all of the points; even some of the good ideas are lost. If nothing is written for everyone to see, people become redundant and make their points more than once. When there is no common set of notes, each person leaves the meeting with his or her own ideas about what was said and what was decided. A few may have taken notes, but these may represent only what was important to each person.

Why Record?

Some of the numerous advantages to recording key points, decisions, and action items are listed below:

- The note-taking process holds people's attention and keeps everyone focused on the work at hand.

75

- The notes become the "group memory," the words, phrases, and diagrams that trigger members' memories about what was said.

- The notes become the working papers of a group in action. They contain ideas, data, opinions, alternatives, pros and cons, and issues.

- Recording people's contributions allows for quick review and recall of what has been said, thus allowing the group to function more efficiently, as every group member can consult the notes whenever necessary.

- When the group reaches consensus, the agreement or decision can be written down and posted.

- Action items and the names of those responsible, time frames, and deadlines can be published so everyone can acknowledge agreement with and support of what has been decided.

The notes can be kept or published as handouts, but their main purpose is to serve as the working papers during the group meeting. The group can decide what portion of the notes needs to be distributed later to group members.

Skilled facilitators become adept at taking group notes, posting, and arranging them. Many of the tools and group methods facilitators use, such as brainstorming, affinity diagramming, and fishbone diagrams, require posting and arranging items in an organized way. The group both creates and uses its own material in a problem-solving process. Group memory is one of the keys to successful group work.

Recording and posting people's ideas also give everyone an equal chance to participate and to influence the course of the meeting. Recording a person's idea, and placing it so everyone sees it, acknowledges its value. The person who contributed the idea can then relax and listen to what others are saying, knowing that it has been recorded.

Recording and posting ideas add objectivity to group decision making. When ideas become too strongly associated with one individual, group members can be swayed. If an idea is recorded and posted with other ideas, it is separate from the originator, making it more likely that the idea will be evaluated on its own merits. Even though there may be occasion to acknowledge or question the originator of the idea, the process of posting all ideas and discussing them still increases objectivity.

Notes can function as meeting minutes as well. They can be transcribed after each session and distributed to group members. Because a lot of data can be generated during a meeting, the group may want to decide which notes can be discarded. For highly important and sensitive meetings, it may be wise to save all the notes, at least for a time. Some groups roll up the flip charts and save them for use at future meetings.

What to Record

Perhaps the most difficult aspect of recording is knowing what to record and what not to record. Knowing how to write ideas on a flip chart is a *skill*. Knowing what to record and what not to record is an *art*. When a discussion is going full swing or a brainstorming session is ripe with creativity, you will not want to miss anything, but you must edit comments and decide what to record. Listen carefully to find one or two key words or phrases that will capture the idea—just enough information to jog people's minds later. Remember, you are not selectively listening; you are selectively recording. Your aim is to hear everything and then glean the key message.

Deciding what to record is difficult when someone rambles and you are not clear what the point is. This is the time to say, "George, you've made several points. Can you sum up what you've said in a phrase or two so I can write it down?" This gives George an opportunity to edit and summarize his own comments. If he cannot, you can offer to come back to him in a few minutes when he is ready. Another technique is to offer to summarize someone's comments: "Beth, you've made several points. Does it capture them if I write . . . ?" or "Lowell, let's see if I've understood your point . . . [paraphrase what you think he said]." If you are wrong, the person has the opportunity to edit and reword his or her comments before they are recorded.

If you are in the process of gathering people's ideas or if you have asked a group to respond to an open-ended question, you will want to encourage participation and validate people's comments by recording everyone's ideas. After you have started to record people's ideas one by one, it is important to record every idea and not leave anyone's idea out. A brief phrase for each idea usually suffices. Occasionally, someone makes a comment that sounds identical or similar to someone else's. *Do not, under any circumstances, neglect to record that comment without first checking with the speaker.* You may be wrong in assuming that he or she is saying the same thing. Let the speaker determine whether it should be recorded as a different idea or whether it is similar enough to someone else's idea to be left off the chart or recorded as a check mark beside the original idea. You can say something like, "Anna, is the point you made the same as the one Jose made earlier? Let's see, here it is [read it]." Anna can then say, "No, my point is different because . . . ." or "Yes, I'm really just saying the same thing Jose did in a different way." Listen to Anna's tone of voice and watch her body language to make sure she is willing to let her idea go uncaptured. If there is any hesitation in her voice, it is better just to say, "Well, Anna, let's put down your idea. I think it's a bit different from Jose's." Use the person's own words to write down the idea, then check to see if the wording accurately expresses his or her idea.

During some discussions, little or nothing has to be recorded. Try to sense when the group just needs to toss around ideas and thoughts. You may just sit down and let the group go for a while. This is a good time to take notes on a note pad and use them to summarize the discussion after a few minutes. An appropriate time will come, when the discussion dies down or becomes too heated, that you can go to the flip chart and suggest a way to deal with the data that has been generated. After listening to a group discussion, you may be able to come up with a tool or method to help the group sort out and evaluate the ideas that have been generated.

Sometimes a group needs time to vent. If this is the case, let it. However, at some point you will need to intervene and suggest a way for the group to move on and be productive. Say something like, "We've taken time to let off some steam about several of the problems we are experiencing. I have recorded several of them on the flip charts. Now let's take a break, and when we come back we will begin to look at how we can move forward to reach the goals we have set." It may not be wise to record the group's frustrations when sensitive or confidential issues are brought up. The whole group should decide. Say "Some of these things you are bringing up are sensitive and confidential. Do you want me to stop recording while you talk, or would it be better for me to record the main points of your discussion?" Even when the group decides not to record the items, you may need to summarize the discussion later and check with the group to see whether your summary is accurate.

Learn the art of capturing a brief phrase in the speaker's own words. One of the most common mistakes facilitators make, especially those who are articulate and express themselves well, is to change the wording when writing an idea on the flip chart. At times this works well, but it is better not to do it too often. Several things can happen when you reword the speaker's comments:

- The speaker feels that his or her own wording was not quite acceptable.

- The speaker becomes annoyed because he or she believes you changed the meaning.

- The meaning actually is changed.

- You miss the opportunity to validate the speaker's idea as it was said.

- You may be offering your own ideas on the topic (thus giving up neutrality).

- Even when you have a more precise, powerful, or lyrical way of wording the idea, the group will value what the speaker said more.

- Rewording comments puts you in a position of power. The group may resent it or lose confidence in itself.

To summarize, there are three main reasons why facilitators (and the group) benefit from using people's own words when recording comments:

1. It validates the speaker and shows that his or her comments are valued.

2. The facilitator maintains a neutral role.

3. There is no chance of altering the meaning of the original idea.

Using Flip Charts

Because of their informality, availability, and flexibility, flip charts have become the most common tool facilitators use to record group input. Flip charts are ideal for recording, reviewing, and amending material as it is generated.

New facilitators often argue that flip charts are bulky, hard to transport, and not always available in meeting rooms. They may prefer a white board or an overhead projector and blank transparencies or may not see the point in recording discussion points publicly. They may assign someone to take minutes or let everyone take his or her own notes. Others find that using laptops and the technique of computer projection is more efficient than flip charts. Those using technologies other than flip charts should consider the advantages of flip charts and find ways to address the deficiencies of other methods, if possible.

Experienced facilitators and group leaders have generally found that the advantages of flip charts outweigh their disadvantages. Following are four main reasons why flip charts are a valuable tool:

1. They are more effective than white boards or transparencies, which cannot hold as much information.

2. They can be placed anywhere in the room as needed to focus group attention.

3. They can easily be kept for later use in another meeting or for transcription of information such as group goals, mission statement, key concepts, process steps, or directions for individual or group activities.

4. They can be altered by the group: ideas can be reworded, material reorganized, or items crossed out.

Using Someone Else to Record

You will find advantages and disadvantages to writing on flip charts while trying to facilitate. Some facilitators are self-conscious about their handwriting, some have trouble writing legibly, and others feel that writing takes their attention away from the group. For these reasons, many facilitators assign someone else to do the recording. Even if you assign a recorder, however, you are still responsible for the accuracy of the information. You may have to slow down the conversation so that all ideas can be captured.

If you do your own recording, you do not have to be as concerned that anything is being left out. You may find that the act of writing what someone said in a brief phrase reinforces your own understanding. This is particularly helpful later, when summarizing the comments. You may prefer to do the writing so you have something to do other than stand in front of the group. You will probably develop methods of highlighting, organizing, and displaying the data that speeds up the recording process and makes the charts more useable.

Be flexible. During a brainstorming session, for example, when ideas are coming very fast, it may be useful to have two people recording, each with a chart. They can alternate recording ideas to keep from slowing down the process. It may be useful to have a recorder when the group is large so that you can roam around the room to draw people in. If you are not sure whether anyone in the group has recording skills, it is usually better to do the recording yourself. If you facilitate an ongoing group or team, you may decide to rotate the job so that members of the group learn the skill. See Figure 5.1 for a summary of the advantages and disadvantages of using someone else to record versus doing it yourself.

Figure 5.1. Recording on a Flip Chart Yourself Versus Using a Recorder

	Advantages	Disadvantages
Using Someone Else	Facilitator: Is free to scan room, walk around, and make eye contact. Can select someone with clear, legible handwriting. Can concentrate on listening and "reading" the group.	Facilitator: Must have legible handwriting, accuracy in capturing ideas, ability to organize data and remain neutral. May miss some key points. May be distracted by coaching the recorder. Must use tact and finesse when making suggestions to the recorder. May lose control if recorder "takes over" and the group becomes confused as to who is facilitating. May need to intervene to remind recorder to check whether comments have been recorded accurately. Misses contributions from the recorder.
Recording Yourself	Facilitator: Can capture and organize the data in own way. Is free to check accuracy with group members. Does not pull a member of the group out of the discussion. Can select what to record and how much.	Facilitator: Has more to do. May have difficulty writing quickly and legibly. May have trouble spelling in this situation. Must stand more.

Role of the Recorder

No matter who does the recording, the role of the recorder is similar to the role of the facilitator—a "servant of the group." In this capacity, he or she does not contribute to the content of the discussion. The recorder's role is simply to capture the key points as quickly, clearly, and legibly as possible. Participants are annoyed if the recorder adds opinions, editorializes, paraphrases, or disagrees with ideas being presented. The role of the recorder is just that—to record. Recorders should be careful not to begin facilitating the discussion and run the risk of taking over. In special cases, the recorder may ask permission from the group to step out of the role and contribute an idea, then go right back into the role.

If you choose someone else to record, be sure the recorder understands the role and coach him or her along the way, if necessary. Coaching the recorder in front of the group should be in the form of a suggestion or question and every effort must be made not to embarrass the recorder. Say something like, "Donna, did you have time to capture that last point of Allen's? I think he said . . . . Is that right, Allen?" Or you might say, "Donna, would you put a dash beside each comment so that it will be easier to code them later?" If someone else does record, be sure to show appreciation for the good work and to thank him or her in front of the group at the end of the session. After you feel comfortable using others to record, rotate the assignment by asking for volunteers. Usually people with poor handwriting will not volunteer, and those who enjoy writing will. Occasionally, someone will volunteer whose recording skills are not up to par. This is a ticklish situation, but at an appropriate time suggest that you would like this person to join the group discussion. At that point, resume recording yourself or rotate the job to someone else.

Ownership of the Flip Charts

Because so much of a facilitator's time is spent writing on flip charts, they often begin to think of them as theirs and guard them accordingly. It is best to think of the charts as belonging to the group. They represent the work of the group and the group memory for that session, and even subsequent sessions. You are a catalyst for creating the notes, but the notes belong to the group.

Encourage and coach the group to take responsibility for the flip charts after the meeting. Generally speaking, do not transcribe the notes, distribute copies, or store the charts. The material on the charts belongs to the group, and its members are responsible for it. Emphasize the importance of the material on the charts and then give the group options for what to do with it. More mature groups and teams will already have a system for doing this, although you may still want to suggest something different, depending on the situation. An ongoing group or team can appoint someone to transcribe the charts after each meeting, or this responsibility can be rotated. The group can decide which charts to keep and which to throw away, with some suggestions from you.

Sometimes you will not ask the group to take responsibility for the material. You may want to use it to report back to the group. In this situation, keep the charts for a time. Or keep the flip-chart sheets safely until the next meeting. In this case, because they contain valuable material that represents hours of hard work, they must be stored safely and not lost!

The best way to organize charts that will be transcribed or used again is to number the pages as each is finished so they can be put in order later. Put the pages in order with the first page on top and roll them with the written words facing out. When they are hung later, they will not roll up and obscure the writing. Use masking tape to keep the roll together or secure the roll with a rubber band and label it in an upper corner of the top page. Charts can also be folded and put in a briefcase (fold so the words are facing upward). Store the charts where they will not be damaged and where you can find them before the next meeting. Many facilitators have been known to stand a tube of important charts behind a file cabinet, bookshelf, or in a corner somewhere—and forget where. It might be helpful to make a note in your planner as to where the charts are stored to avoid a mad scramble and panic just before the next meeting!

Other Uses for Flip Charts

In addition to recording ideas, plans, and decisions, facilitators use flip charts to enhance and increase the productivity of group sessions. This has been covered thoroughly in *Flip Chart Power: Secrets of the Masters*, by Bonnie E. Burn (1996). Following is a brief review of how to enhance your facilitation with flip charts.

To Welcome Participants

Use a prepared flip chart to greet participants when they come into the meeting room. Placed near the entrance of the room, this greeting gives a positive impression and lets people know they are in the right place.

To Display Objectives and Agenda

Use prepared flip charts to state the objectives of the session and outline the agenda. You may wish to use two flip charts, one for the objectives and one for the agenda. These can be left attached to a flip-chart pad to be referred to when ready or posted in the room before the session. Be sure to draw participants' attention to them during the introductory part of the meeting.

To Give Directions for an Assignment

Use a flip chart to give directions. It is easy for people to forget what to do if there is more than one step to an assignment. Whether you are asking group members to complete something individually or instructing them to do a small-group activity, it helps to have directions written briefly on a flip chart where people can see them.

To Focus Attention

The value of strategic, open-ended questions was emphasized earlier. An excellent nonverbal technique is to write out the open-ended question at the top of a piece of flip-chart paper. (This can be done before or during the session.) This gives people a place to focus and helps them remember the question. When people stray from the subject, direct the group's attention back to the question by referring back to the flip chart. "We've strayed a bit. Let's get back to our original question, which was . . . [read from the chart]."

To Teach or Inform

Use a prepared flip chart to reveal important points in a concept or process you are introducing. These could be points for working together as a team, a procedure you are asking the group to use, or charts, plans, or models the group is using in its work.

To Stay Focused on the Goal

If you are working with an ongoing group, bring a flip chart with the group's stated goals and time frame for the project to the meetings. If the group has a mission statement, it should be available on a flip chart or overhead as well. A skilled facilitator knows when it is a good time to review the mission and goal statements—at the beginning of the meeting or perhaps when the group is bogged down in confusion or disagreement or has reached an impasse. Referring back to the group's original goals and mission statement refocuses the group and provides new insights.

To Use as Group Process Tools

Flip charts are used to implement group processes, such as prioritizing items, categorizing ideas, grouping ideas, making group diagrams and charts, organizing data, filling in information, and so on. Find ways to use flip charts in practical and creative ways to help the group be productive.

To List Items for Future Discussion

Flip charts can serve as a place to hold items that come up that need attention but are not part of the meeting's objectives or agenda. Label a chart with words such as "Parking Lot," "Items for Future Discussion," or

"Holding Tank." When an item comes up that should be dealt with later, it can be recorded on the chart and in the minutes of the meeting. Later, when the agenda for a future meeting is being planned, these items can be incorporated. Ask the group at the end of a session whether it wants to discuss any of the items at the next meeting. Caution the group about tackling too much in one meeting, but this way the items do not go unnoticed.

Organizing and Handling Flip Charts

In a very short time, a group can generate a lot of material. You must organize the material and decide how and when to post the charts. Here are a few suggestions for organizing the material while it is being generated and then while it is being reviewed and evaluated:

- When writing a list of ideas, problems, or possible solutions on a flip chart, separate the ideas so that they can be easily distinguished from one another.

- Use a number, bullet, dash, or other symbol before each idea to set it off from other ideas. Consider using a long dash before each idea in a list so that you have a place to label the item later if the items need to be categorized, prioritized, or voted on.

- Switch pens to alternate colors between ideas. (Use only two colors, as too many color changes can be confusing.)

- Number each page in the bottom right-hand corner before you tear it off and post it. If you anticipate generating several pages of material, number the sheets ahead of time.

- Decide ahead of time where and how you will post the charts. Try to keep them in order on the walls.

- Assign someone to help you post the charts and to make sure they are in order.

- Keep pieces of torn masking tape ready along the edge of a table or the flip-chart easel. This will keep the pace from slowing down while you tear tape and post charts. Consider buying a masking tape dispenser or asking someone to tear off pieces of tape as you need them.

- Check beforehand to see whether there are ways to hang flip charts in the room. Some rooms are equipped with a strip of cork or a metal clip for hanging them. Bring pushpins and practice using the metal clip. Sometimes shorter people must have help posting charts where everyone can see.

- Occasionally windows, drapes, or pictures leave almost no wall space for posting charts. This is especially true in executive-style conference rooms. You may need to use straight pins to attach the charts to the drapes. (Put some in your briefcase for this type of situation.)

- Use pushpins if masking tape will not adhere to the surface.

Using More than One Easel

For some facilitations, it is helpful, or even essential, to have more than one flip-chart easel available. For example, during a brainstorming session, two people can record ideas, each at a different easel, writing down alternate ideas. During small-group work, each group may need an easel or at least a spot on the wall for one or two flip charts. After a group's work is complete, everyone can gather around to review what was written or each group can bring its easel to the front of the room to present its work. Think ahead about what method will work in each situation.

Organizing Voluminous Notes

If the walls are covered with charts and there is still work to be done, you must decide the most efficient way to deal with the charts.

- One way is to tape charts that deal with the same topic on top of one another in order from top to bottom. This can be done during a break. If the group needs to refer to material on any of the charts, hold up the sheets to reveal the needed information.

- Another way, although a bit messier, is to leave the original charts on the wall in order and begin posting new charts just above them when the walls fill up. If necessary, you or group members can still find material that was generated earlier.

- Sometimes the charts are too messy to serve any useful purpose, so you may need to copy key material onto a new chart, with help from group members.

- If a large list of items has been prioritized, and many items failed to make the top priorities, a new chart should be created showing the top-priority items in order. The old charts can be saved, but the new chart will help the group proceed with the next task.

A useful organizational technique is to label the first chart with the topic or question being discussed. When introducing a new topic or question, label a new chart with a new heading. That way when group members are reviewing material, they can easily see which topic was being discussed. When one topic or question generates more than one chart, abbreviate a heading for each additional chart. Another technique is to change colors for different discussions. This might become difficult over the course of a long meeting, as there are only a few dark colors that can be read well.

Ideally the room will be large enough to hold most of the charts needed for a session. For multiple-day meetings with many sheets, have someone transcribe the flip charts before the next session and distribute them as handouts. When a group needs several meetings to work on a task or topic, the flip charts can be saved and used from meeting to meeting or they can be transcribed.

The Art of Charting

Adding a few artistic touches to flip charts enhances a facilitation and may even make it more productive. Facilitators who are not particularly artistic can still be excellent facilitators, of course. Some superb facilitators use only a black marking pen, chart paper without lines, a scribble, and a scrawl that literally sprawl over the chart, but because they are skilled in verbal and nonverbal techniques, their flip charts work! However, groups generally respond positively to color, and everyone, including the facilitator, can become hopelessly lost when flip charts are disorganized, too messy, and poorly posted.

Therefore, some attention to flip-chart art can benefit almost all of us as facilitators. This does not mean that you must spend a great deal of time learning complex coloring techniques or graphic design to be a facilitator. Art for facilitators is basic.

- First, learn to *print* in large letters, clearly and legibly. People who say their handwriting is terrible are often referring to their cursive. Facilitators with beautiful, round, and clear cursive are the exception. It is best to print, as printing is easier to see from a distance. With a little effort, people can print legibly. The main rule is that the writing *must* be legible. Here are a few tips on printing:

  - To write large, use the whole arm, not just the wrist, and make the open spaces of letters fat, not skinny. This makes them easier to read.

  - Use a uniform printing style with letters all slanting in pretty much the same direction.

  - Combine capital letters and lowercase letters. Using all capital letters makes text hard to read, and capital letters usually take longer to write, thus slowing down the progress of the group.

  - Try to keep the size of letters consistently large.

  - To make print larger, turn the marking pen so you are using the widest part of the tip.

- Ask for help from the group if you have trouble spelling a word.

- Use abbreviations and acronyms when possible, being careful not to use too many or to use ones people will not recognize or decipher easily.

- Use color appropriately and sparingly. A minimal and strategic use of color greatly enhances the readability and usability of flip charts.

- When using color to enhance flip charts, remember the following:

  - Use the darkest colors (black, purple, dark blue, brown, and dark green) for the main text.

  - Use the brighter and lighter colors for highlighting or underlining text or to make certain words stand out.

  - Use two or, at most, three colors on a page.

  - When listing ideas, alternate colors between ideas, using a pleasant combination of two darker colors, such as blue and black, green and blue, purple and black, purple and blue, purple and green, brown and green, or blue and green.

  - Use a different color to code items, to tally votes, or to tag items for reference.

Flip-Chart Equipment and Supplies

Facilitators have a wide variety of chart paper, easels, and marking pens to choose from, and each facilitator has his or her own favorite products.

Chart paper comes in a variety of weights, quality, and price. The one-inch, blue-lined, grid paper helps you to write straighter and is useful for drawing charts and models when straight lines are needed. Some chart pads tear easier than others, some bleed through more easily than others, some are a dull newsprint color and others are bright white, and the thickness of the sheets varies considerably. It pays to shop around and find a paper you enjoy working with.

Many easels are on the market in a wide price range. It is well worth it to invest in easy-to-use, sturdy easels that will hold up. The tripod style designed for small chart paper or posters is not suitable for facilitation. These do not have a solid back to support writing; they wobble and can easily be knocked over. Some easels on the market are difficult to fold and have complex methods for inserting the paper pads. The best easels have the following qualities:

- Flat, sturdy backs that allow you to write without the pad bending. (Unfortunately, this does make the easel heavier and more difficult to carry.)

- Legs that fold easily for storage.

- A mechanism at the top that makes it simple for one person to attach a pad of paper. Some have clamps, slides, or pegs for the paper and some have screws to tighten the frame over the chart. It is difficult for one person to hold a chart while placing the screws into the frame.

- A carrying case that zips and has a handle, which makes it possible to transport easel and paper without the paper flapping in the breeze. Again, the easel, chart paper, and carrying case can make a rather bulky and heavy load, but it is better than not having a handle for either the easel or the paper.

- A trough or tray for holding a few marking pens. Some have bins attached to the back to store extra marking pens.

- Pegs for holding rolls of masking tape.

- Telescoping legs that allow the height to be changed are a nice touch, also.

If your organization's budget allows, buy plenty of good-quality easels of the same type. Facilitators in your organization will become accustomed to the same type of easel, and there will be an easel in every meeting room. When there are not enough easels, people are apt to hoard them while someone else has none. Since some easels work noticeably better than others, the "good" ones are always in demand.

Marking pens come in permanent or water-based ink in a variety of colors, sizes, and even aromas. Permanent markers are made of waterproof ink that cannot be washed out. The ink from water-based markers can be washed out of clothes and off from wood, plastic, or glass. By now, most of us have seen scented markers: orange smells like an orange; black, like licorice; red, like cherry; magenta, like raspberry; blue, like blueberry, and so forth. These markers are water-based and therefore safe to use when writing on chart paper posted on walls. Permanent markers will bleed through the paper and can leave marks on the walls! Most permanent markers are no longer made from toxic materials, but may still have an offensive odor and can stain your clothes and make permanent marks on wood, glass, and plastic. Permanent markers do seem to have the advantage of lasting longer and making darker marks. You may find it best to take some of each type and vary their use. It is best to have plenty of markers handy during a facilitation, as they tend to dry out when used a lot.

Some other essential supplies are listed below:

- Masking tape

- Safety pins

- Pushpins

- Rubber bands

- Scissors

- Adhesive tape (for taping papers together, but not for use on walls—it pulls off the paint!)

- Sticky notes

- Notepad and pen

A few typical problems facilitators have with flip charts and suggestions for dealing with them are given in Figure 5.2.

Do not let all of this information about easels, pens, printing, and flip-chart logistics overwhelm you. Recording techniques are fairly easy to

Figure 5.2. Dealing with Flip-Chart Problems

If	Then
• You have trouble finding a flip-chart sheet you want to refer back to.	• Make a tab out of masking tape and label the tab.
• You spend too much time facing the flip chart.	• Stand on the side where you can easily see people over your shoulder, and participants can read the flip chart as you write. • When reading from a chart, don't stand too close to it. Move off to the side or back of the room and your voice will not get lost talking to the chart.
• You trip over the legs of the easel.	• Give yourself plenty of room to move in front of the easels. Use sturdier easels that will not fall over should you bump into them.
• One piece of paper is too small for the activity you are conducting.	• Post two or more pieces of paper side by side on the wall. For timelines and work that requires a wide space, turn two or more pieces sideways and tape them together on the wall.
• You run out of paper toward the end of a meeting.	• Use a sheet of paper you have written on earlier that is not needed at the moment. Turn it over and tape it with masking tape.
• You plan to use permanent markers to prepare flip charts ahead of time, but they bleed through to the next sheet.	• Write on every other sheet or save paper by placing a blank sheet of paper behind the sheet you are preparing. Attach the blank sheet to the easel with masking tape. Use this blank sheet over and over by moving it each time you prepare a new chart.

learn. You will no doubt develop the basics of using flip charts fairly quickly and can add the polish later.

In summary, knowing how to record and use the material a group generates is an essential skill for facilitators. Flip charts are to the group what a notepad is to many professionals: they contain essential material the group needs to do its work and provide a method to use the knowledge productively. To be effective at recording, remember to do the following:

- *Do* record and post people's ideas.

- Record *everyone's* ideas.

- Use a *brief phrase and the speaker's words* to capture what was said.

- *Organize* material on the charts for easy reference.

- Write *clearly* and *large* enough for everyone to see.

- Use the charts as *working papers* for the group (make changes as needed).

- *Save* and transcribe what the group needs; throw away the rest.

As you become comfortable using the flip charts to facilitate and document a group's work, you will undoubtedly acquire your own methods for creating, handling, and organizing them. When you experience the value of using the charts as group memory, you will understand why facilitators cannot go far without good recording skills.

Reading the Group

Skilled facilitators develop the ability to "read" a group and make necessary adjustments to the group process. You always have the option to alter the course of group work if it is in the best interests of the group, and the group's goals, to do so. Adjustments range from simply having the group take a break to using a different group method or actually ending the meeting. In some cases, you will check with the group to see if it agrees with your recommendation. In other cases, you will simply give directions to the group and proceed, changing the planned process. In some cases, you might explain to the group why you are recommending a different process.

Just because a facilitation is not going as planned, however, does not mean that the process must be changed. Sometimes the process must continue despite difficulties. With experience, you will know when to change and when to stick with the plan.

How to Read the Group

Continually watch for signals for how individual group members, or the entire group, are reacting to the facilitation. These signals tell you whether to slow down or speed up the pace of the session, whether to change the process, whether to take a break, or whether to ask the group what is going on.

Some signals are fairly easy to read; others are more difficult to decipher. For example, when a group member is confused, his or her face will show it through a wrinkled forehead, slight frown, or facial strain. ("Manuel, you look confused. Do you have a question about what we are doing?") When group members are tired, bored, or frustrated with the process, they are likely to slump in their chairs, stop paying attention, or withdraw. They may yawn, look at the clock, or begin to put away their notebooks, planners, or other materials. On the other hand, when energy is high and group members are fully involved in what is going on, they may sit forward in their chairs, be attentive, interrupt others, raise their voices, make emphatic gestures, and stay involved.

Read the group to test whether the process is working or whether to make adjustments. There are two ways to make adjustments: (1) Simply tell the group what is going to happen next ("Let's take a break now. You've worked very hard on this task.") or (2) ask the group what it wants to do next ("People seem tired. Are you ready for a break?"). When you are fairly certain you are reading the group correctly, just tell the group what the next step will be. However, if you are not certain, ask the group. This gives people a chance to participate in the process and helps you adjust to meet the needs of the group.

Another reason for reading the group is to ensure that the discussion or process being used is productive and that all group members are aware and involved. A quick question ("Is everyone clear about the process?" or "Is everyone ready to begin?") will help you determine whether everyone understands, but a quick look around the room at people's faces will sometimes give a more accurate answer. Some people will not speak up if they are confused, but will show it on their faces.

When energy dies down during a discussion, a brainstorming session, or an activity, this may be a sign that the group is ready to move on. It may also be a sign that the group has hit a snag or difficulty. An observant facilitator will sense whether it is time to move on or to seek guidance from the group:

- "Are you ready to move on to the next step in the process?"

- "Do you want to work on this some more, or is it time to move on?"

- "Have you completed this task to your satisfaction?"

- "I sense some reluctance to continue. What is going on for the group?"

Some signs that the process is working well are:

- People show signs of being alert, such as good eye contact, leaning forward, making contributions, listening intently, and nodding their heads.

- The group is generating plenty of data fairly quickly.

- People are enthused and energetic.

- The discussion is lively, and most of the contributions add value to what has already been said.

- People contribute solutions, ideas, and exploratory questions.

- Most people are contributing.

- There is periodic humor and laughter.

Some signs that the process is not working well or is dying down, which may indicate that it is time to change the pace, are:

- Fewer and fewer people are participating.

- People are finding excuses to leave the meeting.

- One or two people are dominating the discussion.

- The group becomes quiet during a discussion or task.

- People's energy levels are low, even though they are contributing. They appear to be just going through the motions.

- Group members continually change the subject or go off on tangents, which may indicate that there is more energy to deal with other issues.

- People act silly and spend a lot of time joking. (Although occasional humor and joking are healthy and a good sign.)

A facilitator can be likened to a sailor or the captain of a ship. The facilitation is the journey. A facilitator can prepare the session, assemble the right equipment and supplies, study the maps, bring along special items or tools in case of emergencies, stock up on essentials, and estimate what will happen along the way. But until the journey is undertaken or until the meeting takes place, he or she can only guess at how it will unfold. Not until the group is assembled and the meeting in progress will you know what adaptations, if any, to make. Just as many factors influence a journey—weather, road conditions, the dependability of equipment, quality of supplies, interaction of people involved, distractions along the way, unexpected dangers—so do many factors affect the success of a facilitation. You may face equipment failure, noise, uncomfortable room temperatures, poor location, refreshments that do not show up on time, and other hindrances to success.

Group Dynamics

One of the most common factors leading to the success (or lack of success) of a meeting is "group dynamics," broadly defined as what is going on both as a group and individually between group members. A group is made up of individuals, each of whom brings history, expectations, and personal needs to the group. Each group generates its own history, expectations, and needs. Both individuals and the group are part of a subculture, usually the organization of which they are a part. In addition, each person is part of a deeper culture, his or her background, values, and beliefs. When groups are composed of representatives from more than one organization, additional perspectives must be considered.

The churning waters of group dynamics can be overwhelming to new facilitators. It is impossible to actually observe all of the dimensions, although a sensitive facilitator will "sense" many of them. The expert can observe group behavior, determine which dimension might be affecting it, and then take various steps to alleviate nonproductive behaviors and to encourage more effective behaviors. Sometimes the facilitator acts like a mirror for the group and points out what is happening. New facilitators may find it difficult to read the dynamics of a group at first, but with experience and practice they will find ways to help a group overcome difficulties.

Many factors contribute to group dynamics. The most common are interpersonal dynamics, political dynamics, project dynamics, physical comfort and environment, and personal agendas. Some common dimensions of group behavior are listed below. First familiarize yourself with this list and then practice observing these dimensions in a group.

Interpersonal Dynamics

All groups must deal with the dynamics of interpersonal relationships. Some of the factors that influence interpersonal dynamics include:

- How well members know one another;
- Whether and how much members trust one another;
- Whether there is past history, either good or bad, among individual members—personal or work related;
- How well members communicate with one another;
- Whether individuals feel comfortable and accepted;
- How well members understand and value diversity; and
- Whether group members have completely different and conflicting goals, needs, or attitudes about what is important.

Political Dynamics

Few groups escape the fact that politics (hierarchy, status, roles, and power) play a big part in organizations. Depending on the culture of the organization or the multiple cultures that may be present in cross-functional and cross-organizational groups, politics may stifle the best and most creative work of a group. Be sensitive to political situations that might hinder group work. For example, if no one "important" or at a significant level in the organization is visibly supporting the group's work, this may lead to low morale. Conversely, if someone with considerable organizational clout and power is watching too closely over the group, this may cause group members to hold back. Group members know that their jobs and reputations, even their careers, can be helped or hindered by knowing how to operate within the political confines of the organization and their fields of expertise. Here are some political questions that may arise for group members:

- Who is part of the group?

- Who is not included in the group?

- Who selected the group members?

- What organizational leaders support the group and its work? Why?

- Who does not support the group and its work? Why?

- Is the group tackling a project that is "blessed" by those higher in the organization?

- Is the group tackling a project that, no matter what the outcome, is unpopular with those influential in the organization?

- What is likely to be the fallout of the group's work if it is successful? If it fails?

- What is the past history of similar groups and similar projects?

- Is the organization facing any political change or upheaval that will aid or impair the work of the group?

- What are the attitudes of the group members toward their work and the political climate?

- Is anyone inside or outside the group likely to sabotage the group's work? Why?

Here is an example of a political situation that often affects group dynamics. In the middle of a reorganization or downsizing, teams may be asked to develop into high-performing or self-managed teams. Learning to work as a cohesive and productive group under such conditions can be quite difficult—actually impossible without the support of influential organizational members. Without such support, group members may find the political climate too risky to put forth genuine effort. They may hold back, doing just enough not to appear rebellious, but not risking anything either. They may not trust the organization to follow through and may not trust that the group's work is important enough to carry on during the turmoil the organization is experiencing.

Project Dynamics

How the group members relate to the project or work at hand has an impact on how they work together. If the project appears to have a high degree of relevance to them and to the organization, they are more likely to become fully engaged in the work, giving it their energy and commitment. If, on the other hand, the project seems unimportant to the group members—or to the organization as a whole—group members are less likely to be enthusiastic or to support the work fully. Facilitators and group leaders must help group members envision how their work can make a difference. Addressing the questions below will help determine the importance and relevance of a project:

- What relationship does the group's project or work have to the overall goals of the organization?

- How important and relevant is the group's work to the organization? To the group as a whole?

- Has this work, or something similar, been done before? What was the organizational leaders' attitude then toward the work? Were the prior group's efforts taken seriously? Were the group's ideas implemented? Why or why not?

- Are group members already on overload? Will the work or project suffer because of that?

- Are resources available?

- What specific support is available to the group for this project (money, experts, time, space, additional people)?

Physical Comfort and Environment

The physical comfort of the group and the appropriateness of the environment for the type of work affect group dynamics also. Group members will generally be more involved and alert when they are comfortable and in a productive environment. Some things that can negatively have an impact on group dynamics follow:

- A room that is too hot or too cold;

- Group members who are tired;

- Group members who are hungry;

- Too many or too few refreshments;

- A heavy lunch, after which group members are likely to be drowsy;

- Uncomfortable chairs;

- Noise and distractions;

- Interruptions; and

- Beepers and cell phones going off and people leaving the meeting.

Personal Agendas

A personal agenda is something an individual wants to happen, whether or not it is in the best interests of the group. A personal agenda may center around a need for acceptance or control or an attempt to influence the outcome of the group's work.

Sometimes people will openly admit to their personal agendas, leaving the group with the option to ignore, acknowledge, or try to accommodate them. If personal needs can be addressed without hurting the overall needs and goals of the group, this is ideal—a win-win for everyone. However, for a group to be effective, personal needs and agendas may have to be set aside.

Often, people are unwilling to reveal their personal agendas to the group. Two things may happen as a result: (1) An individual may not have his or her personal needs met and, therefore, may not be satisfied with or supportive of the group, and (2) an individual may try to manipulate the outcome of group decisions to meet personal needs. This may reduce group creativity and halt progress.

Recognize personal agendas by paying attention to the following:

- Group members competing for status, power, and influence within the group, revealing a personal need to lead or control. This may not necessarily hurt the group's progress, as groups need members who can lead. However, if the desire to lead runs counter to what the group needs, it becomes a hindrance.

- Group members distracting the group with pet peeves and side issues. In this case, the personal agenda is to complain and solicit group understanding and support. Sometimes the need is simply to complain and be heard.

- Group members with their minds made up before the group works on the problem, desiring to have their own solution implemented.

- Group members vested in believing that "if it hasn't worked before, it won't work now." The personal agenda here is to prove that what happened in the past still stands.

- People resisting being part of the group. The personal agenda is not to be in attendance. Some behaviors that may indicate such a personal agenda are withdrawing, missing meetings, coming late and leaving early, and verbally stating that one should not be in the group.

- Group members appear to resist being part of the group, but the real need is to be drawn in, to be included, to be assured that they are wanted.

People bring many personal agendas to group work, and you must expect personal needs to surface or exist just below the surface much of the time. Facilitation tools and methods can help to dissipate or accommodate personal agendas. One of the exciting aspects of group work is that personal agendas can be dealt with openly and honestly and handled so that both individual and group "win."

In addition to the factors discussed above, there are other factors that influence the dynamics of any group. People work together in a group on seven different levels, according to Hunter, Bailey, and Taylor (1995a). The ability of a facilitator to distinguish among these different levels develops gradually with practice and experience. The seven levels you may observe in working with groups are listed below and described in more detail on the following pages:

- The physical level;

- The thinking level;

- The emotional level;

- The intuitive level;

- The energy level;

- The ritual or spiritual level; and

- The synergistic level.

The Physical Level

This level takes into consideration the physical needs of the participants. Plan to meet physical needs in advance and check periodically with the group to see if members are comfortable.

The Thinking Level

This level deals with the thoughts participants share with one another. Encourage open dialogue; a safe environment in which to express thoughts, ideas, and concerns; and participation from everyone. Select processes and structure the session so that thoughts are creative, focused, and constructive.

The Emotional Level

This level is concerned with how people are feeling and whether they feel free to express feelings openly. Encourage group members to share their feelings by asking questions that draw them out and by showing empathy. ("How did you feel about that?" "Was that difficult to do?" "I can understand how that might upset you.") Recognize when people are not "owning" their feelings and are blaming others. Encourage people to express their true feelings. ("When that happens, how do you feel?") Allowing people to express feelings as well as thoughts and opinions creates the atmosphere of trust and openness essential for a group to perform well.

The Intuitive Level

This level deals with sensing what is going on for people and involves taking the risk to say what is *not* being said. You may sense that people in the group are not really saying what needs to be said, so bring this up to the group. Group members may choose to remain silent, but you have opened the path for them to speak.

The Energy Level

This level deals with how awake and tuned in the group is. Read the energy level and any shifts in it within the group and make decisions regarding group process.

The Ritual or Spiritual Level

This level deals with tapping into the higher purpose of the group and developing practices that allow and encourage ways to deepen the group's experience. Rituals may be developed to recognize that the group is making a meaningful contribution, both outside and within the group. Instead of focusing solely on tasks, help the group develop a sense of unity and a feeling of inclusion for all members. Include group members in developing ways to acknowledge the higher purpose of the group.

The Synergistic Level

This level deals with the group working collaboratively to reach levels of achievement that can only be reached when individuals work together. Synergy occurs when a group's achievement is greater than those of individuals working separately. A key responsibility you will have as a facilitator is to foster group synergy.

Most groups tend to operate well at the thinking level, but are unaware of other levels. A group that operates only on the thinking level will not bond, which requires a shift to the emotional level. Many work groups are unaware of the necessity to bond as a group if they are to be effective.

Two additional levels in a group are worth mentioning: the social level and the learning level.

The Social Level

This level deals with how group members interact socially with one another. Do members meet informally over lunch or coffee? Are all members included in social gatherings? Are members comfortable with one another in social settings? Provide opportunities for group members to socialize during breaks or at the end of the meeting. This will give them a chance to build trust and develop relationships that make it easier for them to work together.

The Learning Level

This level deals with what the group is learning as a group and as individuals. Most group experiences give members a chance to learn something about teamwork, about the subject matter or issue the group is working on, and about themselves as individuals as well. As a facilitator, you are in the unique position to foster learning by allowing time for the group to reflect on its own progress and experience. Simply ask a question and lead a discussion focused on learning:

- "What have you learned so far about working together as a group?"

- "What have you learned about this subject that will help you in the future?"

- "What has working together on this project taught us?"

Although facilitators are not expected to be aware of all levels at once, it is important to know what they are and that what is going on at different levels may significantly affect the group's productivity and sense of well-being. Help the group at each level, as needed. Take the pulse of the group by occasionally asking yourself how the group is doing on the various levels.

Plan activities and processes that will address various levels over the course of a group's work. In *Teamwork from Start to Finish* (Rees, 1997), ten steps that teams can take to achieve results are outlined. Teams that follow the ten steps will address many of the levels of group work. For example, taking time to evaluate and discuss how the team is functioning helps the team deal with the thinking, emotional, learning, and physical levels of its work. Writing the team charter addresses the synergistic level during the important step of team goal setting. Celebrating team milestones addresses the social and ritual levels.

Reading the group requires keen observation and ongoing analysis. When groups are blocked because of ineffective group dynamics, you must intervene to help the group get back on track.

CHAPTER 7

Facilitating Consensus

The basic facilitation skills presented in earlier chapters—verbal skills, non-verbal skills, recording skills, and reading the group—all come together when facilitating the group decision-making process. Much of a facilitator's work is in moving a group toward consensus.

Understanding Consensus

Consensus is a point of maximum agreement so that action can follow. It represents a win-win solution for both group members and the organization they serve. For a group to implement a decision, the members must support it 100 percent. Whether or not group members are in full agreement, they must agree that the decision is the best possible one in this case and support it whole-heartedly.

Try to help groups create solutions that will meet as many members' criteria and expectations as possible. These are the solutions that group members are likely to support fully. To facilitate a group reaching consensus, first help the group decide if the decision is important enough for the group to pursue consensus. Consensus is highly valued and necessary when buy-in and support are essential for successful implementation and when the quality of the decision is important. For less important decisions, the group may decide to delegate the decision making to a subgroup or an individual. After a group decides to try to achieve consensus, proceed with a process to help the group achieve this goal.

Problems with Consensus

Facilitators must be aware of problems associated with consensus: (1) Achieving consensus takes time, especially for complex decisions and projects, and (2) consensus requires the proper use of rational and structured methods, as well as the resolution of conflict along the way. Because groups face many different types of problems and decisions, you must be equipped with a variety of tools. The facilitator and the group together must carefully engineer a balance between dragging out the process and rushing through it to a hasty solution.

Reaching consensus requires skills on the part of group members as well, and you may be placed in the role of explaining and teaching those skills. Because consensus is essential for much group work to be successful, encourage groups to put forth the effort to reach consensus.

The Flow of Consensus

Skilled facilitators use a process that may be repeated several times during a facilitation or over the course of several group meetings to solve a problem or make a decision. This process has a fairly predictable flow. After a decision goal is identified, the group generates ideas, clarifies them, evaluates them, narrows down the alternatives, and comes to a decision.

For example, a group that is trying to solve a problem may first need to generate a list of what everyone thinks the problem is. The group may make a list of problem statements and then discuss and evaluate the list. At some point the group will narrow down the list to a single problem statement on which to focus its energies. This is the end of "round one" in the decision process. The next round may find the group generating ideas as to the possible causes of the problem, which will then lead to discussion and evaluation, and finally a narrowing down to the main cause or causes of the problem. After the cause(s) of the problem have been identified, the group may then generate a list of possible approaches to take in solving the problem. The group may decide to skip this step and begin generating solutions to the problem, which will then be discussed, evaluated, and narrowed down to one or two solutions to implement. During each stage of the process, you will use basic techniques and checks for consensus as described below.

Generate

State the goal of the exercise. ("Let's start by listing all the ways you can think of to state the problem. Just what is the problem?") Turn to the flip chart, pen in hand, and begin listing people's ideas. To help the group generate ideas, ask clear, open-ended questions; repeat the question, if necessary; and be silent long enough for people to think. It helps to have a blank flip chart and marking pen ready, signaling to the group that you are ready to begin. Write the question on the flip chart to focus the group.

Write down ideas as people volunteer them. If there are silent members, encourage them to contribute by saying things such as, "Do others have any ideas to add?" or "What other ideas are there?" If someone is silent who has experience or expertise that might relate to the issue at hand, say something like, "Karem, you have worked in the order-processing area for quite a while. What do you think is the problem?" If no one in the group comes up with an idea after ten seconds or so, ask if they would like you to give them an example. Then write your example on the flip chart.

Allow individual work. For more thought-provoking questions it may be best to stimulate the generation of ideas by having individuals work silently on their own at first, jotting down their ideas on a piece of paper. (This is sometimes the first step in the brainstorming process, which will be described in more detail in Chapter 8.)

Use small groups. Another method for generating ideas in a large group is to divide the group into subgroups of three or four people each and have each group come up with ideas. Ask each group to read its ideas to the large group, eliminate duplicate ideas, and combine similar ideas. This takes more time, but can be an effective opening activity when the group is facing a difficult task. Because each group will build on its own ideas, there is likely to be a greater variety of ideas this way. When the group begins to wind down, begin closing this activity by asking, "What other ideas are there to add to this list?" Before moving on, check with the group to see if everyone is ready: "We've generated a lot of ideas. Is everyone ready to move on?"

Clarify

Give the group a chance to clarify the meaning of any items on the list. Ask a simple closed question: "Do any ideas on this list need clarifying?" This is not the time to evaluate and discuss any item in detail. Remind people not to start discussing the merits of an idea while still clarifying its meaning. During this discussion ask open-ended and closed-ended questions to make sure everyone in the group understands the meaning of the ideas that were generated. Before going on to the next step, bring the group to consensus by asking, "Does everyone understand the meaning of the ideas listed? Shall we move on to the next step?"

Evaluate

The next step in the consensus process is to discuss and evaluate the merits of the ideas. There are several methods to help groups evaluate ideas and data in an orderly manner. Facilitators are generally more skilled and experienced with these various methods and can suggest one to the group that will work. Some of the methods to evaluate ideas and data are described in detail in Chapter 9. Once again, before moving on to the next step, check with the group: "Are we ready to decide which ideas to keep and which to discard?"

Discard

This step is sometimes combined with the previous step, "Evaluate," as evaluation can include discarding items that do not fit defined criteria or are not seen as important. Groups can use many different methods to discard ideas; some will be covered in Chapter 9.

Decide

Lead the group through the process of eliminating ideas that will not work and narrowing down idea(s) that have the most promise. Many methods exist to help a group come to a decision. Some of these will be covered in Chapter 9. Sometimes the best ideas have to be defined or explored further by discussing them while you jot down main points on a flip chart. If this requires a good deal more work, ask the group, "Do we need to spend more time defining these ideas before we make a decision?"

The tools presented later in this book support this basic consensus decision-making process. These tools help groups generate and organize ideas and evaluate or narrow down a list of ideas. The consensus process—generating, clarifying, evaluating, discarding, and deciding—is the cornerstone of much of what facilitators do. This process is the foundation on which tools are applied. Part 3 of this book presents a variety of tools and methods facilitators can use to help groups reach consensus.

PART 3

Facilitator Methods and Tools

Over the years, various methods and tools have been developed to help groups be productive. Many are familiar to groups and teams because they work well and have been used extensively. A basic set of group methods and tools, which experienced facilitators should have in their "toolkits," is included in Part 3. Most of the tools are visual—logical processes that help groups generate, organize, and evaluate data and ideas. They allow material to be displayed so that an entire group can see and work with the same information at the same time. Some of the tools help groups make decisions; others focus on troubleshooting problems; and others help groups select effective strategies to accomplish goals.

Numerous group processes are used by facilitators today, and only a representative sampling is covered in this book. The processes chosen for inclusion met the following criteria:

- Basic;

- Easy to use;

- Work with a variety of groups;

- Cover common situations;

- Support a variety of problems; and

- Support the typical tasks groups accomplish (set goals, assign roles and responsibilities, brainstorm, make decisions, solve problems, implement plans, and so on).

The methods and tools are organized into two broad categories:

- Tools for Generating and Organizing Material (Chapter 8)

- Tools for Ranking and Evaluating Material (Chapter 9)

Two or more tools are often used in sequence. For example, brainstorming, a creative activity that generates a lot of ideas, must be followed with some method to organize these ideas, such as affinity diagramming. Organizing the ideas in turn leads to discussion and evaluation, which in turn generally leads to selecting and making decisions, for which a decision matrix or a quadrant diagram might be used.

More than one tool may need to be applied for any group task such as setting goals, writing a mission statement, establishing decision criteria, planning, making decisions, improving processes, solving problems, implementing plans, or making recommendations. Facilitators must know the purpose of each tool and how to use it, as well as the task and experience level of the group, before deciding which methods or tools will work best in a given situation. New and experienced facilitators alike can ask themselves questions such as:

- "What is the task facing the group?"

- "What must the group do next to move toward its goal?"

- "What tool(s) will best help the group achieve its task?"

- "Is this tool best for this group? If not, what might work better?"

Using a particular tool works well only if it is appropriate to the task at hand and increases the potential for group productivity. It is important that the tool be used at an appropriate time, that it be used correctly, that group members understand its purpose, and that clear directions be given. Facilitators learn with experience how to allocate adequate time for a particular tool. Using a particular tool is not an end in itself. The reason is to obtain the desired results. The tool is only an aid in the process and, if it does not work with the group or the problem, it should be adapted or another process substituted. When deciding whether to use a particular tool, weigh the desired outcome against the time, resources, and energy required.

In addition to specific tools, a good facilitator uses simple interventions to help lead group meetings and coach groups in their work as a group. Chapter 10 addresses common difficult situations a facilitator may face when facilitating a group, with suggestions on how to intervene. Chapter 11 provides facilitators with suggestions, methods, and tips for resolving conflict in both one-on-one and group situations.

CHAPTER 8

Generating and Organizing Material

When group members are empowered to work together to solve problems, plan projects, make decisions, supervise their own work, and improve work processes, they work with many kinds of material: data, ideas, opinions, and information (both subjective and objective). Much of the time the facilitator helps the group generate material, organize it, explore it, and evaluate it. Just as an individual working on his or her own must seek, find, and lay out material in a way that makes sense, so must the group. Somehow ideas and data need to be generated, recorded, and presented in such a way that everyone can see, understand, and work with the material simultaneously—which increases the likelihood that productive synergy will occur.

In Chapter 5, Recording Techniques, the topic was using flip charts to record the group's output. In addition to basic flip-chart skills and techniques, there are numerous other tools designed to help facilitators and groups come up with the ideas, data, and other material they need to do their work.

In most meetings, or certainly in a series of ongoing group meetings, facilitators use more than one tool. In some instances, no specific tools may be necessary; a skilled facilitator may simply record and post ideas to help the group reach consensus. Most facilitators learn to use both the basic skills to lead discussions and a variety of tools for different group tasks. Variations exist for most of the tools, and they may be called different names by different facilitators. In addition, many facilitators have created their own tools or favorite versions of the standard tools presented here. Experienced groups and teams also have their favorite tools and often suggest using one they think will work for a particular problem. The following tools for generating and organizing data will be described in this chapter:

- Brainstorming

- Structured rounds

- T-charts

- Affinity diagrams

- Fishbone diagrams

- Timelines

- Flow charts

- Matrix diagrams

Brainstorming

What It Is

Brainstorming is a structured process that encourages the generation of a large quantity of ideas in a group setting. All ideas are recorded, and no judgments or evaluations are made. It is perhaps the most popular technique used in groups to expand the thinking process. Brainstorming works on the premise that even crazy and wild ideas should be listed, as they may spark new and practical ideas that would otherwise not have surfaced. Participants in a brainstorming session are encouraged to contribute any ideas, no matter how irrelevant, and to build on one another's ideas.

Why Use It?

The three main reasons to brainstorm are (1) to foster creativity by encouraging people to think beyond the conventional; (2) to record all ideas, then clarify and discuss them later; and (3) to take advantage of synergy that occurs when people think creatively together.

When to Use It

Use brainstorming to look at all aspects of a problem, to list possible solutions or alternatives, to imagine the impact of a decision, and to explore possible goals. Brainstorming helps people think beyond boundaries and stretches their imaginations. Using this technique keeps people from jumping to a decision about an idea without considering it or weighing it against other ideas. It is a good tool to equalize the influence of all members in the group; everyone's ideas are posted and considered, no matter how "off the wall" or politically incorrect in a particular organization.

How to Use It

People often think of brainstorming as any activity that generates ideas, when in fact true brainstorming is a structured process with specific rules. Many brainstorming sessions are not run according to the rules. True brainstorming allows people to submit ideas, but not to evaluate or critique them until later.

To facilitate a brainstorming session, follow these steps:

1. Focus the group on a specific topic and brainstorming goal. State the topic and the goal in clear terms and give an example of the type of ideas you are looking for. Try to avoid broad, sweeping topics that may generate ideas that will not prove useful.

2. Post the topic and brainstorming goal on a flip chart that everyone can see.

3. Post and review the Guidelines for Brainstorming in Figure 8.1.

Figure 8.1. Guidelines for Brainstorming

<u>Guidelines for Brainstorming</u>

1. All ideas are OK. Don't censor your ideas.

2. Aim for quantity, not quality.

3. "Wild" ideas are OK. They may generate usable ideas.

4. Do not discuss or evaluate ideas at this time.

5. It's OK to build on others' ideas.

6. Say "pass" when you run out of ideas.

4. Set a time limit that allows plenty of time for ideas to flow but will not drag. Set the tone for an energetic, lively session to keep people's minds from wandering. A brainstorming session can last five minutes, thirty minutes, or even longer. It might begin by telling participants to bring their ideas to the meeting. It may also continue over several sessions, depending on the size and importance of the issue.

5. Answer any questions the group has before beginning.

6. Give people a few minutes to think quietly and write down their ideas. Set the stage for creativity by encouraging people to record any idea, no matter how wild or irrelevant it may seem. Ask them not to censor their contributions.

7. Write all the ideas on a flip chart for everyone to see, and post the charts when they are filled.

8. Ask people to contribute ideas that are not already on the list and to "piggyback" on ideas when possible.

There are two ways to gather ideas: (1) a "popcorn" approach in which anyone can volunteer an idea at any time; the facilitator must write quickly and make sure all ideas are recorded (this can get a bit difficult to facilitate but keeps the energy and creativity flowing) and (2) a "round-robin" approach in which each person contributes one idea at a time, going in order around the room, "passing" if they have no more ideas to contribute. (It works well to start with a round-robin approach and move to the popcorn method after you have gone around the room once or twice.)

List all ideas as close to the participant's wording as possible. Ask people with lengthy ideas to shorten them. Record all ideas; it can be determined later which ideas are redundant or similar to one another.

Don't use brainstorming when people are tired or at the end of a meeting. Reserve it for when people are fresh and energized. Avoid using brain-storming as the only way to generate material. Overuse of this technique will cause people to devalue it and approach it with less enthusiasm and creativity.

Structured Round

What It Is

A structured round, also known as a "round robin," ensures that everyone has a chance to speak on an issue and that everyone will listen to others without interrupting or immediately responding to the speaker's comments. The technique was developed because of several premises:

- During unstructured discussions, group members are often busy think-ing about their own comments and generally do not listen attentively to what others are saying.

- During most unstructured discussions, a few people do most of the talking and some people never speak.

- People relax and listen better when they know that they will have a turn to speak soon.

- Hearing what everyone has to say will help the group make progress.

Making sure everyone speaks about an issue reinforces the idea that everyone's input and involvement are valuable. This helps equalize the influence of everyone in the room and can be used quickly and informally. It can also be a structured activity, as described below.

Why Use It?

The main purpose of structured rounds is to give each person time to state his or her thoughts without interruption, which helps the whole group develop a position on the issue. This increases the chance that the group will be productive. Second, structured rounds give everyone a chance to speak and be listened to (without judgment) on a topic, which increases teamwork and reinforces the fact that everyone's involvement is needed.

When to Use It

Use a structured round when the group must address a complex issue thoroughly and come to agreement. Use it when an unstructured discussion is not productive, when there is confusion and/or disagreement, when several people are silent, when one or more are dominating the discussion, or when it is time to summarize where everyone is on an issue so the group can move on. It can be used to articulate all the alternatives or solutions people see at that time or to hear everyone's understanding of a particular topic before discussing it further.

Do not use structured rounds to come up with new material. Structured rounds are for more complex situations in which the thoughts each person presents are critical to the group's understanding of an issue.

How to Use It

1. Tell the group the purpose of the structured round and give directions. Clearly state the issue the group will focus on, write it on a flip chart, and post it for all to see. Tell the group that each person will speak in turn, going around the room. All others will remain silent and listen as each person speaks.

2. Decide whether to give a time limit to each person. (If a time limit is set, appoint a timekeeper.)

3. Go from person to person in order around the room. Group members may pass during the round. However, it is a good idea to encourage everyone to speak and to point out the value of hearing from everyone.

4. After the round is finished, invite those who passed to speak. They may speak or choose to pass again.

5. Write down the main points of each person's comments.

6. When the round is finished, summarize the group's comments and indicate points of agreement and/or disagreement. Someone in the group may be asked to summarize. Then ask the group if everyone agrees with the summary.

During a structured round, you may need to remind group members not to interrupt or speak out of turn. Some topics may call for several rounds, so that people can respond to what they have heard others say, elaborate on the issue, and revise their original statements. When several rounds are conducted, begin with a different speaker each time.

T-Chart

What It Is

A T-chart is a simple tool to organize material into two columns. A T-shaped bar is drawn, with room for two headings at the top, and material is sorted into the columns, as in the sample in Figure 8.2. The T-chart can be created while the group is coming up with ideas.

THE FACILITATOR EXCELLENCE HANDBOOK

Figure 8.2. Sample T-Chart

How things are now	How we would like them to be
•	•
•	•
•	•
•	•
•	•
•	•
•	•

Why Use It?

A T-chart helps the group to be more focused and organized about an issue. It helps people think in two dimensions; sometimes without a T-chart, people discuss only one dimension of a plan or idea. T-charts are also useful for comparing and contrasting information and presenting the information in a visually clear way. Another advantage is that T-charts are a quick and convenient way to organize two-dimensional material as people come up with it.

When to Use It

Use a T-chart to compare and contrast information or to show relationships. Use it to help people see the opposite dimension of an issue. A T-chart helps groups:

• To see the pros and cons, advantages and disadvantages, or strengths and weaknesses of a particular approach;

- To identify the issues faced when making a change: one column represents what happens if things stay as they are, the other what happens if a change is made;

- To show changes over time: (1) one column indicating how things were at a point in the past, the other how things are now, or (2) one column showing how things are now, another how people want things to be in the future;

- To compare and contrast two approaches or decisions;

- To delineate the different duties or responsibilities of two people, two groups of people, two functions, and so on;

- To broaden people's thinking by showing them another dimension or the opposite of something, for example, when people are bogged down in the negatives or disadvantages of an idea, ask them to also come up with the positives or advantages as well; and

- To organize and list information by categories: use the left column to show the category and the right column to list supporting details.

How to Use It

1. Explain the reason for using the T-chart: to help make a decision, solve a problem, understand a change, or identify strengths and weaknesses. If necessary, tell the group how making the T-chart will help it achieve the stated objectives for the meeting or how its use supports the group's overall goals. Say what the purpose is: to stimulate further thought and creativity or to develop a comprehensive set of data.

2. Draw the T-chart and its headers on flip-chart paper. If there will be a lot of data, place two easels side by side, one for each column, or

post two flip-chart sheets side by side on the wall. If the material requires more than one page, post completed pages and label each new page. Use bullets to indicate the beginning of each new idea.

3. Ask the group to come up with material that fits in each column. Record each idea in the appropriate column. The group may believe that a particular idea belongs in both columns. If so, place it in both columns and make a note as to why it appears in both. For example, some items may be viewed as both a strength and a weakness.

4. Review the purpose and goal of the activity and determine whether the goal has been reached. Summarize what has been written.

5. Determine any actions that need to be taken.

Variation

A three-column chart can be used to compare and contrast three dimensions to an issue or to compare and contrast several subtopics under a main topic. See Figure 8.3 for a sample.

Affinity Diagram

What It Is

An affinity diagram allows a group to come up with a large amount of material without concern for categories or interrelationships. After ideas have been generated (usually through a brainstorming process), they can be arranged to show which items have affinity (a natural relationship or likeness) to one another. The process allows group members to move the items around and regroup them until the desired relationships and categories are formed.

Figure 8.3. Sample Three-Column T-Chart

	Hierarchies	Teams
Culture	Rigidity Control "Can't Do" Bureaucratic	Flexibility Commitment "Can Do" Situational
Organization Structure	Hierarchical Tall	Teams Flat
Information	To management Filters down Selective Infrequent Prepared, presented	Shared Directly to team Inclusive Frequent On-line
Basic Unit	The individual Single skill, expertise Specific task	The team Multiple skills Whole job
The Work	Specialized Highly defined job Focus on technical expertise	Broad Project-based assignments Blend of technical/team expertise
Manager's Role	Director High control Delegator Sole authority Coordinator	Coach, facilitator Shared control Participant Shared authority Boundary-spanner, resource-finder

Why Use It?

An affinity diagram helps a group organize a lot of information in a short amount of time. It involves the group actively in organizing its own material. An affinity diagram makes it possible to visualize the complexity and relationships of a lot of information. It serves as a stepping stone in deciding how to approach a change, a plan, or a decision.

When to Use It

Use an affinity diagram when there is a lot of information to be categorized, to stimulate creativity in the group, and to involve all group members at once. Use it when facts, thoughts, ideas, and opinions are in chaos and need to be recorded in some useful, organized fashion.

How to Use It

1. Identify the problem to be addressed and state the goal of the activity, for example, "We are faced with making a decision that will affect our entire department's productivity. Our goal for this activity is to identify everything we must consider in relation to this decision."

2. Direct group members to record each idea on a separate 3" x 5" sticky note or index card. If available, distribute medium-tipped marking pens for people to use so that items will be easier to read. Ask each person to record his or her idea briefly and to print as legibly as possible.

3. Collect cards or notes as people brainstorm and place them randomly on a large table or on the wall so they are visible to everyone. Encourage people to continue brainstorming and to build on one another's posted ideas.

4. After all ideas have been recorded and posted, ask the group to gather around the ideas and, *without talking*, begin to group related ideas together. If someone wants to move an idea to a different group, it is all right to do so. *It is important that people do not talk during this step.* If an idea does not fit into any category, instruct people to place it by itself. When an idea seems to belong in two groups, someone should make an extra card.

5. When ideas have been grouped and the energy level of the group slows down, allow the participants to talk. Instruct them to create headings for each grouping that sufficiently capture the meaning.

Write the heading on a card and place it at the top of the group using a different color marking pen or card for the headings. If there are subheadings, instruct the group to create cards for them as well (use a third color) and to organize the ideas below appropriate subheadings.

6. Ask the group to review the completed affinity diagram and comment about it. Make suggestions to the group for using the material, or ask group members what actions need to be taken next. It is important not to rush the process. It may take time to group and regroup the data, and the discussion at the end is valuable and should not be rushed.

Fishbone Diagram

What It Is

This technique allows a group to display visually the causes or contributors to a problem or goal. The fishbone diagram allows material to be easily organized under major headings and subheadings by adding "bones" at appropriate places on a fish-shaped diagram. Originally called the Ishikawa Diagram, after its creator, Kaoru Ishikawa, the purpose was to display cause-and-effect relationships visually. Used in manufacturing environments, standard large categories (represented by the large bones of the fish) were Methods, Machines, People, Materials, Measurement, and Environment. Groups should be encouraged to use or adapt these categories, if appropriate, or to create new categories of their own. See the sample in Figure 8.4.

Why Use It?

The fishbone diagram helps people organize and view material that might otherwise be lost. Being able to see the cause and effect graphically enhances the understanding of a particular issue and encourages groups not

Figure 8.4. Fishbone Diagram

Fishbone Diagram

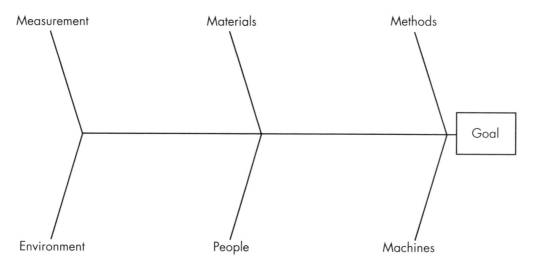

to overlook factors that affect a problem or goal. It allows people to understand more fully an entire operation and identify and acknowledge factors
that may be taken for granted. It becomes valuable data for the group.

When to Use It

Use a fishbone diagram whenever you need to show cause-and-effect
relationships, generally for one of the following two outcomes:

- To identify what is needed to achieve a certain goal or desired
  outcome.

- To identify the possible causes of a problem.

The fishbone diagram can be used to initiate and structure a brainstorming activity or it can be used following a brainstorming activity to organize
the ideas generated. It can also be used following the creation of an affinity diagram. The fishbone diagram becomes a way to further organize and
present the data.

How to Use It

1. Facilitate the group to agree on a problem statement or a desired outcome (goal). Abbreviate the problem statement or goal and write it in the box at the "head" of the fish. Draw a long arrow horizontally toward the box, as in the sample in Figure 8.5.

2. Brainstorm (on a separate sheet of flip-chart paper, if necessary) the major categories of the problem or goal area. There are usually from three to seven. Depending on the nature of the problem or goal, categories differ. To stimulate the group's thinking, list what the traditional Ishikawa categories were: Method, Machines (equipment), People (manpower), Materials, Measurement, and Environment. The group can then decide if these are appropriate or if other categories are more suitable. Write each category in a box (above and below the main horizontal line) and draw lines ("bones") from each category box to the horizontal line, as shown in Figure 8.6.

3. After helping the group identify major categories, encourage people to think about all the possible causes of the problem or about all the factors necessary for achieving the goal. As each cause or factor is identified, determine with the group what category it falls under, and record it on the appropriate line. If there are subcauses or subfactors, they can be written as branches or small "bones" off the appropriate line. Encourage the group to come up with subcauses or subfactors by asking, "Why does this happen?" or "What causes this to happen?" If there are main branches with only a few ideas,

Figure 8.5. Beginning Fishbone Diagram

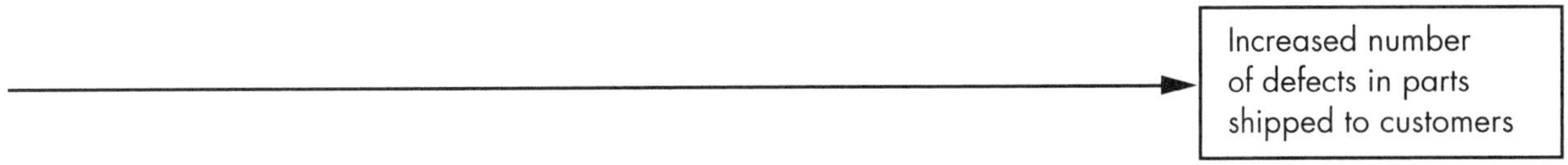

Increased number of defects in parts shipped to customers

Figure 8.6. Sample Categories for Fishbone Diagram

Fishbone Diagram

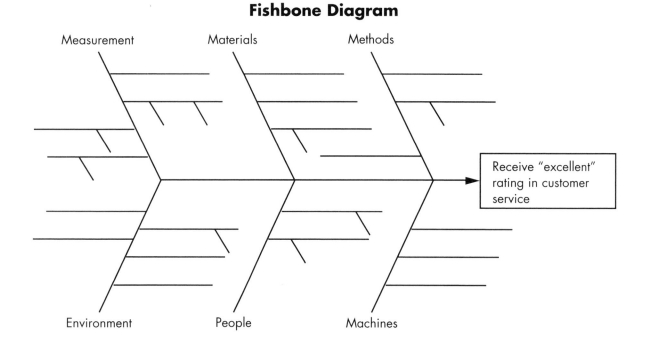

ask the group to consider these categories further. For example, ask, "How are measurements contributing to the problem?" or "How will environment contribute to our success?"

Variation 1

Give people time to brainstorm quietly and to jot down their ideas. Then facilitate a discussion of what the major categories might be. After these have been decided and written on the diagram, give each person a marking pen and have everyone write his or her ideas where they belong. Ask them to read others' ideas for a particular category first and try not to duplicate ideas. When everyone has finished, ask people to read all the contributions to the diagram. Then facilitate a discussion to help the group summarize what they see, fill in categories with only a few ideas, and decide what actions to take next. Generally, a completed fishbone diagram will illustrate which categories or subcategories need attention.

Variation 2

Begin the fishbone diagram during a meeting. Then post it in an area where group members can add to it over a period of time. Bring the filled-in fishbone diagram to the next meeting and facilitate a discussion to help the group summarize what they see and decide what actions to take next.

Variation 3

Rather than focusing on a goal, focus on what the group does *not* want to happen. For example, if the goal is "team success," conduct the activity with "team failure" as the outcome. This will help the group identify potential barriers to team success and cause people to see what must happen if the team is to succeed. A new diagram can be made afterward focusing on team success, using the team failure fishbone to stimulate thinking.

Timeline

What It Is

A timeline represents time as a distance along a line. Relevant information is inserted to indicate what has happened or must happen in the future.

Why Use It?

A timeline is a powerful tool to show either pertinent historical data, factors that lead up to an event, or steps in sequence. Groups can use timelines to understand what has occurred in the past, to predict or plan the future, to record progress, or to understand relationships between events.

When to Use It

Use a historical timeline when the group needs to reflect on the past so that it can plan the future. A historical timeline gives the group a chance to see what everyone remembers about events in the past. Use a future timeline to help a group envision where it needs to go—to plot actions and achievements. The timeline can also be used as a team-building tool to help team members understand one another better. In this case the facilitator uses the timeline to stimulate thinking about how people felt and thought in the past and to share hopes for the future of the team.

How to Use It

1. Have plenty of flip-chart paper and wall space. Tape sheets in a long line on one wall (use more than one wall, if necessary). Draw a horizontal line in the middle of the sheets and add marks to show periods of time (years, months, weeks—whatever is most effective for the work at hand). Each equal period of time should be represented by an equal distance on the line. Write dates along the line.

2. Facilitate the group to fill in the timeline. If you are using a historical timeline, it is helpful to have someone in the organization with accurate historical data fill in the major events ahead of time or bring the data to the meeting for reference. Generally, it works best to reserve either the bottom or the top of the timeline for the historical data, leaving the other portion free for adding qualitative, descriptive material or other details. If using a future timeline, you may need to conduct a brainstorming and organizing activity first to determine what needs to go on the timeline. Then facilitate the group to decide where each item goes on the timeline. You may include both historical and future data on the timeline, in which case you will need to clearly mark the present as a point on the line.

3. Write in the data or ideas as they are generated, or use sticky notes on which people have written ideas. It is especially helpful to use sticky notes when creating a future timeline so that you can make changes easily.

4. To use the timeline for a team-building activity, have each person sign his or her name near the date he or she entered the group, department, or organization—whichever is most appropriate. With team members' help, add organizational changes or milestones. Ask people to add what they thought or felt during some of the changes or events, and then lead a discussion about how the group or the organization has been affected. Such a timeline can be a catalyst for deciding and planning a team's future direction, in which case you can lead activities to help the team envision the future.

5. Save the timeline and perhaps put it on a computer graphic program if it is important to the ongoing work of the group.

Flow Chart

What It Is

A flow chart highlights steps in a procedure or project to show how the project proceeds through time and to illustrate how the tasks relate to one another. Flow charts range from simple to complex.

Why Use It?

A flow chart is an effective way to display the key steps in a process, illustrating how those steps relate to one another. It is a good way to give people common reference points and language for planning or implementation.

When to Use It

Use a flow chart to plan the steps of a process or to improve a process by altering an existing flow. An ideal flow chart can be drawn and then compared with the actual. Many processes lend themselves to flow charting: an office move, a manufacturing process, an administrative process, or a new project from inception to completion. Flow charts are valuable when various groups are involved in the process and when work is handed off from one individual or group to another.

Types of Flow Charts

Top-Down

Different types of flow charts are suitable for different needs. A *top-down* flow chart shows major steps in boxes across the top of a page. Only the essential substeps are listed beneath each box so that the group can identify potential problems or simply understand the process flow. See Figure 8.7 for an example.

Detailed

A *detailed* flow chart shows major steps and also indicates places along the way where decisions must be made, approval received, or answers obtained before moving on. Some processes do not merit the time-consuming work of illustrating steps in this manner, but when detail is important, as when overseeing a complex project from beginning to end, a flow chart such as the one shown in Figure 8.8 is invaluable.

Deployment

A *deployment* flow chart indicates not only the flow of a process but who is responsible for each step. The major steps of a process are listed down the side of a page and the key players (groups or individuals) responsible are listed across the top of the page. As the work flows downward on the page,

Figure 8.7. Sample Top-Down Flow Chart

Process to Train Team Leaders

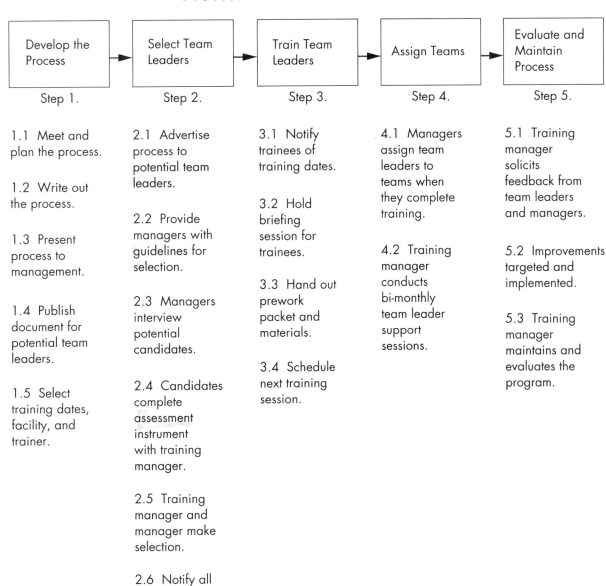

Develop the Process	Select Team Leaders	Train Team Leaders	Assign Teams	Evaluate and Maintain Process
Step 1.	Step 2.	Step 3.	Step 4.	Step 5.

1.1 Meet and plan the process.	2.1 Advertise process to potential team leaders.	3.1 Notify trainees of training dates.	4.1 Managers assign team leaders to teams when they complete training.	5.1 Training manager solicits feedback from team leaders and managers.
1.2 Write out the process.	2.2 Provide managers with guidelines for selection.	3.2 Hold briefing session for trainees.	4.2 Training manager conducts bi-monthly team leader support sessions.	5.2 Improvements targeted and implemented.
1.3 Present process to management.	2.3 Managers interview potential candidates.	3.3 Hand out prework packet and materials.		5.3 Training manager maintains and evaluates the program.
1.4 Publish document for potential team leaders.	2.4 Candidates complete assessment instrument with training manager.	3.4 Schedule next training session.		
1.5 Select training dates, facility, and trainer.	2.5 Training manager and manager make selection.			
	2.6 Notify all candidates of status.			

Figure 8.8. Sample Detailed Flow Chart

Team Leader Selection and Assignment Process

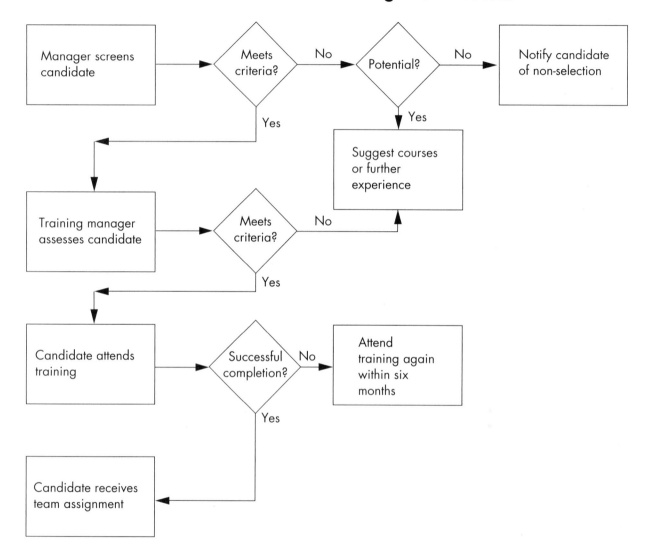

boxes are drawn to indicate who has ultimate responsibility for each step. (See Figure 8.9 for a sample deployment flow chart.)

Work-Flow Diagram

Another type of flow chart is a *work-flow diagram,* which shows the layout of a work area and uses arrows to indicate how a particular work process

Figure 8.9. Sample Deployment Flow Chart

Deployment Flow Chart
Development of New Training Program

Activity	Allen	Sue	Bianca	Chan	Bill
Do needs assessment	●	●			□
Design program	●	□	●		
Create training manual and materials			□		●
Train trainers		●	●		
Schedule and coordinate pilot offering		□		●	
Solicit feedback from participants		●	□		
Revise design of program	●	□	●		
Revise materials			□		●
Coordinate subsequent offerings of program		□		●	

● Major responsibility   □ Secondary responsibility

flows from person to person and area to area. A work-flow diagram can be used to illustrate the movement of materials, paper, people, or information and is useful when a group is confused about a process, needs to improve efficiency, or wants a quick way to explain or teach a process to others. (See the sample in Figure 8.10.)

How to Use It

Because a flow chart is a detailed account of a process, those who actually perform the process should construct it. No one else will know or understand all of the steps involved. Customers, suppliers, supervisors, and other groups can give valuable feedback about the content. It is a good idea to show the flow chart to others between working sessions to obtain their comments and reactions. The basic steps for constructing a flow chart are given below:

1. The first step is to define the process. Write it clearly at the top of the sheet. Decide where the process starts and ends, and make it clear to everyone what the boundaries of the process are.

2. Next, determine the purpose. Will it be used to understand, plan, improve, or teach a process? The purpose will determine whether to represent the way things actually are or the way they should be and will dictate the level of detail needed.

3. Then determine the type to use: a top-down chart, a detailed flow chart, a work-deployment chart, or a work-flow diagram.

4. Brainstorm all the steps in the process. Use sticky notes or 3″ x 5″ cards, one for each step. Help the group decide whether to brainstorm the major steps first and the substeps later, or to brainstorm all the steps that come to mind and sort them into major steps later.

5. Lay out the steps in the format chosen in Step 2. If cards or sticky notes are used, steps can be arranged and rearranged on a table or

Figure 8.10. Sample Work-Flow Diagram

Work Flow for Receiving and Shipping Orders

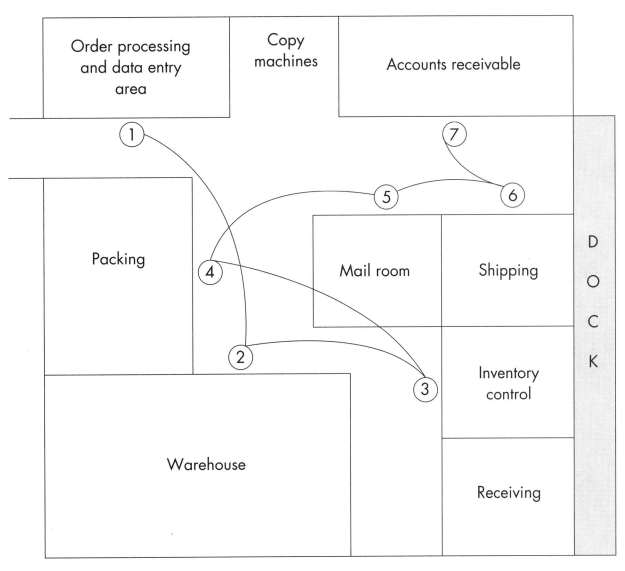

wall. Lead any discussion about where some steps belong and why. Although the group should try to reach consensus on where to put each step, unresolved issues should be noted on a flip chart.

6. If creating a work-deployment chart, add the names and indicate responsibilities *after* the process flow has been determined.

7. As the flow chart is being created, group members will remember steps that were forgotten. Add these to the chart. Stop from time to time and ask the group if all steps have been included. Ask pertinent questions to help the group recall all of the steps: "Does anything else need to happen here?" "What happens between these two steps?" Allow time for reflection between the creation of the flow chart and its publication. Plan a second session to review the chart. If necessary, ask people to gather more information or to think about how the process actually occurs.

8. If the purpose of creating a flow chart is to improve a process, the next step is to stimulate the group's thinking about how the process could be improved. Ask the group to consider the entire process first: "Is the process cumbersome at some points?" "Does it lead to errors or delays?" "Is the process efficient overall?" "Where do we run into difficulties?" "Where does the customer have problems with this process?" This big-picture view of the project will help target critical areas for improvement. Later, less-critical areas can be examined and improved.

9. Make sure everyone can see the entire flow chart all of the time. The best way to develop a flow chart is with several sheets of flip-chart paper laid out on a wall or table. Overhead transparencies and white boards are generally not large enough. After arranging index cards or sticky notes, group members can draw the boxes and arrows right on the flip chart.

Variation

Instead of brainstorming the steps, walk the group through each step until all the substeps are determined. Start with the first step and determine the actions required to carry it out. Build the flow chart as each step is identified. If you anticipate a lot of changes and additions, use sticky notes for each step and move them around as the group proceeds. The actual flow chart can be drawn later.

Matrix Diagram

What It Is

A matrix diagram shows the relationships between one group of items and another. Because information is laid out in columns and rows, the relationship between two pieces of information can readily be found and compared to the other relationships displayed.

Why Use It?

A matrix diagram facilitates the organization and retrieval of several pieces of information at once. It can become a productivity tool for teams and groups because necessary information is quick to find and easy to understand. A matrix diagram can also alert groups to problems or opportunities after they have seen the information displayed graphically.

When to Use It

Use a matrix diagram when one group of items relates to another and people must understand this relationship in order to communicate about or alter it. Common uses of a matrix diagram include charting responsibilities of a group of people, scheduling activities or tasks, and evaluating several options against a set of criteria.

How to Use It

1. Determine what dimensions of information are interrelated.

2. Draw a matrix grid.

3. Fill in the columns and rows with their respective headers, as in Figure 8.11.

4. Decide what symbols will be used to describe the relationship between two pieces of information. Some common symbols are used in Figure 8.11.

5. Fill in the matrix after discussing each relationship item by item.

6. Summarize and/or discuss the information on the matrix and decide what action steps to take.

All of the above methods help groups generate and organize material so that it is visible to everyone and laid out in a format with which the group can work. They help groups quickly brainstorm and organize ideas without getting bogged down in the tedious process of recording them. They can accommodate small or large amounts of data. If group members come up with more ideas as the work proceeds, these techniques allow for their addition. The tools adapt easily to flip-chart paper that can be used at an easel or posted on walls as needed. If desired, participants can be invited to add to the various charts or diagrams during a break or between group meetings. Each of these basic methods for sorting data groups generate is a valuable tool for facilitators.

Figure 8.11. Sample Matrix Diagram

Team Meeting Responsibilities

	Team Facilitator	Team Leader	Team Member	Team Recorder
Coordinate team meetings	○	□	○	
Oversee content of team's work	○	□		
Prepare agenda	△	□		
Bring in facilitator		□		
Attend team meetings	△ as needed	□	□	□
Structure team meetings	□	△		
Ensure balanced participation	□		△	
Provide methods to reach consensus	□			
Notify team of time, date of meetings		□		
Record people's input	□			△ post-meeting
Coordinate and preserve documentation		○		□
Bring supplies to meetings		□	△	
Contribute to discussions		△	□	□
Listen to and draw out teammates		□	□	□
Keep focused on the meeting goal	□	□	□	□
Contribute agenda items		□	□	□
Distribute meeting minutes				□
Contribute professional skills, experience, and knowledge	□	□	□	□

□ = primary responsibility

△ = secondary responsibility

○ = must be informed

CHAPTER 9

Ranking and Evaluating Material

After a group has generated and organized material, it is ready to begin the process of evaluating the material, to decide on the best alternative, focus the issue on a few significant concerns, or rank order items. Several processes can be used to narrow down a long list of options or to make a decision. The following methods will be described in this chapter:

- Multi-voting

- Ranking and prioritizing

- Nominal group technique

- Force-field analysis

- Quadrant diagram

- Decision matrix

Multi-Voting

What It Is

Multi-voting allows a group to select the most important or preferred items from a list with a minimum of discussion. Those items that move to the top of the list can then be explored in depth. Multi-voting is done through a series of votes, with low-ranking items eliminated after each round.

Why Use It?

Many issues are so complex and broad that long lists of items emerge during a brainstorming session. Multi-voting is a quick way to eliminate items and determine those on which group members want to focus.

When to Use It

Multi-voting is used after a brainstorming session or to narrow down any long list.

How to Use It

After a brainstorming session, post all the flip charts for the group to see and follow the process below:

1. Ask the group if any two or more items are so similar that they can be combined. Combine any items the group chooses by using the most representative wording and drawing a line through the duplicates.

2. Clearly number (or letter) all remaining ideas.

3. Decide how many votes each person will have. A good rule of thumb is to allow each person a number of votes equal to one-third of the total items on the list. For example, if there are thirty items on the list, each person has ten votes.

4. Have each group member vote for items by listing the item numbers (or letters) on a piece of paper.

5. Collect the pieces of paper and tally the number of votes for each item, placing the number of votes beside each item on the flip chart.

6. Eliminate the items with the fewest votes. If there is no obvious separation between items, simply eliminate any that fall in the lower third of the ranking.

7. Repeat this step until there is an obvious favorite or until there are a few clear favorites at the top of the list.

8. Stop the voting and have the group discuss the results. If there is one clear favorite, ask the group if and why this represents the best choice. If there are several top choices, determine with the group whether one choice must be selected. If so, ask the group to discuss the pros and cons of each of the top choices and reach a decision by consensus as to which idea is best. If necessary, use one of the other methods described in this chapter to determine the best choice.

Variation

Lead a brief discussion after each vote so that the group thinks about the results. Use questions such as, "What surprises you about the results?" "Does anyone object to items being eliminated? If so, why?" or "Do we need to discuss the top items before we vote again?"

Caution

Multi-voting *does not guarantee consensus*. Lead a discussion following the process to determine whether the group has reached consensus, making sure each member can support the decision 100 percent. Do not use multi-voting when data collection, analysis, and decision criteria are necessary because it does not allow for much (if any) discussion of items prior to voting.

Ranking and Prioritizing

What It Is

Ranking and prioritizing is a way of narrowing down many options to a few that the group believes merit further consideration. Ranking and prioritizing combines discussion with voting to help groups eliminate all but the most worthwhile options. Although this method gives members a chance to "vote" on one or more preferred options, the outcome of the voting does not determine the final decision. After a round of voting is finished, the group discusses the results until it reaches consensus. It differs from multi-voting in that it centers around discussion of the prioritized items after each vote and asks members to select and prioritize their top choices only.

Why Use It?

Ranking and prioritizing is an effective and efficient way to narrow down a list of ideas. After ideas are clarified and discussed, members have a chance to vote for their preferences, which moves the group to the next round of discussion. Without some way to prioritize a list, group members may waste time trying to reach consensus. Ordering the list weeds out enough items to help the group focus.

When to Use It

Use ranking and prioritizing after a brainstormed list has been posted, all ideas are understood, and some discussion has taken place about which items deserve further attention. *Do not begin ranking ideas before group members have had a chance to discuss and defend their ideas.*

How to Use It

Use ranking and prioritizing along with a well-facilitated discussion of the ideas. Encourage discussion by asking questions first to open up the thinking of group members and later to help them zero in on preferred ideas. After adequate time for discussion, move the group into a round of voting, as described below:

1. First, make sure all brainstormed ideas are posted and can be seen and read by everyone. Ask if group members would like clarification on any ideas. If ideas do need clarification, ask the contributor of the idea to explain it further. During this first step, ask group members not to evaluate the ideas but to clarify them.

2. After the ideas are understood by everyone, start a discussion with an open-ended question such as, "Which ideas would you like to discuss further?" The ensuing discussion will highlight both ideas that group members find unsuitable and ideas that appear desirable. Let the discussion continue as long as there is energy and interest or until people begin to cover points that have already been made.

3. Now is a good time for a short break if the discussion has gone on for a while. Mention to group members that they will have a chance to select their preferred options when they return. This gives people time to think about and discuss ideas during the break.

4. Explain the voting method you will use and give group members a few minutes to cast their votes. Here are several ways to gather votes:

   • Give every person ten points and a marking pen. Ask people to distribute ten points among their preferred items, using ten check marks, one per point. If someone wishes to use all ten points on one item, that is allowed.

- Give each person sticky dots in place of check marks to cast votes.

- Have each person select his or her top three (or four or five . . .) items and place one check mark by each.

5. After check marks or dots have been placed, tally the points and note the top-ranked items. The flip charts are often messy at this point, and it generally helps to start a clean sheet of paper with the top-ranked items listed in priority order from the idea with the highest number of votes listed first and so on. Frequently two or more ideas receive the same number of votes, so it helps to write the number of votes received beside each item. Ask the group how many top items they wish to list (usually five to seven is sufficient, unless there are clearly four or fewer that stand out).

6. Before discussing the top-ranked items, it is important to ask people to share reasons for selecting the items they did. Start with the top-ranked item and ask, "Of those who chose this item, what were some of your reasons for selecting it?" After one or two people have spoken, move on to the next ranked item and so on through the list. This helps people clarify and understand how other people viewed the idea and why they selected it.

7. Next, ask if anyone who selected an idea that did not end up on the top-ranked list would like to discuss his or her reasons for selecting it. This gives people a chance to point out the value of ideas that did not make the top-ranked list. If no one volunteers, move on to the next step. If someone speaks in support of an idea, ask the other group members whether they would like to add that idea to the list. Add any agreed-on items to the list.

8. If the top-ranked list is still too long, conduct another round of voting. Allow only one vote per person if the group is trying to select one item. Allow two or three votes if the group wants to determine the top two or three items. Some methods include:

- Ask individuals for their vote(s) so that everyone can hear the votes.

- Use the check mark or dot method as in the first round.

- Use a round-robin approach to give each person a chance to explain why he or she is making the choice.

9. After the second round of votes is tallied, summarize the results and continue to move the group toward consensus. If most people are leaning in a certain direction, ask the group if everyone can support the highest-ranked item(s) 100 percent. Check with those who did not vote for these items to make sure they will support what the rest of the group has selected. Say something like, "Breck and Natalie, if I remember correctly, you voted for a different option. Can you support this selection 100 percent?"

10. If consensus is reached, record the decision and check with the group to see if any further discussion is needed. If someone cannot support the decision, ask what he or she would like to see changed or added. Ask the rest of the group to come up with a way of stating or implementing the decision that will satisfy everyone's needs. Reword the idea or decision and check again for consensus. If this fails, the group is not ready for consensus. Compliment the group on its work so far, highlight where the disagreement seems to be, and ask the group if it is willing to work at the next meeting to reach a consensus.

Nominal Group Technique

What It Is

Nominal group technique is a process for generating and prioritizing ideas, concerns, and tasks. It includes both the brainstorming of ideas and procedures to rank them.

Why Use It?

The nominal group technique provides structure so that everyone has an equal opportunity to contribute and to influence the outcome of a decision. It allows members to remain anonymous during the voting process. Members are given time to brainstorm individual lists and to select their own preferred items. Using this technique reduces the time it takes to reach consensus by discussion. It is versatile and can be used in several phases of problem solving or decision making.

When to Use It

Use the nominal group technique when a lot of information must be recorded and prioritized or when there are a number of alternatives, ideas, or problems from which to select. It is especially effective in group meetings, but can also be used in a series of one-on-one meetings at which each person's input is received and taken into account. Because it is more structured than a discussion and allows less time for interactions, it is a good tool to use when group members do not know one another or when some group members might not otherwise speak up. It is particularly helpful at the beginning of a problem-solving session to identify important issues. Some other applications follow:

- Developing a problem statement;

- Generating possible causes of a problem;

- Selecting key areas for attention; or

- Evaluating any list of brainstormed ideas.

How to Use It[1]

1. Determine the topic and write it where everyone can see it. The topic can be stated in the form of a question or problem state-

---

[1]Note: The first three steps are a simple brainstorming process.

ment. *Examples*: (a) How to respond more quickly to customer requests? or (b) What goals must we achieve in the coming year?

2. Ask each group member to write down as many ideas as possible, working independently without talking to others.

3. When people have finished brainstorming individually, go from person to person, asking each group member to volunteer one idea from his or her list.

   - Record all ideas on flip charts without concern about redundant ideas.

   - Encourage people to add new ideas to their lists as they think of them.

   - Keep the round-robin process going, allowing members to pass when they have no more ideas.

   - Continue until all ideas are on the flip chart.

   - Give each idea a letter of the alphabet for ease of reference later. If there are more than twenty-six items, continue with AA, BB, CC, etc.

4. Discuss the list to make sure that everyone understands all the items. Ask everyone to look over the list and ask for clarification if needed, rather than reading each idea and asking for understanding; this usually takes too long and slows down the momentum of the group. Allow people to add new ideas as they think of them. Be sure to identify each of the new items with a letter also. If someone suggests combining or categorizing ideas, explain that the purpose is to prioritize ideas, which will not be possible if they have been put into categories. However, if two people agree that their ideas are identical, combine the two ideas into one. Make sure the wording represents the full meaning of both statements.

5. Give each group member a stack of 3″ x 5″ cards. Determine the number of cards as follows: if there are fewer than twenty brainstormed ideas, give group members four cards each to select and rank the top four items. If the list has from twenty to thirty-five items, use six cards and have members select and rank six items. Use eight cards for thirty-six to forty items; use ten cards for forty-one to fifty items. If there are more than fifty items, see if any group members want to eliminate less-significant items they have contributed. (No one is allowed to remove someone else's item from the list.)

6. Ask each person to select the most important items in the context of issues or problems facing the group. Tell people to write one item per card, along with its letter identifier. Next, ask each person to rank the choices by assigning points to each card as follows: if using four cards, assign four points to the most important item, three points to the second most important, and so on; if using six cards, assign six points to the most important item, five points to the second most preferred item, and so on. Instruct group members to write the points they assign to each item in the upper right-hand corner of the card. Show an example (see Figure 9.1) of one or two completed cards on a flip chart. Collect the cards when everyone has finished.

7. Tally the cards while the group takes a break. A quick way to do this is to sort the cards according to the items (using the letters assigned) and add up the points each item received. Post the rank order on a flip chart with the item receiving the most points first and so on. Include the top four to twelve items—more if it better represents the results.

8. Lead a discussion of the results. Make sure that group members understand the reasons why the items were selected as high priority. Ask if there is an item that did not make the top list, one that merits further discussion and consideration. Allow time for the group to briefly discuss these items.

Figure 9.1. Sample Card Ranking

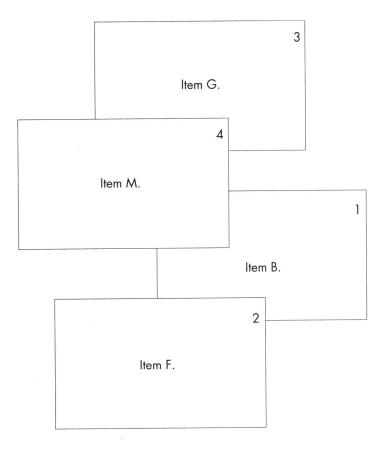

9. On the basis of the discussion and the first tally, members are allowed to change their first selections. Give each member a new stack of cards, the same number you handed out previously. Ask each person to refer to the original list, select the items he or she now considers the most important, and write each item and its letter on a 3" x 5" card.

10. This time instruct each person to assign a value of 100 to his or her highest ranked item and then give a value from 1 to 99 for each remaining item to indicate its relative importance to him or her. Tell people to write the value in the upper right-hand corner of each

card and not to use any number more than once. Give an example such as that shown in Figure 9.2.

11. Tally the new rankings and record the new prioritized list on a flip chart, with the highest ranked item on top and so on. Show the numerical results of the second round.

12. Lead a discussion about the results: "What does this final list indicate?" "Based on the results, how should we proceed?" "What might have happened if we had not used this technique?"

Figure 9.2. Sample Point Distribution

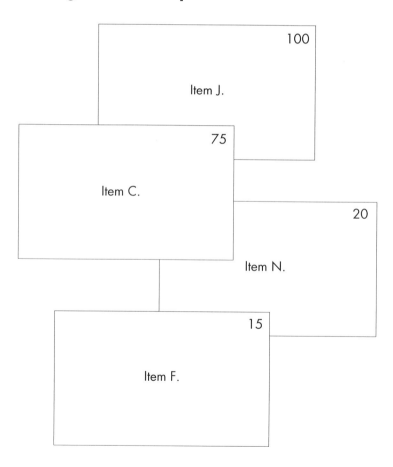

The group must now determine whether further discussion is necessary. Facilitate the discussion until you are reasonably certain the group has reached consensus. Ask the group to set a time to determine specific action steps to carry out the decision or to proceed with the next steps.

Some disadvantages of using the nominal group technique include:

- It requires thorough knowledge of the steps and an ability to give clear directions and tally votes properly.

- It takes time to tally the scores.

- When pressed for time, there is a tendency for facilitators (and group members) to slight the discussion time and rely too heavily on voting.

The nominal group technique is not simply a voting process, but also a structured, narrowing down process to allow for discussion of the most important items.

Force-Field Analysis

What It Is

Force-field analysis is a visual representation of the positive and negative forces at work when moving toward a goal. In any effort to reach a goal or to implement change, there are enabling and opposing forces. To reach the goal, the enabling forces must be strengthened and the opposing forces diminished. Looking at problems and goals in this way helps people bring about desired change. Force-field analysis is a complete process that can take a group from beginning to end in identifying and solving problems, or in reaching goals.

Why Use It?

People tend to overlook the forces that may affect success and rush into the planning phase before considering the environment or "field" in which they will be working. Force-field analysis highlights both the assets and liabilities people have for reaching a goal and helps them make realistic plans. It also can highlight why progress is not being made.

When to Use It

Force-field analysis can be used in the following situations and is especially helpful when issues seem complex and deeply rooted:

- When planning a solution;

- When launching a project or a team effort;

- When identifying the causes of a problem; or

- When identifying problems in a particular process.

How to Use It

Explain to the group that force-field analysis is a way to identify a strategy for success. The five major steps in the process are as follows:

1. Describe the current situation—the status quo, the way things are today.

2. Define the desired situation—the objective(s) the group would like to accomplish.

3. Brainstorm the driving and restraining forces in relation to the desired objective(s).

4. Develop a strategy for a solution by determining which of the driving forces to strengthen and which of the restraining forces to weaken.

5. Check the strategy to see whether it will move the group toward its goal.

Here is how to facilitate a group through the five steps above:

1. Ask the group to define the problem or the status quo—the way things are today. Ask the following questions: "What is the situation today?" "What problem exists?" "What contributes to the problem?" Record responses on a flip chart and post them.

2. Next, ask the group to read over the responses and to come up with a definition of the problem. Write the group's definition and post it beside their previous responses.

3. Ask the group to think about what the situation would be like if the problem were solved: "If we overcame the problem, what would be the desired situation?" "Can the desired situation, the objective, be acted on? Can it be measured?" "Are there any time constraints?" Note what is said along with the description of the desired situation. Post the description of the desired situation.

4. Now ask the group to brainstorm all the forces it can think of that will help it achieve its objective(s): "What forces can you think of that are likely to help us reach our objective?" Label a flip-chart page "Status Quo" and then draw a line down the middle of the sheet.

5. Ask the group for the "driving" forces, list them on the left-hand side of the sheet, and label them "Driving Forces." Record all ideas and do not discuss or evaluate them.

6. Next ask the group to brainstorm all the forces it can think of that might keep it from achieving its objective(s). List these on the right-hand side of the same flip-chart sheet and label them "Restraining Forces." Figure 9.3 provides an example. If the lists are long, use more than one flip chart.

7. Draw a dotted line representing the desired situation and label it "Objective." Include a phrase briefly describing the group's objective, if desired. (See the example in Figure 9.4.) Explain to the group that you have drawn a "field" representing the desired objective and the possible enabling and hindering forces that might affect success.

Figure 9.3. Sample Force-Field Diagram

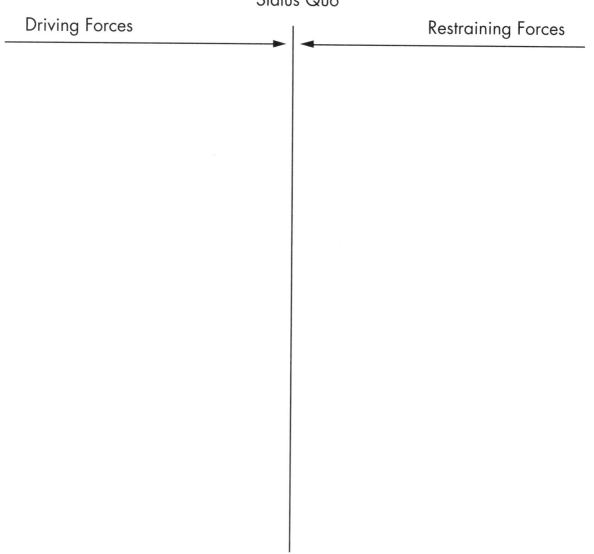

Figure 9.4. Sample Force-Field Analysis

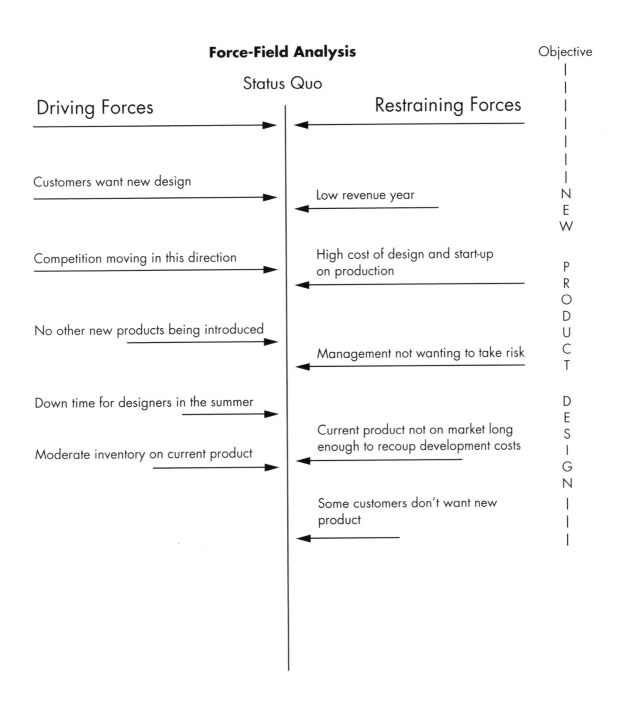

8. After the brainstorming process, give the group a chance to ask questions about the meaning of any of the items. Add more ideas if they come up. Post the force-field diagram where everyone can see it.

9. *Optional step.* Use ranking and prioritizing (see pages 154–157 in this chapter) to help the group identify which forces are more powerful than others and thus have the biggest impact on the group's achieving (or not achieving) its objectives. Precede this with a discussion. Tally the votes and indicate the importance of items by placing the number of votes received beside each one. An alternate method is to show the relative importance of each by varying the length of the arrows, the longer arrows representing the more powerful forces, the shorter arrows the less powerful forces. (See Figure 9.4.)

10. Tell the group that there are three types of forces generated: (A) forces that can be controlled by the group, (B) forces that the group can influence but not completely control, and (C) forces over which the group has no control. Lead a discussion to help the group identify these. List each on a flip chart.

11. Look at the list of A items—those driving and restraining forces the group can realistically do something about. Decide which driving forces the group will attempt to strengthen and which restraining forces the group will attempt to weaken. If the group completed Step 9 above, encourage people to put considerable effort into those issues that can make the biggest impact on its success.

12. Assign subgroups and/or individuals to suggest actions to accomplish these strategies. Have subgroups report back to the large group and assign action items.

13. *Optional step.* The group members may wish to discuss ways to influence the B forces they have listed. This can be a beneficial discussion and may also lead to action items for the group.

Quadrant Diagram

What It Is

A quadrant diagram is a method to determine which solution best meets two goals at once, such as low cost and high benefit. Ideas are discussed and placed on a quadrant in relation to how they rank in relation to two factors. Quadrant diagrams help groups see how a particular solution may be desirable in one way and undesirable in another. Solutions that have the most potential are those that fall in the most desirable cell (for example, low cost/high benefit).

Why Use It?

Use a quadrant diagram to compare alternatives to one another while graphically portraying how each rates on two dimensions.

When to Use It

Use a quadrant diagram to compare potential solutions to one another in relation to key factors. Some common key factors are listed below:

- Cost/benefit

- Effective/achievable

- Impact/effort

- Cost/time needed (to implement)

How to Use It

Discuss the issues involved in selecting a solution to the problem. Decide which two factors to evaluate and draw a four-quadrant diagram. Label the quadrants, like the example in Figure 9.5. After drawing and labeling the quadrant, follow these steps:

1. Brainstorm criteria the group will use in its evaluation. For example, if the group is using an effective/achievable matrix, define what is meant by "effective." Ask, "What aspects of effectiveness are the most important?" Define "achievable" also: "Just what do we mean by 'achievable'?" "What are we looking for?" Post the results of the discussion for the group to see during the next steps.

2. For each potential solution, ask the group to consider where it falls in the quadrant. For the example above, ask the group: "How effective is this potential solution? Where does it fit on the effectiveness continuum?" Next ask, "How achievable is this potential solution? Where does it fit on the achievable continuum?" When the group

Figure 9.5. Sample Quadrant Diagram

Sample Quadrant Diagram

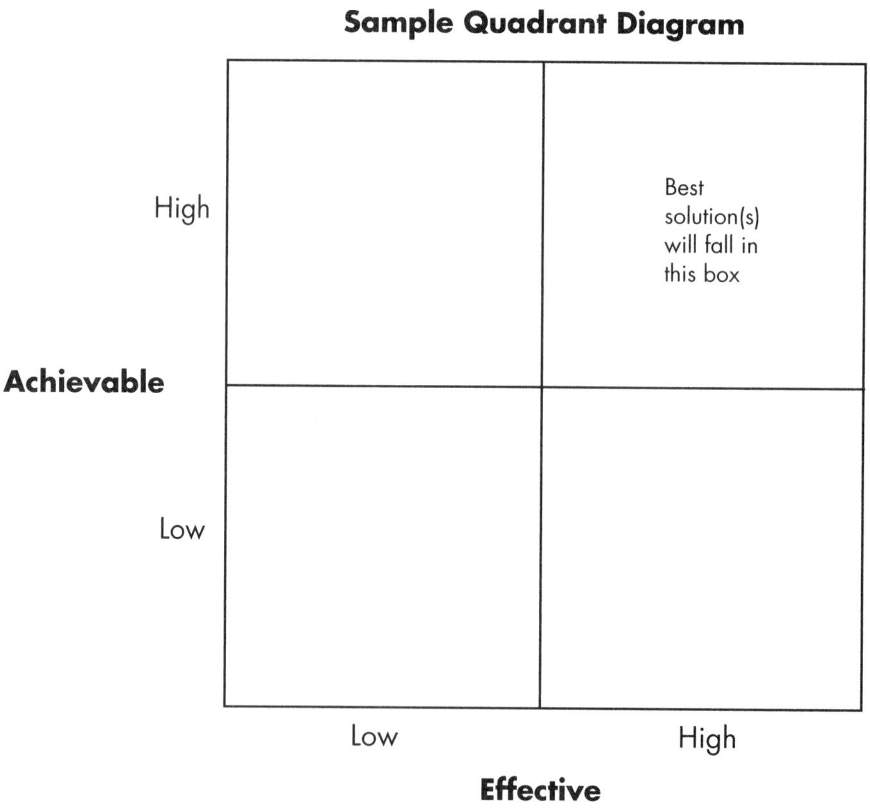

determines where the potential solution should go, place a symbol in the appropriate quadrant. If the group wishes to refine further, place the symbol to the far right or left of the box or higher or lower in the box, to represent the group's evaluation of that idea.

3. Continue evaluating each potential solution in this manner, showing where each fits in the quadrant.

After all potential solutions have been evaluated, those that fall in the most desirable quadrant represent the best alternatives.

Figure 9.6. Sample Labeled Quadrants

Sample Quadrant Diagram

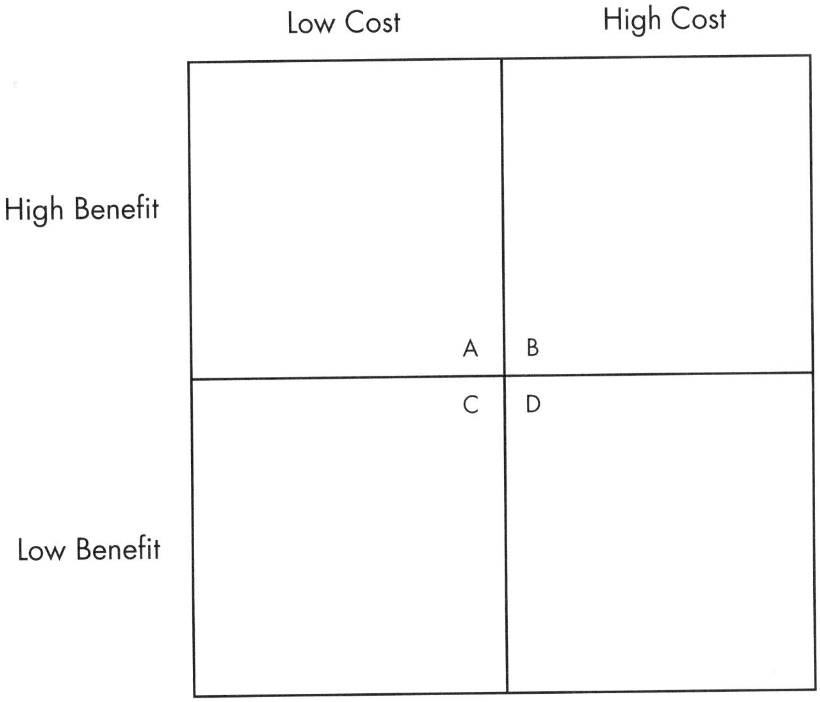

A = Best Solution
B = Costly Solution
C = Undesirable Solution
D = Worst Solution

In the example in Figure 9.6 the quadrants A, B, C, and D have been la-
beled to clarify which represents the most desirable solution and to label
their priority. (Note that this example is set up differently from the one in
Figure 9.5.)

Decision Matrix

What It Is

A decision matrix is used to evaluate possible solutions against a predetermined set of criteria. The criteria are listed down the left side of the matrix
and the potential solutions listed across the top. A decision matrix allows a
group to consider all solutions against the same set of criteria and to
record evaluations in one place.

Why Use It?

A decision matrix forces a group to determine the criteria it will use to
judge a list of options and to evaluate each option against those criteria.
The process is particularly useful when there are many criteria or standards
that a solution must meet. It helps the group keep track of how each solution was ranked against the criteria. The decision matrix does not necessarily represent the group's final decision, but it helps the group reach a point
at which it can make a high quality, informed decision. The process of
working through a decision matrix forces the discipline of gathering more
information and asking more questions about each alternative, if necessary. The process causes people to see options from several perspectives
and removes preconceived notions about what the solution should be.

When to Use It

Use a decision matrix for important decisions that must meet many criteria and for which multiple solutions are available. A decision matrix
would work well in the following situations:

- A group is deciding on software that all members will be using and that will affect the productivity of the group. Several packages are on the market.

- A group is deciding on which vendor to use for a line of products essential for success. Several vendors are bidding for the business.

- A team is selecting one or two new team members from a list of applicants.

- A small catering company is deciding what make of vehicle to purchase for its deliveries.

- A department wishes to publicize its services and must select the most effective method from many.

How to Use It

Lead the group in setting criteria against which to evaluate each choice. Divide the criteria into two categories: (1) *must have* and (2) *desirable*. Agree that any alternative that fails to meet a must-have criterion will be discarded. All remaining alternatives (those that meet all of the must-have criteria) will be compared according to how well they meet the desirable criteria. Here is how to facilitate the process:

1. First ask the group to brainstorm a list of characteristics of an ideal solution or choice. Record these on a flip chart.

2. For each criterion listed, ask the group to determine whether it is a characteristic the solution *must have* or whether it is simply *desirable*. Label each characteristic: M (must have) or D (desirable).

3. Ask the group to weight each desirable criterion according to its importance. Use a scale of 1 to 5 (or 1 to 10), with the highest number signifying the highest importance. Each desirable criterion will then have a number that indicates how important it is to the final decision.

Figure 9.7. Sample Decision Matrix

Sample Decision Matrix
Selecting a Team Member

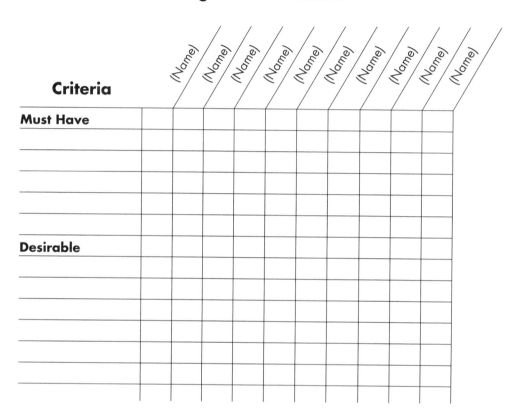

4. Draw a decision matrix on the flip chart like the one shown in Figure 9.7. List the must-have criteria first down the left side, followed by the desirable criteria. List the alternatives (or a symbol or an abbreviation that represents each alternative) across the top.

5. Ask the group to rate each alternative as to whether it meets the must-have criteria. Do not consider the desirable criteria at this point. Eliminate any alternatives that do not meet *all of the must-have criteria*.

6. For the remaining alternatives, determine to what extent each meets the desirable criteria, using a scale from 1 to 5, with 5 signifying that the alternative meets the criterion very well and 1 signifying that the alternative meets the criterion only to a minimum extent. Multiply the number that represents the importance of that criterion by the number signifying the extent to which the alternative meets that criterion. Write both numbers and show the score (e.g., 3 × 5 = 15) in the corresponding box. Continue until all remaining alternatives have been evaluated. The result should resemble the sample in Figure 9.8.

7. After each alternative has been considered in relation to all the desirable criteria and given a score, determine the total score for each alternative and write it at the bottom of the matrix in a "Total" row. The alternative with the highest score best meets the established criteria. (*Note:* The alternative with the highest score is not necessarily the final decision. However, this is a rational approach for weighing one alternative against another.)

8. The next step is to look at the highest scoring alternative and determine whether this really does seem to be the best decision. Ask the group: "Were any criteria overlooked?" "What intuitive response do each of you have about the results?" "Does this seem like the right decision? Why or why not?"

There are some disadvantages to a decision matrix. It focuses on a rational process and requires criteria that can be measured. It does not take into consideration group members' feelings and intuition about decisions, nor does it allow for the addition of new alternatives after the rating process has begun. Sometimes a better solution is to combine two or more alternatives or to seek another alternative altogether. The danger comes from locking in the alternatives too soon. The process works best when the alternatives have been well-researched and subjected to creative "tinkering."

You can overcome these disadvantages by asking the group to include qualitative or intuitive criteria as well as rational, measurable criteria. For

Figure 9.8. Sample Completed Decision Matrix

Selecting a Training Program

Criteria			Option A	Option B	Option C	Option D
Must Have						
Cost less than $400/person			yes	yes	no	yes
Design work complete			yes	yes	yes	yes
Can use internal trainers			yes	yes	no	yes
Skill-based			yes	yes	yes	yes
Proven track record			no	yes	yes	yes
	Weight*					
Desirable	1–5	Weight**	1–5			
Easy-to-use materials	4			4 x 3 = 12		4 x 2 = 8
Vendor furnishes updates	5			5 x 4 = 20		5 x 1 = 5
Half-day sessions possible	3			3 x 2 = 6		3 x 5 = 15
Uses interactive methods	5			5 x 3 = 15		5 x 5 = 25
Videotaping of participants	2			2 x 0 = 0		2 x 1 = 2
Real-world applications in exercises	3			3 x 5 = 15		3 x 3 = 9
12 people max per class	3			3 x 5 = 15		3 x 1 = 3
Total Score:			veto	83	veto	67

Best
option

* Weight each desirable: On a scale from
1–5, how important is this desirable?
5 = very important; 1 = slightly important.

** Weight how well each option meets the
desirable criteria: On a scale of 1–5, how
well does the option meet the criteria?
5 = very well; 1 = slightly well.

example, one criterion might be "group enthusiasm" for the alternative. You can tell the group that it will have the opportunity to combine or alter the alternatives later.

Another way to facilitate a decision matrix, especially if there are many alternatives and a long list of criteria, is to have subgroups work on each alternative and give scores for that alternative to the large group. If you use this process, allow the large group to change the score if necessary to best represent the entire group's opinion. This is a good method if the process of evaluation will require data gathering, phone calls, and other research outside of the meeting. A subgroup can bring the data back to the large group.

Sometimes, as alternatives are being evaluated, a new criterion is suggested. Ask the group if it wishes to add this criterion to the list. If yes, add it and evaluate each alternative against the new criterion.

The above methods are designed to help groups come to consensus through an orderly process of ranking, prioritizing, eliminating, and/or evaluating. They foster thorough evaluation of ideas and help groups resolve conflict as part of the consensus process. They can be adapted to a variety of problems and decisions, simple or complex.

This information becomes the focusing point for the group. Should group members come up with more information as the evaluative work proceeds, the techniques allow for the ongoing addition of that information. Like the tools in the previous chapter, these tools adapt easily to flip-chart paper, which can be used at an easel or posted on walls. Small groups can gather around the charts to carry on a discussion and to alter or move information around as needed.

The methods presented in this chapter are invaluable to facilitators. Without them groups have trouble dealing with large amounts of material, exploring and narrowing down options, resolving conflict, and reaching satisfactory consensus. Use these effective tools whenever possible to make your work easier as a facilitator, to increase your skill level in using them, and—most important—to increase group productivity.

CHAPTER

Facilitating Difficult Situations

There are a number of difficult situations a facilitator may face, and it is worthwhile to note some and discuss how to deal with them. First, *it is important to follow the basic guidelines in other chapters of this book to prevent as many problems from occurring as possible.* Despite careful planning and experience at facilitation, difficulties may still arise. Some must be dealt with on the spot in a meeting; others can be dealt with over time. With experience, facilitators will learn to anticipate and circumvent some of these situations, and become more skilled at deciding when and how to intervene.

Difficult situations can arise in relation to one or more of the following:

- Meetings

- Group dynamics

- Environment

- Leadership and management

- Resources

A good facilitator makes an effort to assess these areas before taking on the job of facilitating a group or a group meeting. An effective facilitator observes, questions, and takes into account what is going on that might affect the group or organization concerned. Plans and contingency plans can then be made to take this information into account.

Meetings

There are many things that can cause difficulties for a facilitator and group members during a meeting. Most of these can be handled or avoided by using good facilitator techniques, as described in previous chapters. Below are a few common difficulties facilitators face during meetings, with some suggestions for dealing with them.

Not enough of the right people are present at the meeting to accomplish the meeting objectives. Ask the group to decide whether it is worthwhile to proceed. If so, have the group members determine how those not present will be linked into the work of the group. If necessary, disband the meeting and reschedule it. Work out a plan with the group to ensure adequate attendance at the rescheduled meeting.

People arrive late or leave early. Don't let late arrivals hold up the meeting. If it is not possible to bring them up-to-date with one or two sentences of explanation, ask someone in the group to take the latecomer aside and bring him or her up-to-date on the progress of the meeting. Stress at the beginning of the meeting how important it is for attendees to stay to the end, when important decisions and plans are often finalized. Ask ahead of time whether anyone must leave early. If so, ask for a volunteer to contact that person after the meeting with an update. When group meetings are focused on key issues, plans, and decisions and when decisions made at group meetings are implemented, people will be more motivated to be present on a regular basis.

There is little interest in the objectives at hand, and more energy seems to be focused on other topics. Sometimes planned meeting objectives are superceded by other pressing needs or concerns of the group. Be aware of low energy in the group, lack of attention to the topic at hand, or continual side-tracking onto other topics. Try to pull the group back to the stated objective. If this doesn't work, it is all right to stop the meeting and relate your observations to the group. Say something like, "There seems to be more interest and concern for topics other than the one we are trying to address today. For the sake of productivity, does everyone want to table the planned objective and set a new one?" If the group agrees, the next step is to re-create the objective on the spot, get the group's buy-in to proceed, and move on. This type of adapting should not become the norm of the group, however. It is important to get the group's help early on in setting the most pressing meeting objectives.

Group discussions are hindered by poor meeting behaviors. Some examples of poor meeting behaviors are people taking calls on their cell phones, people coming and going during the meeting, side conversations that disturb the meeting, people using their computers during the meeting, and so forth. As a facilitator, it is important to state meeting norms up front, or have the group do so. If people then stray from these norms, it is the facilitator's job to bring them back. Say something like, "I'm observing some distractions that are hurting the progress of the meeting. The norms we set for the meeting are . . . [review the relevant norms]. Can we agree that we need to follow these guidelines for the remainder of the meeting?"

Lack of balanced participation. When some people are silent most of the time, or when one or a few people do most of the talking, the meeting participation is imbalanced. The facilitator has many tools to address imbalance and achieve fuller participation. Use eye contact and body language to draw in everyone. Occasionally call on someone, especially if you know they have expertise or opinions on the matter. From time to time, use the structured round (or "round robin") technique described on page 125 in Chapter 8 to hear briefly from everyone on a particular topic. Design subgroup work that gives everyone a chance to participate. Use facilitator methods and tools such as nominal group technique and affinity diagram, which are designed to elicit inputs from everyone. If most of the participation is coming from one area or side of the room, you can say, "I'd like to hear from this other side of the room," or, "Let's hear what this group over here has to say."

If someone is *dominating* the conversation, it is the role of the facilitator to find ways to draw out everyone's ideas. You can thank the person for his or her comments and note that they have been recorded; then look around the room and ask, "What ideas do some of the rest of you have in relation to this topic?" Or, "That's an interesting point; are there others who would like to comment?" Sometimes a person poses a problem because he or she *rambles,* strays from the subject, uses far-fetched analogies, or gets lost without reaching the point. When a rambler stops for breath, refocus attention by briefly restating the relevant points he or she has made, thank the person for his or her comments, while also indicating, "Let's return to our main subject."

A different problem occurs when someone just will *not talk.* Try to determine what is motivating the person (such as boredom, indifference, timidity, feelings of superiority or insecurity, or cultural taboos against interrupting others or speaking out). Seek suitable ways to involve the person. For example, respond positively to that person's comments during a Structured Round. Ask a direct question that you know that person can answer, or ask for his or her agreement or opinion on views expressed by others. Be careful not to embarrass or draw too much attention to the person, as this may cause him or her to shut down even more.

Uncooperative individual(s) blocking the progress of the group. When someone refuses to listen to others and continues to *harp on his or her own ideas,* the group bogs down and momentum is lost. The facilitator can point out that the idea has already been recorded and say something like, "Are there any other ideas or points people have to make?" Another situation is when someone is *definitely wrong* and continues to come up with obviously incorrect comments. The group will become annoyed, since wrong information gets in the way of productivity. This situation must be handled delicately. As a facilitator, you can intervene with, "I understand how you feel. That's one way of looking at it, but can we reconcile that with the true situation?" More directly, the facilitator can say, "What are some facts you have to support what you are saying?" Or, "You certainly have a right to that opinion, but I think there are other viewpoints we are considering today as well." Sometimes an individual will be *obstinate*, refuse to budge, and will not go along with the group's point of view. Acknowledge that different viewpoints are healthy and say something like, "I'm sure you have a reason for your point of view, but I'd like you to try to consider the rest of the group's viewpoint for now, since that will help us move forward."

The group gets stuck. There are many ways a group can get stuck or bogged down during a participative meeting. The facilitator can use several techniques to move a group forward when it gets stuck. When the group is bogged down in detail, ask it to move on to generalities: "We seem to be getting stuck on detail. Can someone give us the 'big picture' of what we are talking about?" Or when the group gets stuck on generalities, move them to specifics: "I'm hearing a lot of generalities; can someone give us some specifics?"

The group may get stuck on an issue that does not relate directly to the objectives. If this happens, tell the group you would like to stop for a few minutes and record the key points of the discussion on a flip chart. Mention that this may be something the group will decide to work on at another time. Then ask the group to come back to the objectives and issue at hand.

Group Dynamics

The facilitator may have to work with a group that has poor group dynamics. Some of the group "attitude" or behaviors to take note of are

- Members do not seem comfortable with one another or are not speaking to one another;

- Members do not know one another very well;

- Personalities "clash";

- Personal agendas take precedent over group goals;

- Cultural diversity or differences of opinion are not tolerated very well;

- Members try to become "favorites" with the leader as opposed to working collaboratively with one another;

- There is lack of energy or enthusiasm for the group's tasks;

- There is poor attendance at group meetings;

- The group is poorly organized;

- There is poor communication among group members and within the group as a whole;

- Group members make negative comments about teams, empowerment, collaboration, and so forth;

- The group is pressed for time to accomplish its goals;

- There is a poor reward system (or punishment) for the group's achievements;

- The wrong people are on the team or in the group; and

- The group has a negative history.

The facilitator can intervene in several ways to resolve some or all of the above problems. Initial meetings can include get-acquainted types of exercises and icebreakers. The facilitator can conduct a group self-evaluation, followed by discussions and decisions about how the group plans to improve. Norms can be formulated (or reviewed and altered, if they exist). While working through these tasks with a group, the facilitator can ensure that differences of opinion are considered "normal" aspects of group work, that diversity is valued, and that personal agendas or personality clashes are not appropriate in light of the group's more important purpose of achieving its goals. Generally, when positive behaviors and norms are discussed, verbalized, decided upon, and recorded for all to see, people begin to police themselves and some of the clashes and personal agendas naturally begin to diminish. Those who do not can be handled offline. The facilitator may need to talk privately with offending parties about how their behavior is affecting the group. These people can be asked to alter their behaviors for the sake of achieving the group's purpose.

Next, the group meetings need to be facilitated with the goals in mind of building purpose within the group. What are the group's goals? What is the group's purpose in the organization? The facilitator can work with the group to renew, revisit, or frame for the first time its overall goals. If formulating group goals is too big a job to tackle, a smaller decision or plan can become the focus of the facilitation. Some groups will do well to list out, prioritize, and tackle their own problems, while the facilitator provides processes to do this.

While working on these concerns, the facilitator can make it a point to use facilitation processes that encourage everyone to contribute (such as affinity diagram, brainstorming, and structured round technique) and set up methods that will involve the entire group in coming to decisions (such as nominal group technique, and ranking and prioritizing). The keys in these types of difficult situations is to get the group working together toward some goal and to get everyone accustomed to all ideas being heard, recorded, and considered. Once group members understand that the entire group is going to be called on to contribute, they are more apt to attend subsequent meetings and demonstrate enthusiasm for the group's work. The object is not to formulate perfect decisions or plans but to get people used to working together.

Facilitators can help a group select norms of communication, systems for communicating in a timely fashion with group members and those outside the group, and ways of communicating about problems that arise. Group members are usually the most competent ones to make recommendations about how to improve group communication. The facilitator can make suggestions while encouraging the group to come up with the most effective and efficient ways to communicate.

Some groups have empowerment issues. Empowerment, the authority to make and implement decisions, has been linked in many organizations with a kind of "lip service" to true empowerment. A group may have been told that it has the power to make and implement plans and decisions when, in reality, it is not allowed to do so. This will kill group spirit very quickly and should be addressed. The facilitator can work with team leaders and members to get clear about the real boundaries and decision authority of the group. This may mean going to management to negotiate more real decision authority for the group.

There are usually some people in a group who do not want empowerment. They may not say this outright, but to them it is not the group's responsibility to make certain decisions. They may not be comfortable with change or with authority and power. These people may sabotage efforts by the group to become empowered. In cases such as this, the facilitator should make sure the group leader or management makes it very clear to the group that change is needed and what is expected from the group. The leadership should describe carefully to the group what will be different, what will be acceptable, and what will be unacceptable behavior. Leadership should show empathy for those who will be uncomfortable with empowerment, while telling them that the new expectations are not negotiable and why. The facilitator can lead group members in a discussion to enumerate both the challenges and the advantages to the new way of doing things and to brainstorm how the group can make the transition with as little "pain" as possible.

Issues concerning empowerment will surface again and again for those who work with groups. Good facilitators know when to stop the group's work and let the group discuss its concerns around issues of empowerment. Facilitators can steer the group in the direction of taking action to clarify and resolve these concerns.

Coming into the middle of a group's work (not present at initial meetings) can cause difficulty for a facilitator. In this case, the facilitator should make it a point to meet with the group leader and some or all of the group members before facilitating. This will help the facilitator know how to design the first meeting with the group. The facilitator should make every effort to ascertain ahead of time which of the above-listed conditions he or she might be facing.

Environment

The term *environment* is broad and covers the arena in which the group works: the organization as a whole; the industry or service the organization is part of; the facility, department, and group(s) in which the particular group works; and even the physical setting(s) where the group works and meets. A good facilitator makes an effort to piece together information about the group and its environment both before and while working with a group.

Here are a few questions that facilitators may ask to evaluate how environmental issues might affect the atmosphere and productivity of a particular group:

- What types of changes are occurring in the industry? In the organization? How might these affect the work of this group?

- What departments, functions, or organizations are represented by this group?

- How does the work of this group relate to the rest of the organization?

- What type of physical setting will the group's meetings be held in? (If unsuitable for good facilitation, can the physical setting be changed and improved?)

When facilitating a group meeting, the facilitator may observe that environmental concerns or roadblocks keep coming up in the discussion. One way to deal with these is to identify and list them as "environmental" and then note which issues are within the power of the group to change. Those that are not can be noted but dropped as a working concern of the group.

The others can become part of the group's discussions, decisions, and action plans.

Leadership and Management

One reason a facilitator is called into a group is that it may not have been working together in a collaborative way. It is not rare to find group and team leaders with technical expertise but lacking in people management and communication skills. Sometimes the leader sees the need for facilitation and sometimes he or she has been talked into calling in a facilitator. Whatever the case, it is a good idea for the facilitator to sit down with the leader before working with the group to ascertain where the group is in its development, what the group's goals are, and what the leader expects or needs from the facilitator. It is important for the facilitator to create trust with the leader and explain to him or her some of the processes that the facilitator may use and why. The facilitator should work out with the leader the role the leader should play in the meetings so that the group will not be hindered in its progress.

The facilitator should debrief the team's meetings with the team leader from time to time and coach the team leader in how his or her behavior affects the group. The facilitator can give suggestions to the team leader and describe specific behaviors that the leader can use to encourage participation, build team cohesion, and increase team productivity.

Another difficulty for a facilitator lies with the espoused versus actual support of management for the team's efforts. If teams are told they should move forward, make decisions, and be empowered but in actuality they are ignored or their decisions not allowed to be implemented, it will be difficult to continue facilitating the team. Team members will sense that management is only giving lip service to their decisions, and team morale will be low. Here are some suggestions for the facilitator:

- Work with the team and team leader to ascertain what the team's boundaries are (this may involve a session or two with management).

- Work with the team to list the areas they will be allowed to make decisions in and those they will not. Keep these visible to the team. If they change, make a new list. (This may call for the facilitator to facilitate a meeting with key managers to determine guidelines for the team.)

- When the team is about to embark on a new project, suggest that the team leader and one or two team members meet with management to clarify what authority the team will be given to decide, plan, and carry out the project.

Resources

Inadequate resources can pose problems for groups and teams and will eventually affect productivity. The facilitator can work with a group up front to determine where it may run into difficulty regarding resources. Some members of the group can be appointed to work on these issues, or the entire group may choose to work on them. When a group or team is working together to accomplish goals, it will need resources, such as time to meet, adequate meeting facilities, and supplies to do its work and to follow up with one another on a regular basis. When group members are overworked and excessive demands are made on their time, the group will suffer. Some ways to deal with resource concerns are

- Identify early on what the group needs in the way of resources to work well as a group and to accomplish its goals. What kind of time, money, and other resources will be required?

- Review what has happened before in similar situations to hinder a group and determine how these can be avoided.

- Find out whether some things need to be "put on the back burner" while the work of the group proceeds.

- Identify who is ultimately responsible for supplying the group with the resources it needs, meet with that person, and discuss how the issue of resources will be handled.

While working with the group, if inadequate resources hinder the group's progress, suggest that a meeting be devoted to coming up with ideas and solutions to the problem. This might be a time to invite whoever is responsible for the resources of the group to attend the meeting and work collaboratively with the group to resolve the concerns.

Difficult situations will arise, despite careful planning and facilitation. With experience, however, facilitators learn to anticipate and circumvent the most common difficult situations and they become skilled at deciding when and how to intervene. Finding out as much as possible about a group before facilitating gives clues about what types of difficult situations might arise. The facilitator can anticipate problems and have interventions and alternate processes in mind. Overall, the best defense is to follow the basic guidelines and processes for effective facilitation, which will minimize difficult situations.

CHAPTER 11

Facilitating Conflict Resolution

onflict is inherent in teams, groups, organizations, and even in most relationships. Whenever people work, live, or socialize together, there is potential for conflict. In work groups, there are numerous opportunities for conflict to arise, since by nature work groups are complex and much is demanded of them. The higher the stakes involved, the greater the likelihood of conflict.

Definition of Conflict

Conflict is defined as "to come into collision or disagreement; to be at variance or in opposition; a battle or struggle; opposition between interests or principles."[1] Simple disagreements that do not halt the progress or impair the unity of a group should probably not be called conflict; but when a disagreement causes ongoing disharmony or hinders the progress of a group, it becomes conflict and needs to be recognized and resolved if the group is to move forward.

---

[1]*The Random House Dictionary of the English Language, College Edition* (1968). New York: Random House.

Causes of Conflict

There are many sources of conflict among individuals and groups. People disagree over *facts*; indeed, people see the same fact from distinctly different viewpoints. People differ over *methods*, both on what to do and on how to do it. They may disagree on overall *goals* or interpret the wording of stated goals differently, thus causing conflict and misunderstanding. On an even deeper level, people differ in their basic *values*, the things they hold dear and important. Conflict may arise from differences in culture, background, or experience; or from poor communication, incompatible personalities, pressure to conform, unresolved problems, unintentional slights or offensive behavior, inadequate conflict resolution skills, and people exerting unwarranted power over others.

Negative Effects of Conflict

Unresolved disagreements in teams and organizations can seriously affect productivity and cohesion. Unless important disagreements are aired, discussed, and addressed in a group setting, the disagreements may not be resolved. When conflict is buried, denied, and allowed to fester without resolution, the negative outcomes can seriously hinder progress and decrease effectiveness.

When there is unresolved conflict in a group, people will behave in various ways, many of them not conducive to better communication or performance. Some people withdraw and withhold opinions, ideas, and even performance. Some try to sabotage the group's or the leader's efforts. Others give in or accommodate others to maintain harmony, thinking that by giving in they will ease the conflict. Some cling to the status quo by not rocking the boat. Others compromise and try to get others to do the same. Still others work to get people to cooperate and move forward. Some people may try to dominate and use various tactics to force a decision to go their way. Even though the group may move forward temporarily, the long-term unity and productivity of the group may be seriously affected if conflict is not resolved so that all parties feel their critical needs have been met.

Because the results of unresolved conflict can be detrimental and even painful to people and groups, the tendency to maintain harmony at all costs is sometimes strong among individuals and in groups. Since conflict—and what often results—confrontation—are uncomfortable for many, people often work hard to avoid conflict. They believe that conflict gets in the way of progress, causes hurt feelings, and makes working together difficult. When conflict is avoided or denied, over time a once small conflict may grow into one that is difficult to manage.

Positive Aspects of Conflict

In most groups, conflict is *normal, healthy,* and even *essential.* It is through disagreements and a diversity of viewpoints that problems get solved, creativity thrives, and improvements are made. Continuous agreement and harmony can actually be dangerous to a group. Avoidance of conflict for the sake of harmony may cause the group to overlook pitfalls that may cause failure, or avoid addressing important problems or ideas that could lead to the group's success.

Conflict can increase motivation and creativity and encourage openness, honesty, and vulnerability within a group. Once feelings and opinions are aired, there is greater likelihood of moving toward a solution, and once the solution is implemented, greater momentum exists to make it happen. Bringing conflict into the open increases understanding of others and paves the way for viable and innovative alternatives to be defined. When conflict is acknowledged and resolution attempted, people must clarify personal ideas and opinions in light of the group's goals and direction. Conflict can open the door not only to agreement but also to *better* agreements.

Once people experience the healthy and productive resolution of conflict, they become more willing to address it early on and to participate actively in resolving it. Those who experience purposeful and successful conflict resolution come to consider conflict an *asset,* an opportunity to improve the status quo and to add creativity and vitality to the group.

How People Manage Conflict

People deal with conflict in different ways at different times. The way they choose to deal with conflict depends in part on what the particular issue is, their personality and upbringing, their culture and its expectations, their experience in resolving conflicts, their individual perceptions, and the perceived and real rewards or punishments resulting from the resolution of the conflict. Kenneth Thomas's (1976) model of conflict handling behavior identifies *five* methods people use to manage conflict: *withdraw, defeat, compromise, accommodate,* or *collaborate.*

When people *withdraw* during conflict, they choose to ignore or avoid the issue. They may adopt the attitude, "Take whatever you can get," or "What's the use? I can't make a difference anyway." They may conclude that the pain of confrontation isn't worth the reward of resolution. They might expect some form of punishment if they bring the matter into the open and try to resolve it. They may learn to rely on others to do the "dirty work" of conflict resolution. Using this method leaves unresolved issues, causes decisions to be made by default, and limits creative input that could lead to genuine improvement of the situation. (On a positive note, this can also be a temporary strategy to allow for a cooling-off period before the conflict is addressed more collaboratively.)

When the *defeat* approach is taken, one person or party tries to take all the gains and "be a winner at any cost." This method is characterized by competition. Although this approach may be necessary when a quick, decisive action is needed or when an unpopular course of action must be implemented, the *defeat* method does not resolve issues in the long run. Cultures or groups in which conflict is handled by the *defeat* method run the risk of being made up of "yes" people. In such environments communication is reduced, relationships are damaged, and commitment is often lacking.

When people *compromise* during conflict, involved parties each give up something to "split the difference." Compromise may be expedient in the following situations: as a back-up mode when collaboration fails, when opponents with equal power are strongly committed to mutually exclusive goals, when time pressure eliminates the possibility of a joint solution, or when temporary solutions are needed until further collaboration can be achieved. However, when compromise is used, no one is fully satisfied, and the solution may be short-lived. Someone is bound to feel that they "sold out." Also, when a focus on immediate practicalities makes *compromising* the norm, a group may lose sight of its larger issues, long-term goals, and values.

When the *accommodate* method is used, conflict is resolved because someone gives into the demands or wishes of the other party. There may be times when this approach is effective or necessary; for example, when one realizes he or she is wrong, when the issue is much more important to the other person, or when preserving harmony and avoiding disruption are especially important. In groups, individuals may accommodate others because they are nonassertive in style, wish to maintain a friendly atmosphere, or perceive that this is a productive way to resolve conflict. However, maintaining harmony through accommodation can cause problems in groups, on a team, or in organizations. Too much deference creates environments where the strongest, most aggressive people take over and where the best solutions may not be found. Those who continually accommodate others will diminish their influence on the group and may not be respected by colleagues or supervisors. Over time, their self-esteem may be undermined, and they may become frustrated at not getting their needs met.

When people *collaborate* to handle conflict, there is an effort to creatively problem solve so both parties can win. The parties involved come to a joint solution that meets as many needs as possible, while supporting an agreed-on, overall goal. Although this approach takes more time and skills to implement, collaboration is important in several instances: (1) when all parties' concerns are too important to be ignored or compromised, (2) when maximum creativity is needed to resolve the issue, (3) when it is necessary to merge insights from different perspectives on a problem, (4) when commitment from all parties is critical, (5) when there are hard feelings that need to be worked through, or (6) when it is important to establish an atmosphere of team spirit, trust, and equality. When collaboration is used, it is important to draw input from people who have the experience, knowledge, and variety of perspectives needed to make a quality decision. Those who are critical to the implementation of the decision should be part of the collaboration as well.

Not all decisions or problems in organizations can or should be dealt with in a collaborative manner, but many of them can be. The quality of solutions is apt to improve when people become skilled at collaboration. Teams can become accustomed to resolving conflict through collaboration so that doing so does not require uncomfortable confrontation. Instead, collaboration becomes a way of working together, part of the normal operating procedures. People can become skilled at knowing when to seek win-win solutions and when to make an effort to reach consensus.

Organizations are beginning to examine the validity of collaborative work systems, entire organizations built on the principle that collaboration is a fundamental principle for success. If collaboration and consensus are more and more important for organizations to succeed, it stands to reason that the structure, systems, goals, and methods of the organization must be framed to support this approach. Facilitators, team leaders, and organization managers recognize that, of the five methods for resolving conflict, collaboration is frequently the best way to ensure that everyone is committed to organization goals and tasks. When people have helped make the decision, solve the problem, and draw up the plan, they are committed at a deeper level to making it stick than if they were simply told, "This is the way it will be."

Facilitator's Role in Conflict Resolution

Facilitators play a key role in helping groups resolve conflict and work in an atmosphere of collaboration and reaching consensus. An important job of a facilitator is to make the resolution of conflict *possible, probable,* and *easier* for all parties. The group meeting is a logical place to resolve conflict, and having someone to facilitate the discussion can be extremely helpful and, in most cases, essential. In fact, most participative, results-oriented (and healthy) group meetings involve some disagreements and conflict. Experienced facilitators anticipate disagreements and plan accordingly. The role of the facilitator is to employ methods to help others come to agreement while maintaining the dignity and respect of all individuals involved.

Good facilitation processes are geared to accept (and even encourage) diversity of opinions and ideas. Simply using good facilitation methods and tools often means that conflict will be addressed and resolved during the course of a regular group meeting. One of the strongest arguments for having a skilled facilitator lead a meeting is that the very process of facilitation automatically makes it easier to bring conflict into the open and resolve it as a matter of course. Teams and groups that are fortunate enough to have meetings facilitated become accustomed to resolving conflict as part of the normal meeting environment.

When disagreements surface during a meeting, it is more likely that they will be worked through if the meeting is being conducted using proven and productive processes (such as those described in previous chapters). If a conflict cannot be addressed as a part of the group's regular meetings, a separate meeting can be planned to address the issue. A skilled facilitator makes an effort to:

- Learn about conflict within a group before facilitating a meeting;

- Anticipate where conflict may arise in a group;

- Recognize points of potential conflict during a group discussion;

- Point out (mirror back) to the group disagreements that might hinder the group's progress;

- Suggest and lead processes to address and resolve differences and conflict;

- Create an atmosphere of openness and trust, so people can air differences freely without fear of recrimination;

- Create an atmosphere of productivity so that people believe it is worthwhile to put effort into working through the conflict;

- Keep the group focused on goals and direction;

- Make the group aware of how harboring or hiding conflict can keep the group from achieving its goals;

- Create an atmosphere that accepts and encourages looking at many sides of an issue for the sake of productivity (versus forcing harmony and cohesion to avoid conflict);

- Provide guidance and clear direction regarding the process the group will use to work through conflict;

- Make sure group members have, or formulate, a goal to focus on;

- Help the group develop its own guidelines (norms) for resolving conflict;

- Use proven group processes and methods for resolving conflict, and adapt these processes as necessary for a particular group or issue;

- Focus people on the ideas and issues, not on personalities behind the ideas and issues;

- Help the group determine which disagreements must be resolved in order for the group to move forward and which disagreements will not affect the group's progress, and point out that some disagreements are healthy and do not require resolution;

- Allow time for all ideas to be heard, understood, and considered;

- Encourage brainstorming and innovative suggestions;

- Help group members understand that conflict is healthy and can lead to innovative problem solving; and

- Encourage group members to bring things into the open for the whole group to solve, not to discuss them outside the group or in "cliques."

How to Facilitate Conflict Resolution

The first rule of thumb for facilitating conflict is to *use basic facilitation methods and techniques.* Just by using good facilitation techniques and methods, a facilitator sets the stage for productive conflict resolution. In fact, when facilitation processes are in place, conflict is surfaced in a supportive manner and is likely to be resolved more efficiently and effectively than if no facilitation processes were used. Frequently conflict arises *because* no one is facilitating or because the group is using processes that run counter to good facilitation. Conflict will be exacerbated when people feel stifled, unheard, ignored, and uninvolved.

Second, an effective facilitator keeps at his or her fingertips various *conflict resolution procedures,* such as multi-voting (see page 152), ranking and prioritizing (see page 154), nominal group technique (page 157), and a process for resolving conflict (at the end of this chapter, page 205). It is a good idea for facilitators to take notes on effective conflict resolution methods they observe, read about, take part in, or learn in training programs or other venues.

Third, a good facilitator is vigilant about setting up an *atmosphere* of open communication, creativity, structure, and productivity. Aware that conflict and disagreement may naturally arise, the facilitator uses positive processes, not to avoid the conflict or disagreement but to work through it as a matter of course. Some of these positive processes are

- Clear meeting or team objectives (agreed on, referred to frequently, posted, published);

- Structure that allows for brainstorming, addressing concerns, surfacing disagreement, setting group norms, and tackling problems in both a creative and orderly way;

- An atmosphere that demonstrates genuine consideration of all viewpoints while still remaining productive (acknowledging real-time and resource constraints);

- Positive feedback to the group when it works through difficult problems;

- Constructive mirroring back to the group to help it understand whether it is adhering to agreed-on goals and norms; and

- Clear record of what the group decided and agreed on (written and published).

Fourth, an effective facilitator is willing and able to *educate* groups about conflict. Making sure people understand how and why conflict arises, how people deal with conflict, and what methods are appropriate for resolving the conflict—all of these will help set up an atmosphere of control over conflict, as opposed to an atmosphere in which people fear conflict because it may destroy group productivity or cohesiveness.

Fifth, a good facilitator *models positive conflict resolution behaviors* while working with a group. Active listening, open questions, repeating back the other person's point of view, and working toward a win-win solution should be natural behaviors on the part of a facilitator.

Sixth, an effective facilitator *ensures that the group accepts ownership* for its own conflicts. The facilitator helps the group identify the conflicts and evaluate the impact it will have if left unresolved. The group takes on the responsibility to work through the issues, while the facilitator brings knowledge, skill, and coaching to the group. Part of this process is to help the group set norms of behavior that will allow disagreement and surface healthy conflict for the sake of creative resolution of problems. The facilitator should be up front about the norms and explain why they are there.

Conflicts may be minor or major in impact, and sometimes it is difficult to tell the degree of importance a particular conflict may have. It may be all right to ignore some disagreements and work on larger concerns. However, even small disagreements may require resolution before the group feels energized to move on. A good facilitator will work with the group to identify these nuances and will continuously use facilitation processes that allow conflict to surface and be resolved.

Seventh, the facilitator works with the group to *identify win-win solutions based on agreed-on goals.* Rather than focusing solely on the disagreements, the group must move beyond those disagreements and focus on the bigger picture: the overall goal and what kind of solution will provide an adequate win for all parties. Without a clear overall goal, there may be no framework within which to work out solutions. Without common goals, personal agendas may take over to fan the flames of the conflict.

The process for resolving conflict (page 205) is an example of how to work through a conflict so that all parties hear and acknowledge the others' supporting points and reasons for their beliefs or ideas. Once all parties' views have been adequately heard and recorded, the activity shifts to setting an overall goal that will satisfy all parties. If a goal can be agreed on, the group has a better chance of working out solutions that will satisfy a majority of people's needs. If people have taken time to understand the diversity of viewpoints at the beginning, it will be easier for them to craft a solution to satisfy everyone.

To help groups move forward during conflict, it is important to point out that reaching consensus does not mean everyone agrees that a particular solution is the best way to go. It is a point of maximum agreement so action can follow. *Consensus is reached when everyone can support a decision 100 percent.* The most effective processes for reaching consensus involve striving to provide as many "wins" for everyone as possible.

When people become frustrated with conflict, they may suggest, or naturally want to pursue, one or more of the following:

- Voting;

- Compromising (a settlement of differences by mutual giving in);

- Appointing someone to dictate the solution;

- Getting everyone to agree on every point (forced unanimity); and/or

- Suppressing minority views and dissent (by showing disapproval when people disagree).

None of these methods leads to positive conflict resolution but will often only make the conflict deeper and more ingrained. To guide groups to reach win-win solutions, facilitators can do some or all of the following:

- Allow plenty of time. Sometimes a group may need several meetings to make a consensus decision.

- Use rational, structured methods such as brainstorming, decision matrix, problem solving, nominal group technique, list reduction, and conflict resolution processes. Check with the group for consensus before you move on. "Can everyone support the conclusions we have come to so far? Are we ready to move on?" Consensus may need to be reached at several points in the process before the group can move on.

- Write out what was decided and post it for all to see. This will clarify what the group has agreed to, provide a decision record, motivate individuals to keep the agreement, and maintain team members' energy and attention.

- Help the team avoid "group think" (the pressure or tendency for members of a group to agree on everything). Ask questions to stimulate creative thinking, encourage divergent viewpoints, and to make sure dissent that may later stall the progress has been expressed. "Are there other alternatives we should consider? What are we overlooking? Have we considered what would happen if . . . ?"

Teaching Others to Use Positive Conflict Resolution Skills

Facilitators have a role in educating others about conflict resolution. Educating others about conflict takes some of the burden off the facilitator and shares the responsibility for conflict resolution with the group. Once people understand the nature and methods of conflict resolution, it is not as difficult or threatening to tackle issues and problems.

The concepts in this chapter can be presented in a brief presentation to groups when the facilitator deems it necessary. A group can be encouraged to address some of its concerns and past experiences with conflict resolution. The material that follows will help facilitators work with groups to become collaborative rather than confrontational systems.

One way to help others become better communicators and problem solvers in conflict situations is to simply ask them to come up with suggestions as to how to proceed when resolving conflict. These can be listed and discussed as part of a brief educational "lesson" at one of the group's meetings, or before a conflict is going to be worked on. The ideas can be discussed briefly, and the facilitator can hand out a list, such as the one in the handout shown later in this chapter, which may add additional insights to what the group has already come up with. Any discrepancies can be noted and discussed. Norms for behavior can then be decided on before moving forward. A "lesson" such as this could be a routine activity for working with a new group. The agreed-on norms can be posted at the group's subsequent meetings and referred to if the group gets stuck in disagreement.

To further educate group members on how to work toward consensus and to come to win-win solutions, use the handout on pages 207–208 in one or more of the following ways:

- Ask group members to read the handout after establishing norms for dealing with conflict. Ask whether the handout brings up any norms they would like to *add to their list.*

- Use the list as a *personal evaluation tool.* Ask each group member to assess his or her conflict resolution behaviors and skills by using the list. Use a number range from 1 to 5 (or 1 to 10), with the highest number representing the highest level of achievement for that particular item. Ask each person to select his or her top three to five items and "star" them as conflict resolution strengths, and select his or her bottom two or three items and circle them as areas for potential growth. Emphasize that conflict resolution skills are critical to people in all walks of life and that any improvements in these areas will benefit each person, not only at work but also in their personal, community, and social lives.

- Follow the above activity with *small discussion groups.* Divide the group into subgroups of three people each (use pairs if it is a small group). Ask each person to relate one or two strengths and weaknesses to the others. Have others in the group suggest ways that this person can use the strengths to an advantage and ways to improve on the weaknesses. Subgroup members can help one another with ideas. Once each person has related strengths and weaknesses to the subgroup, instruct the subgroups to come up with at least two good ideas to share with the larger group. The ideas should represent *ways all group members can facilitate the healthy resolution of conflict.* Reconvene the large group and discuss the ideas.

- Use the list as *a group evaluation tool.* Ask group members to rank their team or group as to how well it achieves each item *as a group.* (Don't have them rate themselves only, but the group or team as a whole.) Use a number range from 1 to 5, or 1 to 10, with the highest number representing the highest level of achievement for that particular item. Collect each person's overall score (either privately or outwardly) and give a score to the group or team. Ask group members to state reasons they think their group scored as it did. Ask them to list the group's main strengths and weaknesses.

- Post these for all to see. Ask the group how it can take advantage of its strengths and what one or two weaknesses it would like to improve on and how. Check to see what group members will do to monitor their own commitment and progress.

A Process for Resolving Conflict

The following step-by-step process facilitates resolving conflict when a group is strongly divided on an issue, especially when the group is divided into two or more "camps." When progress is stalled because of unresolved conflict, this is a great process for getting people to move forward. The purpose is to make sure each "side" hears and understands the points presented by the other side. It involves writing out (or repeating back) what the "opposing" side has said. The turning point is when all sides have heard one another out and together they come up with a common goal, one that everyone agrees they will work toward. From then on, the process follows traditional brainstorming, discussion, and prioritization processes until the group comes to a joint, win-win solution.

- *Step One.* Announce the situation or problem to the group. Lay out as many facts and as much information as is necessary to prepare the group to make a decision.

- *Step Two.* Lead a discussion to find out where people stand on the issue. What do they think is the solution? Try to draw everyone out. Ask people not to get into discussions at this time but simply to state their opinions and ideas. Do not record the ideas, since you will be asking the groups to do that in Step Three.

- *Step Three.* Break into groups based on viewpoint and have groups feed back to one another what they have heard the "opposing" sides say. Ask the groups to write out the ideas on a flip chart for everyone to see. Ask these groups not to berate the ideas or reasons of the other side, but to simply present them and show they have heard and understood the other side's point of view. They are not agreeing with it; they are demonstrating their skill and maturity in *hearing and understanding.*

- *Step Four.* The listening groups then give feedback to the presenters, letting them know whether they presented the opposing opinions accurately and whether any were left out. If any were left out, the presenting group should write these down in the words of the person(s) whose idea or opinion it is. During this step, it is important that all sides have their ideas written out or heard accurately. Discussion is still not allowed, other than to clarify that the ideas have been heard accurately.

- *Step Five.* Form subgroups that are "mixed," with members from both "sides" in each subgroup. At this point people with different opinions will be working together. The subgroups each come up with what they think is the overall, common goal of both sides of the issue. They must take into account the organization they are serving, as well, if this is the case. Each subgroup presents its goal statement to the other group, and the facilitator works with both subgroups to determine the common goal of the larger group.

- *Step Six.* Once a goal is agreed to, the entire group brainstorms as many solutions as it can think of to reach the goal, taking into account the arguments posed by both sides. Follow traditional brainstorming

Handout

Team Member Behaviors
and Skills for Reaching Consensus

One of your abilities as a team member is to help your team reach consensus in a creative, productive way. The goal is not to avoid conflict (there should be healthy conflict) but to work through the conflict to arrive at the best solution possible. Accept the attitude that you are working cooperatively to make the best decision in support of the purposes, goals, values, and mission of the team or organization. Strive to be a "consensus seeker." Consensus seekers strive to make sure all parties get as much of what they want as possible to achieve the overall goal. They become genuinely concerned that all parties feel a "win" and that everyone will support the decision 100 percent.

When team members learn these skills, the conflict that naturally occurs in teamwork is likely to be more focused on the content of the decision, which is healthy, and less focused on interpersonal differences and lack of good team communication skills. In fact, these skills are the very ones teams need to work through conflict. The goal is not to avoid conflict completely, but to avoid unproductive behaviors that create more conflict or keep the team from making progress.

Here's how you can be a consensus seeker, use productive behaviors for resolving conflict, and help your team reach consensus:

1. Avoid arguing for your own solution.

2. Give full attention to your team members.

3. Ask questions to make sure you have understood others' main points.

4. Clarify your understanding of another's viewpoint by stating that person's views back to him or her, without criticizing.

5. Find merit in the other person's view.

6. Avoid interrupting or defending your own ideas until you have understood what the other person has said.

7. When interrupted, kindly ask people to let you finish making your points: "Please, I'd like to finish making my point."

8. Don't hold back when you disagree or have another idea.

9. Don't agree or change your mind just to avoid conflict. Instead state your own ideas clearly, firmly, and without being overly emotional.

10. Once you have made your point, avoid harping on it. Let your idea stand on its own merit.

11. Aim for the expression of a lot of ideas. Build on other people's ideas.

12. Draw out quieter team members by asking them what they think.

13. Use differences of opinion as an opportunity for creativity rather than a hindrance to decision making.

14. Avoid jumping to solutions when there appears to be initial agreement. Instead, ask questions to keep people thinking of alternatives. Discuss the reasons for agreement and determine whether other viable possibilities have been overlooked.

15. Try not to get personally invested in your own position. Keep the end goal in mind, and don't take it personally if the team decides to take another approach.

16. Don't stall the process. Offer suggestions instead of simply disagreeing or criticizing someone else's approach.

17. Support only those solutions you can live with.

18. Keep the end goal in mind, which is to reach a mutually agreeable solution that will satisfy everyone's needs as much as possible.

so that all ideas are presented first without discussion, discrediting, or reinforcement.

- *Step Seven.* Clarify the brainstormed ideas, eliminate any that are unworkable, and discuss the merits of the remaining ideas.

- *Step Eight.* Use a prioritization process to find the top few ideas that are the most appealing to the group.

- *Step Nine.* The top ideas are evaluated, perhaps tested, or more data are collected.

- *Step Ten.* The group decides on which idea is the best, combines more than one idea, or rejects all ideas and looks for a better one.

Resources

The following are helpful resources for facilitators on the topic of resolving conflict:

- Gibson, C., and Cohen, S. (Eds.) (2003). *Virtual teams that work: Creating conditions for virtual team effectiveness.* San Francisco: Jossey-Bass. See Chapter 15, "Conflict and Virtual Teams."

- Leonard, D., and Swap, W. (1999). *When sparks fly: Igniting creativity in groups.* Boston: Harvard Business School Press. Focuses on facilitating the creative process, which in turn empowers groups to deal effectively with conflict, avoid "group think," and reach the best solutions. The chapter "Creative Abrasions" is a valuable discussion of the importance (and challenges) of bringing diversity (people with different viewpoints) into groups to promote creativity.

- Levine, S. (1998). *Getting to resolution: Turning conflict into collaboration.* San Francisco: Berrett-Koehler.

- Parker, G. M. (2003). *Cross-functional teams: Working with allies, enemies, and other strangers.* San Francisco: Jossey-Bass. Chapter 12, "The Team

Working Together," enumerates healthy team processes that help manage conflict successfully in cross-functional teams.

- Tagliere, D. A. (1992). *How to meet, think, and work to consensus.* San Francisco: Pfeiffer.

- Tague, N. R. (1995). *The quality toolbox.* Milwaukee, WI: ASQC Quality Press. Presents numerous tools to help groups reach consensus.

PART 4

Designing Effective Facilitations

After you are comfortable facilitating discussions, and as your skills improve, you will no doubt be called on to plan and facilitate an entire meeting—anything from a simple one-hour meeting to a three-day offsite meeting. At this point you will need design skills, since much of the success of a facilitation of any length or importance lies in the appropriateness and effectiveness of its design. The "design" is simply the flow of activities and timing laid out in outline form with notes for the facilitator. The design itself is not shown to the participants, but a brief representation of it becomes the agenda, which is usually posted or distributed at the session.

In Chapter 12, we will look at the general principles of How to Design a Facilitation. Chapter 13 is a discussion of Organizing and Enhancing Group Work and Chapter 14 will teach you about Opening and Closing Activities.

How to Design a Facilitation

The "design" of a facilitation refers to the objectives or goals of the session, the flow of activities, the breaks, the refreshments served (if any), the grouping and regrouping of the participants, the opening and closing activities, and even the location of the meeting. Skilled facilitators expect to be involved in the design of a meeting they will be facilitating. In fact, if you are ever asked to facilitate a meeting that has already been designed, beware, as you will be working at a great disadvantage. It is best to agree only to facilitating some of the discussion and not the entire meeting. Or, you may influence the design of the meeting so that it lends itself to facilitation.

Ten Steps for Designing a Facilitation

Designing a facilitation requires certain defined steps. At the same time it is a creative process that may or may not always fall into place. Follow the ten steps below with some flexibility, allowing time for the creative process to work. The steps are:

1. Define the purpose of the meeting.

2. Decide who will attend the meeting.

3. Diagnose the situation.

4. Write results-oriented meeting objectives.

5. Set the timing of the meeting.

6. Decide where the meeting will be held.

7. Decide whether pre-work is necessary.

8. Determine what processes will be used.

9. Choose opening and closing activities.

10. Assign responsibilities for arranging the meeting.

Each of the ten steps is described in detail below. As a facilitator, collaborate as much as possible with the client, gaining his or her understanding and approval at each step. Advise the client how to proceed, and make joint decisions. As a facilitator, sense the readiness, willingness, and ability of the client to collaborate on the design.

Define the Purpose of the Meeting

The foremost consideration of any facilitation is the purpose or goal of the meeting. Ask questions such as "What will this meeting achieve?" "What do we need to accomplish at this meeting?" "What would happen if the meeting weren't held?" "Is the meeting really necessary?" "What tangible outcome or results will we aim for at this meeting?" In other words, what decision will have been made, what tangible product will everyone have (a plan, a decision, a list, a problem solved, a recommendation made)? Tangible evidence is important, because it can be shown as proof of what was accomplished. People have serious doubts about meetings today; most meetings are simply not as productive as they could be. As a facilitator, one of your main goals is to help a group be productive. One of the most effective ways you can do this is to focus from the beginning on what needs to be accomplished by this particular group during this period of time.

Sometimes the client is vague about the purpose of the meeting and will say something like, "To get together, to get to know one another better, and to find out what's going on in the department" (or region, organization, or team). This may indeed happen at the meeting, but a tighter, more focused goal needs to be spelled out. Work with the client to determine a product the group can walk away with: a list of action items, a priority list of problems, a plan, or a decision. The possibilities are numerous.

Decide Who Will Attend the Meeting

In order to accomplish the meeting objectives, who must attend? This is a critical question to ask in designing a facilitation, because those who will be involved in authorizing and/or implementing the objective must be at the meeting.

Diagnose the Situation

Work with the client to diagnose the situation as thoroughly as possible. Hopefully, the client will make time to answer questions about how the situation relates to the overall goals of the organization. Ask for information about who will be attending the meeting and their relationship with one another and the organization. The more information the facilitator has about the group and the task, the better he or she will be equipped to design a productive session.

The diagnostic phase can be quite daunting, and it is often neglected by the inexperienced facilitator. Sometimes it seems that the group is facing all kinds of difficulties and trouble and that the path ahead is riddled with problems. At other times, the client minimizes problems, and the facilitator walks into a rat's nest. Solicit enough information about the group to move forward with a plausible design. Find out enough to design a facilitation that stands a good chance of helping the group meet its objective. Keep in mind, however, that the group will have only a few minutes or hours to work. Keep some perspective, as one facilitation is not going to solve all of a group's problems.

Asking the client a few key questions will help immensely. Here are a few suggestions:

- "How does this group fit into the overall organization?"

- "Have the group members worked together before? How well do they know one another?"

- "How long has the group been together?"

- "Who is new to the group?"

- "Describe the mix of people: levels in the organization; age distribution; ratio of women to men; cultural, ethnic, and/or educational backgrounds; length of time with the company."

- "Who is responsible for the work of this group? Who outside the group is interested in the results?"

- "How well do group members get along/work together?"

- "Have any recent changes affected the group and/or individuals in the group? How might these affect the goal of the meeting?"

- "What are group members' expectations of the meeting?"

- "What attitudes are group members likely to bring to the meeting?" (Will people be hostile or accepting of the purpose of this meeting?)

- "Is anything happening before or after the meeting that might affect the group members' behavior?"

- "If this meeting is wildly successful, what will happen?"

Write Results-Oriented Meeting Objectives

After establishing a goal or purpose for the session and reaching an understanding of the group and the situation, in collaboration with the client, determine the specific objectives of the meeting. Typically people create an agenda at this point. However, agendas alone do not work, and in fact are the cause of many dysfunctional meetings. Objectives work! "Objectives focus the group, drive the outcome, and serve as a measure of performance and productivity" (Rees, 2001, p. 147).

The ability to write a strong, clear, results-oriented meeting objective is an important skill. Of course, a meeting may have more than one objective, in which case all objectives should be results-oriented and clear. The group should feel that objectives can be achieved during the meeting and should be able to measure the meeting's success by determining whether the objectives were met.

Many meetings lack momentum and direction because the agenda consists of only a list of topics to be discussed. The key to a meeting's success is to be clear about the purpose for discussing each topic. Is there a decision to be made? Information to be shared? Brainstorming needed? Approval desired? These *outcomes* then become the objectives of the meeting. The objectives are a powerful tool to keep the group focused and productive. If a particular objective cannot be achieved, the group still feels a sense of productivity simply from making it a priority at the meeting, tackling it, and at least identifying why it cannot be achieved at this time. When an objective is achieved, the group feels a solid sense of satisfaction and accomplishment.

To write a clear, results-oriented meeting objective, first picture the outcome that will be achieved. Ask, "What will we end up with to demonstrate the results of the meeting—a plan, a decision, a recommendation, a brainstormed list, a set of criteria, a mission statement, a set of guidelines, a new policy?" Write the objective so that it describes what the group will be doing and the outcome. Use whatever words or phases are needed to clarify the objective. Some examples follow:

- Create the first draft of our team's mission statement.

- Revise existing customer guidelines so they are clearer and easier for customers to use.

- Outline the major steps of the project and estimate time and resources needed for completion.

- Create a responsibility matrix showing who has primary responsibility for departmental tasks, who has secondary responsibility, and who receives information related to that responsibility.

Objectives should be posted during the meeting to focus the group. Avoid vague words such as "discuss," "update," or "review." If the objective is stated as "discuss our current standing with customers," the only outcome mentioned is the discussion. Discussing does not necessarily lead to results or action. The objective could be reworded to say "discuss our current standing with customers and decide one or two key actions to take to improve customer relations." To give another example, the objective "review progress on the ABC project" could be reworded to say "review progress on the ABC project and list immediate actions that need to be taken to ensure success." This identifies a result or outcome for the meeting.

Set the Timing of the Meeting

After the participants have been identified and the specific objectives written, the next step is to determine the timing of the meeting—the length of the meeting and the best time to hold the meeting in light of the objectives and audience. Meetings frequently take longer than anticipated, sometimes because they are not managed well, and sometimes because there is insufficient time for discussion, idea generation, and decision making. Facilitators must be skilled at estimating how long certain activities will take and how much time people will need to deal with each issue.

Decide Where the Meeting Will Be Held

The nature of some meetings requires participants to be away from work interruptions and in a more neutral atmosphere. Others require that people be accessible to the workplace. Many meetings simply must be held at the workplace to save time and money.

Decide Whether Pre-Work Is Necessary

Do meeting participants need to prepare for the meeting ahead of time? What can participants do before the meeting to save time at the meeting or make it more successful? What should members bring to the meeting? Does the meeting planner or facilitator need to gather information before the meeting?

Determine What Processes Will Be Used

This is the heart of design work. Know what processes work best for certain situations and select processes that meet with the client's understanding and approval. Determine, given the stated objectives, what processes will help the group achieve them: brainstorming; a problem-solving model; small-group work; an informative presentation; a short training session; charts, diagrams, small-group reports?

Choose Opening and Closing Activities

Opening and closing activities are important to group work. They bring the group together at the beginning and send it off at the end. They serve to solidify and unite people toward a common purpose. They frame the work of the meeting, give it value, recognize it, and even affect the group's productivity. The opening and closing activities are critical to a successful meeting, and skilled facilitators plan them carefully. (See Chapter 14 for more on this topic.)

Assign Responsibilities for Arranging the Meeting

Although the facilitator is seldom the one to actually arrange the meeting (notify participants, reserve a facility, order refreshments, assemble supplies), it is important to clarify these responsibilities with the client. This will minimize misunderstandings as to who is bringing what supplies, when and how people will be notified, and so forth. A well-planned meeting does not just happen; even clients experienced in planning meetings will benefit by coaching from the facilitator. You may want to ask clients the following list of questions:

- "Who will notify the participants and when?"

- "Who will make arrangements for the meeting room/facility and the refreshments?"

- "What supplies are needed?" (Make a list of these: flip charts and paper, marking pens, overhead projector, masking tape, etc.; and determine who will bring them to the meeting.)

Take nothing for granted. I have arrived in rooms without any of the supplies I requested, and I have arrived in rooms with tottering easels and only a few sheets of paper. As a result I always carry a portable easel and paper in the trunk of my car and arrive with fresh marking pens and masking tape. Most meeting rooms are used by so many people that it is not unusual for supplies to be missing, even if the meeting planner requested them. It pays to come prepared. Coach the meeting leader to make sure the room has at least two flip-chart easels and extra pads of paper. Always speak with the meeting planner one or two days before the meeting and remind him or her of your needs. Ask, "Do you foresee any problem getting these in the room?" just to emphasize their importance.

Collaborating with the Client

Collaborating with the client on the goals and design of a facilitation will increase the chances for its success. The client has information the facilitator needs, and the facilitator has expertise the client needs. Some clients prefer and expect to have little involvement with the facilitator, except to give a few instructions in a brief conversation. Facilitators in this type of situation must draw out clients to obtain their buy-in and opinions on at least a few key items. If the client has little or no involvement in the planning, it may indicate that he or she really is not very interested in the results or expects you to understand and deliver his or her expectations with little interaction. Either way, the chances for a successful meeting are lowered. Generally speaking, the client should be willing to spend at least an hour to plan a brief meeting. If longer meetings are being planned, the client should expect to make several hours available to work with you. This may include an initial meeting, several phone conversations, fax exchanges, and preparation of materials or data. If the client is unwilling or unable to spend the necessary time, encourage him or her to postpone the meeting until time is available. Say something like, "I really want to work with you on this meeting and make it a success. However, to design an effective meeting that will be worth everyone's while, I will need about two hours with you between now and the meeting. I may also need you to be available by phone if I have questions. If that is not possible, I suggest we postpone the meeting until we have sufficient time to work together. Is that possible?"

For some meetings to be successful, you might need to interview (in person or by phone) those who will be attending. Be sure to ask the client for time and permission to do this, and then make every effort to speak to everyone. Let the client know what you will be asking and ask everyone the same questions. They will probably talk among one another. Trust will be higher if you treat everyone equally.

Some clients may want to refine the design and co-facilitate the meeting. This requires a different level of collaboration and more hours of work for the client. The client must be coached so that his or her involvement supports the desired outcome. Other clients may not be sure how much they need to be involved with the planning and design aspects. Use this opportunity to suggest ways the client can contribute.

I like to involve the client initially until I have diagnosed the situation and written a rough draft of the goals for the session, sometimes with more than one approach or options. I present this to the client for reactions. Based on our discussion, I confirm the arrangements (dates, times, and other logistics) and put the basic design in writing, as shown in the sample confirmation letter and outline in Figure 12.1. No matter what level of collaboration you have with the client, discuss the design briefly with the client to make sure the client agrees with the approach. Explain how the design supports the overall purpose of the meeting. In some cases, you may need to ask more questions of the client to determine whether a particular design or activity will work.

After these discussions have taken place, revise the design and add necessary details to it, creating what I call "Design Notes," such as the ones in Figure 12.2. These become your notes for facilitating the session, and, along with notes made during the session, a record of how the facilitation went. These are a valuable resource for designing future facilitations.

Figure 12.1. Sample Confirmation Letter to Client

Dear Ann,

This letter is to confirm our arrangements for a Team-Building Session on May 23, 2005, from 8:00 a.m. to 5:00 p.m.

I am planning to work with your team for approximately five hours to help it meet the goals stated on the attached outline. I will be present, however, for the entire session and will lead the introductory icebreaker. The cost for the session will be . . . .

As I mentioned, we will need two flip-chart easels and pads of paper and a room with plenty of wall space and areas for people to move around. I will bring marking pens, masking tape, and any handouts or other supplies needed.

Please look over the enclosed outline and let me know whether it meets with your approval. I am looking forward to working with your group.

Sincerely,

Fran Rees

Enclosure: Outline of Facilitation

Sample Outline of Facilitation

Team-Building Session
May 23, 2005
Suggested Outline

Objectives for the Session

- Become better acquainted with one another;

- Increase your knowledge of teammates' jobs and roles;

- Understand how each person's job relates to overall team goals;

- Clarify and discuss individual and subteam responsibilities, and create a Team Responsibility Matrix; and

- Identify opportunities for increased effectiveness as a group.

Outline

8:00 a.m.	Welcome and Introductions Icebreaker: Paired Interviews
8:45	Departmental history, goals, and future direction
10:00	Break
10:15	Introduction to Team-Building Session and to "Roles"
11:00	Individual exercise: Role Clarification
11:20	Small-group role discussions and feedback (in mixed subteams)
12:00	Lunch
12:45	Subteams meet to: Discuss roles as in above exercise; and List major responsibilities of the subteam on a matrix chart.

1:30	Everyone mills around room to:

Read other subteams' lists; and
Write comments on blank paper next to each list.

1:45	Subteams reconvene, read comments, and revise lists
2:15	Break
2:30	Subteams report to large group
2:45	Complete Responsibility Matrix

Work in large group or subteams—whatever process will be the most productive and beneficial. Add team members' names to charts posted on wall. Indicate those individuals who:

- Have primary responsibility
- Have secondary responsibility
- Must approve decisions

4:15	Wrap-up discussion

- Areas that need further clarification or discussion.
- Opportunities for increased effectiveness.
- Determine action items and persons responsible.
- Round-robin feedback on how the session went.

5:00	Adjourn

Completing the Design

After a draft has been agreed to by the client, complete the design by making detailed notes so that you can facilitate all the activities of the session, assemble materials and supplies, prepare handouts, and make any flip charts that need to be prepared before the session. Here is a brief checklist to use when completing your design:

1. Add final details to the design and prepare design notes.

2. Make a copy of the design notes for use during the session.

3. Prepare handouts and make copies.

4. Prepare flip charts.

5. Assemble folder with important client information.

6. Pack training case or briefcase with materials needed.

With practice, you will write design notes that will give you just the information you need to facilitate an effective session. Ask other facilitators for their tips, and take a look at their design notes when possible.

Bring a folder of notes made during your discussions with the client (and the participants, if interviews were conducted), along with the client's phone number, pager number, and any other important client information, such as names of those attending, official name of the group or department, etc. Always carry a good-quality master copy of handouts with you, in case more people show up and extra copies are needed. Packing the training case is part of the final design work. Preparing the materials is not enough; you have to arrive with all the materials you will need!

Use the sample design notes in Figure 12.2 to help you plan and design your facilitations. Create your own format and make sure it works for you.

Figure 12.2. Sample Design Notes for Team-Building Session

Design of Team-Building Session
May 23, 2005

Objectives for the Session

- Become better acquainted with one another;
- Increase your knowledge of teammates' jobs and roles;
- Understand how each person's job relates to overall team goals;
- Clarify and discuss individual and subteam* responsibilities and create a Team Responsibility Matrix; and
- Identify opportunities for increased effectiveness as a group.

Time: 7½–8 hours

Materials Needed

- Two flip-chart easels with paper (preferably with one-inch blue grids)
- Water-based marking pens in several colors, in two sizes: large for writing on flip charts and medium point for the opening exercise and for the comments exercise.
- White correction fluid
- Masking tape (or other method to hang flip-chart paper on walls)
- Scissors
- Adhesive tape

Handouts

- Role Clarification Activity
- Instructions for small-group work
- Sample Responsibility Matrix

---

*In this particular example, there are three subteams, each with different areas of responsibility. Some of the work during the session is done within subteams.

Flip Charts

One prepared flip chart for each of the following:

- Goals
- Agenda
- Norms
- Drawing of matrix and how to construct it

Activities

8:00 a.m.   *Welcome and Introductions*
              Exercise: Paired interviews using stars

1. Hand out one sheet of blank paper and two to three medium-point marking pens to each person. Have each person draw a large star with five points and fill in each point of the star with facts that could be used by another person to introduce him or her to the group. (Give some suggestions to the group: "You might indicate things you love, a hobby you have, a personal goal, places you have lived, and so on.")

2. After five minutes, have people choose partners and exchange information on their stars. After three minutes, instruct them to change partners and do the same again. After three more minutes, instruct them to change partners and do the same again.

3. Ask each person to introduce his or her last partner by giving that person's name and three facts about him/her from three different points on that person's star. (Allow one minute per introduction.)

8:45   *Departmental direction and goals*
            Timeline exercise and discussion

Note: This portion will be led by the group's manager.

10:00   *Break*

10:15   *Introduction to Team-Building Session and to "Roles."*

- Goals
- Agenda
- Norms

1. Explain the difference between position and role: A position is the actual job one holds as defined by its relationship to other employees and to the system as a whole (generally a hierarchical relationship); a role includes those activities and behaviors that one is expected to demonstrate while holding this position.

2. Write the words "role confusion" on a flip chart and ask, "What can happen if an individual is not clear about his or her role?" List the responses. Ask, "What can happen if team members are not clear about one another's roles?" List the responses.

3. Mention that the goal of this session is to determine the role parameters within which each person operates. The purpose of this process is to minimize any misunderstandings within the team. This activity is meant to provide the team with a nonthreatening setting in which to examine mutual expectations, demands, and responsibilities.

11:00   Individual exercise: "Role Clarification"

Mention that the first step in this process will be to discuss each person's individual role. Hand out the Role Clarification sheet and ask each person to take a few minutes to complete the individual exercise.

11:20   Discussion of individual roles

Divide the group into the three subgroups so that each includes members from each of the three departmental subteams. Using the Role Discussion Exercise sheet as a guideline, each subgroup should discuss its members' roles, one by one. Allow seven to ten minutes per person. Encourage the person whose role is being discussed to listen actively, ask questions if necessary, and take notes. The goal is to solicit feedback on the way others see the role, not to alter or defend the role.

12:00   Lunch

12:45   Departmental subteams discuss roles and responsibilities

1. Bring the small groups back together into one group. Ask how the role discussions went.

2. Mention that the next assignment will be done in departmental subteams. Instruct subteams to discuss each person's role briefly (as presented in the previous exercise) and then to work together to list the major responsibilities of the subteam.

3. Show a sample matrix chart and instruct each subteam to create its own matrix chart in the fashion shown. Ask them to fill in the responsibility portion of the chart. Remind them that they will have to use two pieces of flip-chart paper to make the complete matrix.

1:30   Written comments about other subteams' charts

Bring people back into one group and instruct everyone to mill around the room and read other subteams' charts. Instruct everyone to remain silent during this exercise. Ask people to write comments on the blank flip charts beside the other subteams' matrix charts (not their own). The comments may include positive feedback, suggestions, or questions (if something is not understood). Hand out medium-sized marking pens for this activity.

1:45   Subteams revise charts

Have subteams reconvene, read the comments made by other subteam members, and revise their matrix charts, if desired.

2:15   Break

2:30   Subteam reports

1. Bring the large group back together and have each subteam report on any changes they made to the charts as a result of people's written comments.

2. Ask people to comment on what they have learned or discovered about the work they have done so far.

2:45   Responsibility assignments

1. Bring the whole group together. Explain that the last step in a responsibility matrix is to indicate the following for each responsibility:

    Who has primary responsibility;
    Who has secondary responsibility;
    Who needs to be informed; and
    Who must approve decisions.

2. Taking one subteam's chart at a time, as a group, look at each major responsibility and determine those individuals who:

    Δ Have primary responsibility
    √ Have secondary responsibility
    0 Need to be informed
    * Must approve decisions

Use symbols, as shown above, to indicate the level of responsibility.

3. After about fifteen or twenty minutes, switch to another subteam's list and do the same. Switch to another subteam after fifteen or twenty minutes again. If there is not time to complete the entire matrix, suggest that the team finish it as an action item at an upcoming meeting.

4:15   Summarize and wrap up

1. Highlight and summarize insights.
2. Determine action items to be attended to. Record and post.
3. Do a round-robin feedback; ask each person to:

    - Name one thing valuable about the session; and
    - Name one thing he or she wishes had been done/happened.

4. Lead the "Positive Messages" exercise (optional).

Distribute a piece of paper to each group member. Ask each person to write a positive message about the group and the experience of working with the other group members. Collect the papers and shuffle them. Redistribute them. Ask each participant to read aloud the paper he or she has received.

5. Thank people for their hard work and compliment them on their progress.

5:00   Adjourn

Facilitator Notes

Things to do after the meeting: (Includes promises made to the client or participants during the session, follow-up calls to the client, filing of design notes, forwarding of feedback to the client.)

1.

2.

3.

4.

Designing On-the-Spot

From time to time you may be called on to facilitate a meeting when there is not enough time to plan it or when group members should be involved in deciding the focus and process of the meeting. Sometimes the group is the best one to decide the agenda, objectives, and priorities for the meeting. It is generally true that the more the group members are involved in planning the meeting, the more commitment there will be to the meeting objectives and agenda. However, there is a certain level of skill required to facilitate this type of on-the-spot planning. Be careful not to let every decision bog down into long discussion. The group must move quickly from planning the meeting into the implementation of it. Here are the steps to follow to involve group members in planning the meeting at the beginning of the meeting:

1. Indicate the general purpose and time frame of the meeting. Announce basic housekeeping details such as food arrangements, breaks, location of rest rooms and telephones, etc.

2. Explain your role as the facilitator and that you will involve the group in setting the objectives and agenda for the meeting.

3. If the group has held a previous meeting, briefly review the decisions made at that meeting and actions taken to support each decision. Note the status of each action item from the previous meeting: complete, in progress, or deleted.

4. Ask the group for agenda items for today's meeting. List these and record the name of the initiator.

5. Ask the initiator to identify what he or she wants to happen: brainstorm ideas, identify solutions, reach a decision, obtain feedback. Ask the initiator to estimate how long it will take to address the agenda item. Most items requiring discussion will take at least fifteen minutes; those that require more than thirty minutes may need to be addressed at a meeting dedicated to that item alone or first worked on by a subgroup before being presented to the larger group. Ask the group members whether they think an item warrants a separate meeting.

6. List the agenda items, name of the initiator, estimated time, and result desired. If there are too many agenda items for the time allotted for the meeting, ask the group to determine what agenda items are the most important. "What items must be discussed today?" "Can any items be delegated to a group member or subgroup to address?" If necessary, let each person select the two or three agenda items he or she feels are the most urgent to address today. Use a check mark to indicate each vote and see what agenda items surface as top priority.

7. For each priority agenda item, first ask the initiator to suggest a process or technique to use. If the initiator does not have a suggestion, suggest one.

8. Check with the group for consensus about the technique and begin the process. Record ideas and monitor the process. Throughout the process, check with the initiator to see if his or her needs regarding the agenda item are being met. If there is a decision to be made or if agreement is needed from the group, follow the process for reaching consensus described in Chapter 7. If there are dissenters, check with them to see if they are directly affected by the decision. If not, ask the dissenters if they are willing to support the decision made by the group anyway. If they are directly affected by the decision, ask the dissenters to propose a decision that will solve the issue.

9. Keep the group aware of the time as it proceeds so there will be time for the other planned agenda items. Typically, a group wants to hammer away at an agenda item until it is solved. However, it is better to move on when the time on one item is up. This teaches a group to reach agreement in an efficient way, rather than dragging out one agenda item and leaving no time for the rest. If agreement is not reached on an item, give the group the following choices: (1) Return to the item at the end of the meeting if there is time; (2) table the item for now; (3) schedule the item on the next meeting's agenda; or (4) delegate the decision to a group member or subgroup.

10. End the meeting with one of the activities recommended for closing a facilitation from Chapter 14.

Designing as a Creative Process

Do not expect designs to fall into place or logically arise out of an initial discussion with a client. The process is more organic than that. Designing a facilitation is a creative process that begins with the first conversation with the client and continues to the beginning of the next design. Designing requires time for questions and answers to take hold in the facilitator's mind, and time for discussions with the client. Facilitators should honor and respect the creative process and work with it.

For me a design begins to evolve during my initial conversation with the client. I ask questions and try to understand the context in which the group works and in which the group's assignment takes place. Next, I ask for some time to come up with some possible approaches and set a time for checking back with the client. During the next few days I begin to stir up creative juices for ideas. I look at books, old files, former designs, and just rattle my brain in general about what might work with this group. I scribble out a few notes and ideas on a piece of paper and brainstorm ideas in the car while driving. After a second conversation with the client, I am usually clearer about what needs to be done and what the client sees as the possibilities and limitations of certain approaches. Next, I outline one or two designs on paper, decide whether I think they will work with this group, and go over them with the client (usually by phone). This conversation usually settles how we will approach the session, and my next goal is to add the necessary detail and planning to the design. Frequently at this point, new ideas crop up that cannot be incorporated. Doubts appear like dust, quietly and stealthily. Will this design really benefit the group? What if this and that goes wrong? What if? What if? What if? Sometimes the doubts hit like semi-trucks in the night: No way will this design work with this group! What was I thinking?

When the design is explained to the group, and the group consents to go forward with it, the flat, rigid design laid out on paper becomes alive and is once again moldable, depending on the group and how its work goes. I seldom work without a basic design, as meetings require a beginning, a middle, and an end, and—because I have much experience with groups and in designing group sessions—I am more effective when armed with a design and some planning. I have been known, however, as most facilitators probably have, to toss out the planned design and create a new one on the spot. This, fortunately, is a rare occurrence.

The best way to learn how to design effective facilitations is through experience and feedback. That is why it is very important to find out two things at the end of a session from the participants: (1) "What was beneficial or valuable to you during this session?" and (2) "How could the session have been improved?" A quick round-robin response, while you listen and record comments—not explaining or defending—gives all participants a chance to evaluate the session and provides valuable information for designing subsequent facilitations. Even though you are often aware of what went well and what did not during a facilitation, the feedback from participants usually offers more information, and it is certainly as valid, if not more so, as your own impressions. Good facilitators welcome the feedback of their participants because they know this information will help them design better and better facilitations.

Another way to improve your design skills is to ask yourself a few questions and jot down the answers after each session:

- "What went well?"

- "What could have been improved or done differently?"

- "What creative ideas came to me during the session?"

- "What did I learn from this experience that will help me in the future as a facilitator?"

With participant feedback and your own notes, you learn by experience what works well and what does not.

Good designs do not just happen; they take careful thought and planning. A good facilitator usually puts more time into the design of a facilitation than into the actual facilitating. Skilled facilitators place value on feedback they receive from those they facilitate and use this information to learn how to design better facilitations.

CHAPTER 13

Organizing and Enhancing Group Work

When designing a facilitation, select a process and a flow of activities that will keep the group working at a productive level while enjoying the experience of working together. Almost any facilitation is a chance to build team spirit or group solidarity, as well as to produce something tangible for the organization. When designing a facilitation, make an effort to:

- Conduct activities that will sustain the momentum and energy level of the group;

- Select an appropriate-sized group for the tasks at hand;

- Use time wisely;

- Balance and vary the types of activities;

- Involve everyone as much as possible;

- Allow time for breaks, lunch, or refreshments and some socializing;

- Help group members relax with one another;

- Allow time for discussion and consensus, as well as an occasional wandering away from the main subject;

- Leave time for adequate opening and closing activities; and

- Select activities that promote team building and teamwork.

Facilitators use many methods to organize and enhance group work that provide variety, increase productivity, and promote good teamwork. Dividing the large group into smaller units, using icebreakers and energizers to liven up the group, and varying the type of activities are a few examples. Group work can be enhanced by altering the size of the group when possible, varying the location where the group works, and moving people out of their seats from time to time. Some of these methods are designed into a facilitation; others are integrated by the facilitator on the spur of the moment.

Optimum Group Size

If facilitated well, even large groups (more than fifteen people) can be very effective. However, much of the substantial work of large groups happens in smaller subgroups. The optimum size of a group dealing with substantial issues and tasks is from five to nine people, especially when consensus decisions must be reached and individual work is done apart from the group meetings. This allows a group to develop a sense of teamwork and everyone to be involved and important to the team. A large group can be divided into smaller teams that work on their own; from time to time the larger group can come together to report findings, pass resolutions, or finalize decisions. Generally, facilitators work with groups of from five to fifteen members. The concepts in this book apply best to groups of this size.

Working with Large Groups

Facilitating large groups requires careful advance planning to create maximum opportunity for participation, while keeping the purpose and goals in mind. When working with groups of more than fifteen people, create an atmosphere of small-group interaction (so that everyone stays involved), while allowing everyone to feel part of the whole group. It is important to do substantive work in smaller subgroups, which then report their findings back to the large group. Time limits have to be set and adhered to and everyone given an opportunity to participate. If consensus decisions must be made, ask subgroups to appoint representatives to meet with other subgroup representatives for the purpose of reaching consensus. Large group facilitations are generally reserved for information sharing and reporting sessions, with "buzz groups" (small discussion groups) and time for question-and-answer periods designed into the session.

Round-Robin Technique

A technique called a "round robin" is useful to ensure that everyone is given the opportunity to be heard on an issue. Round robins are especially useful on these occasions:

- To explore an issue the first time around;

- To explore an issue when there is confusion or lack of agreement;

- To check with each person to learn how he or she thinks or feels about a particular issue; or

- To hear quick feedback on the group's progress so far (to check what each person thinks about how the meeting is going, how the discussion is going, how important the issue is, etc.).

Round robins can be used at any time during a facilitation, but should not be relied on too extensively, as this will defeat the purpose and power of the tool to equalize the influence of everyone in the room, to hear from everyone, and to force people to listen to everyone else's opinions.[1]

---

[1]More detail on using the round-robin process for discussion and evaluation of ideas is presented in Chapter 8.

Dividing the Group

It is not always productive to keep the whole group or team together to work on every group task. Some tasks are better accomplished in small groups, in pairs, or by individual group members. Not all work can be divided up, however, or the feeling of group or team will be lost. It is up to you, with the help of the group, to come up with the best ways to organize the group for its various tasks.

Some of the advantages and disadvantages to keeping the group together for all discussions and decisions are listed below:

Advantages

• Everyone hears every idea and argument;

• A sense of "team" is built;

• For consensus, it is essential that everyone be together; and

• The facilitator can observe everything that is going on.

Disadvantages

• Quieter members may not speak up;

• There is less opportunity for everyone to contribute;

• Some tasks are difficult in the larger group, such as detail work; and

• Staying together in one group can be monotonous for some.

There are advantages and disadvantages to subgroup work as well:

Advantages

• Work can be spread out among subgroups;

• Everyone can be more involved;

- More real issues and concerns may surface, as people may feel freer to speak up; and

- It is less likely that one or two people will dominate.

Disadvantages

- Too much subgroup work can create cliques and break down the feeling of "team";

- Subgroups may take sides against one another;

- Some subgroups may not be productive if left unsupervised; and

- The facilitator may feel pressure to be in several places at once.

Facilitators have several options for dividing up a group: (1) A group can stay in the meeting room, but be divided into buzz groups of three or four people each to discuss a topic; (2) subgroups can be formed to meet separately to work on a problem or assignment between large group meetings; (3) if breakout space is available, subgroups can be formed during a large group meeting to work either on the same assignment or on different, complementary assignments; or (4) the large group can be divided in half and each half given the same or different assignments.

Whenever the group has been divided, your role is to make sure the small groups have directions and material needed for their work and know when to return to the large group. Give clear directions to subgroups as to what should be reported back to the large group. It is helpful to have each group summarize its work on a flip chart that can be presented to the larger group. When the subgroup work is completed or the time is up, bring the large group back together and lead a reporting session to bring everyone up to date on what occurred in the small groups. As each group reports on its task, it is important to be brief and to allow some time for questions and comments from the other subgroups. One way to make good use of time when subgroups report back to the large group is to have the first subgroup read all of its ideas or decisions. After that, ask the rest of the subgroups only to report ideas or decisions that differ from what the first group reported. This gives everyone a quick overview and keeps the entire group alert during the reporting process. Sometimes, it is not necessary to have groups report back. For example, after allowing a few minutes for buzz groups to discuss a question or an issue, simply bring everyone back together and lead a discussion. After everyone has had time to formulate ideas in buzz groups, the discussion will usually be lively and prolific.

Figure 13.1 shows some general guidelines for deciding when to divide the group and when to keep the whole group together.

Figure 13.1

If	Then
The group is relatively large (10-15 people) and the task is lengthy and requires focus and detail work	Divide the group into small groups of 3-5 people each and assign each group a portion of the larger task. When you bring the large group back together, allow those who didn't work on a particular task to make comments and add their ideas.
The group is relatively large (10-15 people) and the task requires getting everyone's viewpoint and involvement at a meaningful level (such as writing the mission statement)	Divide the group into 3 or 4 small groups and have each group list items they would like to have included in the mission statement. Post the ideas for all to see. Then have the large group write the mission statement from those ideas.
The group has been working together for a long time	Give people a chance to work in small groups: buzz groups, task groups, etc.

There are many ways to divide a group. Some are quick and easy; others are a bit more complicated. Choose the way that best suits the group, your abilities, and the time available. If your group seems lethargic, dividing it up can serve as an icebreaker to wake up everyone.

Here are a few *efficient ways to divide up a group:*

- Have participants number off (one, two, three) and then have all of the one's form a subgroup, all the two's form a subgroup, and so on. (Read the instructions below for how to have people count off so you do not embarrass yourself by ending up with the wrong size and number of groups!)

- Divide the group in half, down the middle, if you only need two groups.

- Go around the room and group people into pairs, groups of three, or groups of four. Using your arm, draw dividing lines between groups.

- Divide the group alphabetically (first or last name). Put all the A through E's in one group, the F through J's in another, and so on. If groups turn out unbalanced, make quick adjustments by asking some people to move to another group.

It pays to plan ahead when you are going to divide a group into subgroups.

First decide whether you want a *certain number of subgroups* or whether you want a *certain number of people* in each subgroup. Sometimes it is important to limit the number of people in a subgroup; at other times, the design may call for a certain number of subgroups and the number of people in each subgroup will not matter as much. The trick is this: *Do not divide the group until you have decided which of the above results you want.* Then follow the appropriate formula below.

Limited Number of Subgroups

Have people count off by the number of subgroups you want. For example, if you want four subgroups, ask people to count off by four: one, two, three, four, one, two, three, four, and so on, until everyone has a number.

Then instruct all the one's to form a group, all the two's to form a group, and so on. For example: if you are leading a group of thirteen people and you want three subgroups, have people count off by three: one, two, three, one, two, three. . . . In this case you will have three subgroups: two with four people and one with five people.

Limited Number of People per Group

If you want to limit the number of people in a subgroup, first divide the number of people in the entire group by the number of people you want in each subgroup. The answer will give you the number of subgroups, so have people count off by that number. For example, if you have sixteen people and you want four people in each subgroup (16/4 = 4), you will end up with four subgroups, so ask people to count off by four. If you have twenty people and you want four people in each subgroup (20/4 = 5), you know you will end up with five subgroups, so have people count off by five.

In both situations, you will have people *count off by the number of subgroups desired*. The mistake facilitators make is to ask the group to count off by the number of people desired in each subgroup. For example, if you used the *incorrect* method with a group of twenty-three people and you wanted three people in each subgroup and asked the group to count off by three, you would end up with one subgroup with seven people and two with eight. The *correct* way to have no more than three in a group would have been to have the group count off by eight, and you would have ended up with seven groups of three people and one with two.

Here are some creative and fun ways to divide up a group:

- Have participants draw colored slips of paper from a hat and group people according to the colors they have drawn. (You will want to have an equal distribution of colors.)

- If dividing the group in half, group people according to their birth year, putting those born in even-numbered years together and those born in odd-numbered years together.

- Post flip charts around the room equal to the number of groups you plan to form. On each flip chart write a word, draw a symbol, or place a color. Ask people to group themselves according to the word, symbol, or color they are most drawn to.

- Mix people up so that each subgroup represents several different functions, geographic locations, or backgrounds.

- If the group has already worked in subgroups, ask people to group themselves with at least one other person they have not worked with before.

Individual Work

Time for individuals to work or think can be designed into a session, or people can be given prework. It can be useful to have people work on their own quietly from time to time. Here are some situations in which individual work can enhance group work:

- *Brainstorming.* Give people time to think quietly and jot down their ideas at the beginning of a brainstorming session.

- *Between meetings.* Ask people to do an individual assignment between meetings that will jump-start the group's work at the next meeting.

- *Evaluating meetings or group work.* Give people quiet time to evaluate a meeting or the group's work. Provide them with some structure, such as a list of questions or a prepared survey.

- *Reading.* Give people individual time to read material presented at a meeting. Then ask open-ended questions to elicit their responses. If the material is too long, ask people to read it before the meeting. Less lengthy material can be read fairly quickly during the meeting, and this ensures that everyone will read it. One or two questions posed ahead of time will help direct people's thinking as they read.

Adding Variety to Group Work

Many other ways can be used to vary the approaches to group work. One simple way is to change the room in which a group meets or meet away from the normal work environment. Another is to have people switch seats halfway through a meeting or change the typical order of the meeting. Instead of designing all the meetings yourself, ask a subgroup or the whole group to plan a meeting. Inviting guests to speak on a particular topic is an opportunity for a group to learn and develop a different perspective on the issue or topic.

If the group wants fresh insights to help it along, bring in a panel of outside experts, customers, or others who can provide new viewpoints and ideas, information, or facts that will help the group. Let the group create a list of questions beforehand that the panel will address.

Icebreakers

Icebreakers are activities that loosen up the group, help people feel comfortable participating, provide a safe way for people to speak up, give people a chance to laugh or move around, and in general "break the ice." Icebreakers can be designed with specific purposes in mind, such as:

- Introducing group members to one another;

- Helping people to think about the topic;

- Giving group members a chance to relax and move around;

- Dissolving apprehensions and beginning the meeting on a positive note;

- Allowing people to have some fun;

- Starting energy flowing;

- Letting down people's reserves;

- Waking people up;

- Teaching or illustrating something;

- Allowing people to participate in a safe environment;

- Unblocking and rejuvenating a group; and

- Fostering creative thinking.

The New Encyclopedia of Icebreakers (McLaughlin & Peyser, 2004) contains over one hundred quick group energizers that will warm up, motivate, and refresh a group. It includes designs for beginning a session, getting acquainted, re-energizing a tired group, enhancing receptivity, and investing people in the purpose and work of the group. Another book, *Warmups for Meeting Leaders* (Bianchi, Butler, & Richey, 1990) is a guide to creating your own warmups for various purposes. The authors distinguish between two types of warmups: social and topical. Social warmups help the group become acquainted and comfortable with one another. Topical warmups help everyone focus on the topic of the meeting. The book includes one hundred warmups for immediate use, as well as tips for designing and conducting your own.

As a new facilitator, you may wish to rely on icebreakers or warmups designed by others. However, it is relatively easy to design your own icebreakers and it may be essential given the topic or situation a group is facing. Here are seven steps to designing and planning an icebreaker:

1. *Determine your icebreaker goal.* What is the purpose of your icebreaker? Do you want to wake people up, dissolve apprehensions or hostilities that may exist in the group, acquaint people, help people focus on the topic, or create a relaxed and open atmosphere? Do not try to make one icebreaker do everything. Decide what is most important.

2. *Decide how much time you need.* Based on your goal, how much time will it take to conduct an effective icebreaker? Will you be

recording people's inputs during the icebreaker? If so, allow time for this.

3. *Select the type of icebreaker.* Will you use a round-robin activity? Will you use a game? Questions to stimulate thinking? An activity such as a problem to solve, a task to complete, or something to make such as a craft or a picture?

4. *Design or find the icebreaker.* Use published resources such as those mentioned earlier, icebreakers you have seen other facilitators or trainers use, those you have used before, or create a new one.

5. *List required materials, equipment, and space.* Does the room need to be set up in any special way? Would it be helpful to write the directions on a flip chart? Are handouts needed?

6. *Think about how to handle the unexpected.* What will you do if several people come in late? How might people be confused or start off on the wrong foot? What if people talk too long? Have you created an icebreaker that is "safe" enough for everyone to participate? Is there any reason why someone may not be able to participate (physically challenged, too new to the group, health issues)?

7. *Plan how to introduce the icebreaker.* You will probably want to give a brief description of the icebreaker, state its purpose, and give directions about how to proceed. (Be as brief as possible.) Be clear about the directions yourself and think about the best way to present them. Determine ahead of time how to divide the group if the icebreaker calls for subgroups or teams.

These seven steps also apply to designing any group activity. First, determine the goal of the activity; then, design and plan to meet that goal; and, finally, assemble materials you will need, plan for the unexpected, and decide how to introduce and conduct the activity.

In summary, facilitators use a variety of methods to organize and enhance group work for the purpose of providing variety, stimulating thinking, building team spirit, and ensuring productivity. It pays to be on the look-out continually for effective group methods that will keep your facilitations interesting and productive.

Opening and Closing Activities

The tone and spirit of a group's work in meetings is greatly affected by the opening and closing activities. To start a group off well requires setting a positive tone for the meeting. Closing the meeting involves leaving the group with a sense of commitment to and clarity about what has been decided. When meetings are opened and closed well, a positive atmosphere and momentum are established that make the group's work satisfying and productive. At the opening of the meeting is an important time to establish group norms and to reinforce the idea that this is *the group's work* and that each person shares ownership for the group's output. At the closing is the time to solidify decisions made, clarify action items, and determine ways to make the next meeting even more productive.

General Guidelines

Although each meeting and each group will require different ways to open and close meetings, certain important tasks must be accomplished at the beginning and end of most meetings. First meetings, when the group has never been together before, and final meetings, when the group is disbanding, require some special types of activities.

When opening a meeting, aim to receive full and focused participation from all the group members as soon as possible. Reserve the first portion of the meeting to welcome people, attend to administrative details, make sure people are introduced to one another, and outline the objectives (the purpose and intended outcome) and flow of the meeting. If the group has met before, set aside a few minutes to clear up any unfinished business from the last meeting. You may want to go over the ground rules for participating and being a part of the group and to elicit individual expectations for the session.

When choosing opening or closing activities for a group meeting, first ask yourself some questions about the group and the situation:

- "What is likely to be the attitude or spirit of the group?"

- "What are the strong and weak points of the group?"

- "What is the group's attitude toward working with a facilitator?"

- "How well do group members know and respect one another?"

- "What is the goal(s) of the activities?" (What do you want the activities to accomplish?)

- "How much time can be used for these activities?"

- "What are the absolute essentials that must be covered?"

- "What will be the group's attitude toward and exposure to the topic at hand?"

- "What difficulties (time, resources, noise, attendance) might come up?"

After you have assessed the situation and the group, you are ready to brainstorm and decide what the flow of the opening or closing activities will be. First make a list of what must be covered and what you would like to cover. Try to find a balance between squeezing the important opening or closing activities into a tight time schedule and dragging them out too long.

Opening a Group's First Meeting

The opening activities of a group's first meeting are critical in focusing the group, setting a positive tone, and gaining commitment from members to proceed. When members are not acquainted with one another, the first meeting provides a chance for individuals to get acquainted and begin to build trust and credibility in the group. The first meeting is also the opportunity to deal with any misunderstandings about why the group is meeting and to establish the importance and reason for forming the group.

Do not assume that group members have been adequately informed before the first meeting as to why the group has been formed or what is expected of it. It is one of your important roles as the facilitator to design first meeting activities that will clear up misunderstandings and help the group focus and start off on the right foot. The best assumption to make when facilitating a group's first meeting is that members are not fully clear about the purpose of the group. Frequently, a group is formed to address an issue and it is up to the group to chart its own purpose and goals. Here are some typical things that need to happen at most first meetings:

- Welcome to the meeting, to the group;

- Introductions of participants, facilitators, and guests (may be in the form of an icebreaker to relieve tension and draw people into the group);

- Brief explanation of roles (facilitator, recorder, group leader, members);

- Agreement on objectives and purpose of the meeting;

- Agreement on suggested ground rules and a chance for participants to add ground rules of their own;

- Administrative details (ending time, break times, lunch arrangements, location of phones and rest rooms, sign-ups for other activities);

- Individual expectations or desired outcomes for the meeting; and

- Flow of the meeting (brief outline of the content and process to be followed).

There is no set order for these activities. However, one rule of thumb is to introduce people to one another and to yourself and others present as soon as possible. Do this after a general welcome and brief introduction to the purpose and objectives of the meeting. Even if members already know one another, conduct some sort of introduction or icebreaker; this gives everyone a chance to speak up and gives you a chance to learn a little about each person. When activities begin before people are introduced (or asked to speak), the energy level of the room drops and people are not sufficiently drawn into the group. Waiting too long to introduce people gives the undesirable message that they are not important. Here is a sample flow of opening activities for a group's first meeting:

1. Welcome

2. Icebreaker (to introduce people to one another)

3. Agreement to objectives and purpose of the meeting

4. Individual expectations for the meeting

5. Explanation of facilitator's role

6. Suggested ground rules and agreement

7. Administrative details

8. Agenda (content and process flow of the meeting)

When gathering each person's expectations for the meeting (Number 4 above), record names and expectations on a flip chart. When everyone has finished, go back through the items quickly and indicate whether the expectation is likely to be met, given the objectives and design of the meeting. Through this process, you make a "verbal contract" with the group about the content and intent of the meeting. Addressing expectations in this manner lessens the chance that people will go off on their own tangents or be disappointed at the end of the meeting. It helps everyone focus fully on the meeting and its intent and helps people to buy into the objectives and purpose of the meeting. At the end of the meeting, briefly return to the list of expectations, asking each person whether and how his or her expectations were met. It is not necessary to review any expectations that you said would not be met at the meeting. There was no "contract" with the group to meet those.

Groups function best when the members have discussed and agreed on a set of ground rules or guidelines for the group's meetings (Number 6 earlier). These become standards of behavior the group members agree to uphold, and they serve as a "verbal contract" members make with one another. Setting the ground rules at the beginning of a group's work together, usually at the first meeting, will give people more control over how they operate as a group. Groups that do not set standards generally fall into bad habits (not starting on time, interrupting one another, not allowing constructive disagreement); these bad habits become a norm for the group. Provide opportunities for groups to set standards, make suggestions to the group, and let the group know when it is not following its own standards.

After a brief introduction to the value of having ground rules, along with a few examples, a group can come up with some initial ground rules at its first meeting. After a few meetings, post the ground rules again (some facilitators post these at every meeting) and ask the group to review them. ("How are we doing with our ground rules?" "Are we keeping them?" "Do we need to change them or add any new ones?") This gives the group an opportunity to correct some of its bad habits. Instead of finger pointing, it becomes a group effort to identify ways to function better by setting new standards. If the group is only together for one or two days, give the group a chance to review its ground rules about halfway through the session. By then the group has had a chance to experience itself as a group and has more information on which to base its ground rules.

Some suggested ground rules are listed below. Always let the group change, delete, or add its own ground rules. The suggestions just start the group thinking and give you a chance to explain why certain ground rules will help the group be more productive.

Typical Ground Rules

- Hear one another out;

- Make an effort to consider all ideas; keep an open mind;

- When confused, ask;

- Be here; return from breaks on time;

- Participate (share ideas/thoughts, ask questions, listen);

- Keep goals in mind; and

- Conflict or disagreement is OK, but we must work constructively toward a solution.

If a group will be together for several meetings (a project team, for example), it is a good idea to have the group list not only its meeting ground rules but also others it wishes to follow. These can be developed at two different meetings, but both should be discussed in the early stages of the group's work.

Examples of Other Ground Rules

- Honor confidentiality;

- Communicate between meetings when necessary;

- Notify group members if commitments cannot be met; and

- Ask other members for support or information.

Opening a Group's Subsequent Meetings

You, perhaps in collaboration with the group, must decide how best to open each subsequent meeting. The main purpose of opening activities is to gain the full attention of everyone in the group and to help members focus and be ready to work on the task at hand. When participants enter a meeting room, they may not be "fully present." Their heads may be filled with concerns, responsibilities, or ideas related to other aspects of their lives. The opening of a meeting can be facilitated so that everyone has a chance to clear his or her mind of other matters and become tuned into the purpose of the meeting.

Generally speaking, the following need to be taken care of at the beginning of each meeting:

- Welcome and introductions of guests or new members;

- Icebreaker (optional);

- Administration (time meeting will end, announcements);

- Objectives and agenda;

- Agreement to proceed;

- Announcements and clearing of items left over from last meeting; and

- Explanation of facilitator's role (if this is his or her first meeting with a group).

Suggest objectives and agenda for the meeting, based on the progress made at the previous meeting and input from group members and the group leader. Present these to the group as "proposed objectives for today's meeting," written on flip charts, and ask for agreement from the group. An agreement to proceed focuses the group's energy and helps people feel ready to work. It allows group members to alter the agenda; the facilitator and the group then work together on a revised agenda, based on any new objectives.

Closing a Group's Ongoing Meetings

Opening activities are meant to focus everyone's full attention on the meeting and its purpose. Closing activities help make sure the results of the meeting are clear and that everyone knows what he or she must do next. Group members also give feedback on the meeting process and plan details of the next meeting. Typically, closing a group meeting involves the following:

- Reading over the written and posted *decisions* that were made during the meeting and checking for understanding and buy-in;

- Reviewing *action items* (who is going to do what by when);

- Acknowledging *items that surfaced for the first time* during the meeting and asking the group how they want to deal with them;

- Making *arrangements for the next meeting*—setting date, time, and place;

- Going around the group to hear *each member's feedback* on the meeting ("What went well?" "What could be improved?"); and

- Occasionally, *informal time* and refreshments, giving members a chance to socialize and/or deal informally with work-related issues.

Closing a Group's Last Meeting

The time comes for most groups to disband and move on. Either the work is done, it cannot be done, or the situation has changed and the group must start over. Ideally, you and the group will be able to have an official last meeting, as this can be an effective way for people to let go of their connection with the group and move on. When a group is not officially disbanded, something is left uncompleted for the members. Whenever possible, it is a good idea to have a closing meeting instead of ending the group meetings with some kind of verbal or written notice. People will feel better about the group and its work, whether it was finished or not, if they have a chance for a closing meeting. Here are some suggestions for what to accomplish at a final group meeting:

- List any miscellaneous work that must be done;

- Have each group member share what he or she found most rewarding and important about being part of the group;

- Allow time for people to express appreciation to one another and to the group leader and facilitator;

- Offer opportunity for members to exchange phone numbers and addresses;

- Return original documentation and materials to group members;

- Give group members a chance to relate what they learned about group work and what they would do differently next time; and

- Present awards, recognition, or gifts to every group member to signify the value of each person's contribution.

Skilled facilitators pay special attention to the way they open and close meetings. When meetings are opened and closed well, a positive atmosphere results, momentum builds, people are clear about the meeting's goals, and the meeting ends with people focused on what they need to do next. The opening and closing of a meeting provide a framework around everything else that happens during the meeting.

The Facilitator in Action

Those who develop basic facilitation skills and who have knowledge of the basic tools find themselves in a variety of situations, from facilitating a simple one-on-one discussion to facilitating several teams or groups across an organization. Part 5 will help you understand the types of situations you may encounter and the skills required, and it will help you determine whether you are ready for a particular situation. Chapter 15 presents a competency matrix for the three levels of facilitation, Chapter 16 is a discussion of meeting facilitation, Chapter 17 provides a discussion of team facilitation, Chapter 18 provides suggestions for how to facilitate a virtual team, and Chapter 19 is a discussion of organization-wide facilitation.

Generally speaking, facilitating a discussion is less difficult than designing, facilitating, and following up on a team meeting; and facilitating a team is generally less difficult than facilitating an organization-wide series of meetings at various levels. There are always exceptions, of course, and the simplest discussion may require advanced facilitation skills, whereas facilitating a team meeting may require only the most basic skills.

Levels of Facilitator Competency

F acilitation skills range from basic to complex. Generally speaking, basic facilitation skills are needed to lead a group discussion or meeting, while more advanced skills are required to facilitate and coach teams. Facilitating major organizational change demands an even higher level of skill. This chapter contains the Facilitator Competency Matrix, a comprehensive list of facilitation skills, broken down into three levels: Level I, *basic skills*; Level II, *team skills*; and Level III, *organization-wide skills*. The levels build on one another; that is, a Level II facilitator must also be proficient in Level I skills, and a Level III facilitator must be proficient in all three levels.

Most professionals benefit from having basic facilitation skills, as they are frequently called on to manage discussions or lead meetings. Team leaders and managers need a higher level of skills to facilitate team development and to communicate and collaborate with those outside the team. People with organization-wide responsibilities need Level III facilitation skills to navigate through organizational visioning, strategic planning, change implementation, politics, and cross-functional collaboration and cooperation.

The Facilitator Competency Matrix was developed from my work as a facilitator over the past fifteen years, from my work with other professional facilitators, and from teaching and observing hundreds of new facilitators. The competencies are listed in order from the broadest professional competencies (such as credibility, judgment, human relations, and business knowledge) to the specific competencies of group process (such as participation management, listening, meeting management, and meeting design). The specific competencies of group process are in turn ordered with the most basic first (such as listening or managing participation) followed by the more advanced skills (such as managing conflict, change management, and building client relationships).

Use the Facilitator Competency Matrix to understand more fully the role of the facilitator in various situations and to understand and plot your own development as a facilitator. The matrix will help you to:

- Determine your current facilitation skill level;

- Highlight areas in which you feel most confident;

- Identify skills you need to develop further;

- Set developmental goals for yourself;

- Determine whether you have the skills required to carry out particular assignments;

- Educate others about the skills required for facilitation; and

- Explain and carry out your role as a facilitator.

The matrix is also designed to be used in organizations that are training and developing facilitators. The matrix will help an organization:

- Clarify what facilitator skills are needed;

- Develop an outline of skills to be taught in facilitator training;

- Determine what can be expected from facilitators at various levels of development;

- Measure the effectiveness of facilitator training; and

- Design feedback measures to evaluate facilitator performance.

Facilitator Competency Matrix*

Definitions of Facilitator Competency

Level I Facilitator
(Meeting Facilitator):

Someone who has completed basic facili-
tation training and successfully designs and facilitates
short group meetings.

Level II Facilitator
(Team Facilitator):

An experienced Level I facilitator who is
also qualified to facilitate the ongoing meetings of a
team or group. Someone qualified to design and facilitate longer, more complex group meetings.

Level III Facilitator
(Organization Facilitator):

An experienced Level II facilitator who is
also qualified to design and facilitate inter-team, and
organization-wide meetings and projects.

*Adapted from the Facilitator Competency Matrix developed by the McFletcher Corporation and Rees and As-
sociates, ©1993.

Facilitator Competency Matrix

Areas of Competency and Experience	Level I Facilitator	Level II Facilitator	Level III Facilitator
Credibility	Demonstrates ability to gain respect and maintain credibility with colleagues, group leaders and members, and managers.	Demonstrates positive influence on team development and productivity.	Has achieved credibility as a team facilitator and as a facilitator of positive change in the organization.
	Builds relationships and credibility before seeking alliances.	Demonstrates ability to gain respect and credibility with team leader and members.	Has received endorsement from managers and teams.
			Has positive influence on inter-team work; promotes employee involvement in teams and organization-wide projects.
Judgment	Demonstrates ability in knowing when and how to maintain confidentiality.	Exercises good judgment and demonstrates ability to maintain confidentiality.	Has been involved working on an organizational issue and demonstrated ability to confidentiality.
	Takes an objective stance. Approaches issues with an open mind.	Understands the need and senses appropriate timing for interfacing with other teams.	Exercises wisdom in bringing ideas and issues to an organization-wide visibility.
			Reserves judgment while gathering data and encourages clients to do the same.

Areas of Competency and Experience	Level I Facilitator	Level II Facilitator	Level III Facilitator
Human Relations	Focuses on the situation rather than on the individual.	Demonstrates ability to design and lead productive meetings at which the group is mixed.	Deals comfortably with high-level management in individual and group situations, both formally and informally.
	Exercises authority and control without arrogance or intimidation.	Deals comfortably with individuals of different backgrounds and from different levels and functions in the organization.	Works with a mix of levels in a way that values and respects everyone.
	Remains neutral, even in highly charged discussions of personal concern or interest.		Facilitates and models the valuing of diversity within a team, in inter-team situations, and across the organization.
	Understands and values diversity of people and opinions. Demonstrates willingness to under-stand workforce diversity concerns.		
Risk Taking	Willing to develop skills to initiate and manage change in the organization.	Shows willingness to intervene and/or initiate change, regardless of position or hierarchy.	Effectively intervenes to initiate change, regard-less of position or hierarchy.
		Willing to expose self to some criticism and scrutiny for the sake of team progress.	

Areas of Competency and Experience	Level I Facilitator	Level II Facilitator	Level III Facilitator
Business Knowledge	Encourages group to understand how its goals and efforts link to overall organizational goals.	Facilitates increased team understanding of overall business issues.	Facilitates linking of business goals across teams and across the organization.
	Applies facilitation methods and processes to support business goals and needs.	Helps team link its own goals to the organization's business goals.	Helps teams and cross-functional groups work together effectively to support overall business goals and needs.
Learning Orientation	Demonstrates willingness to learn and adapt.	Continually builds on Level I skills.	Continually builds on Level II skills.
	Willing to say "I don't know."	Learns along with the team.	Demonstrates interest in and commitment to continual growth as a facilitator.
	Learns along with group members during a facilitation.	Learns from past experience with teams.	Learns and tries new approaches to organizational efforts.
	Is self-motivated to continue learning facilitation skills and concepts.	Is self-motivated to continue learning about teams and team development.	
Self-Management	Is comfortable with own educational background and work experience.	Is willing not to be needed by the team.	Able to facilitate conflict resolution without becoming emotionally hooked on the issues.

Areas of Competency and Experience	Level I Facilitator	Level II Facilitator	Level III Facilitator
Self-Management (cont.)	Holds self in positive regard, even in difficult circumstances.	Is able to show both strength and vulnerability to the team.	Works not to be needed by the client eventually.
	Is aware of own strengths and weaknesses. negatively.	Manages own work load so as not to affect the team	
	Asks for help or advice from another professional when needed.		
	Able to express own needs and opinions without forcing them on the client.		
Workload Management	Ability to manage own time and workload effectively.	Demonstrates skill in helping a team manage its time and workload.	Ability to facilitate workload management across teams and organization-wide projects.
	Ability to link own work with that of others.	Manages own workload and facilitation responsibilities effectively.	
		Ability to link team's work with that of another team.	

Areas of Competency and Experience	Level I Facilitator	Level II Facilitator	Level III Facilitator
Presentation Skills	Explains in an orderly fashion and presents the rationale behind things.	Presents thoughts, ideas, and information clearly and concisely to a team.	Presents thoughts, ideas, and information clearly and concisely to a team in inter-team situations and organization-wide.
	Presents and develops subject matter in an interesting, easily understood way.	Gathers information and presents it to the team in an orderly, relevant fashion.	Designs and presents information across teams and organization-wide.
	Verbalizes own and others' ideas well.	Gives team members guidance on giving effective team presentations.	
Role Understanding and Application	Demonstrates ability to move from role of presenter or team member to role of facilitator.	Acts as both meeting facilitator and coach to the team.	Is comfortable and skilled at moving into different roles as the situation demands (e.g., meeting facilitator, coach, trainer, presenter).
	Presents self as neither dictatorial nor overly flexible.	Adapts role style as situation demands.	Molds the role of facilitator to serve the organization and accomplish its mission.
	Understands and applies the role of a facilitator and explains the role to a group.	Understands and applies the role of a facilitator and explains the role (and other team roles) to a team.	

Areas of Competency and Experience	Level I Facilitator	Level II Facilitator	Level III Facilitator
Role Understanding and Application (*cont.*)	Understands the difference between presenting and facilitating. Knows when to employ each for best results.	Understands and supports the role of the team leader. Knows how to blend with that role.	
	Knows how to function both as a presenter and a facilitator. Knows when to "change hats."	Collaborates with the team leader for best possible blend of facilitator and leader roles.	
		Helps team define a process for working together.	
		Helps team leaders and team members take on new roles to develop the team.	
Group Skills and Experience	Has experience working effectively with groups and teams to accomplish goals.	Has ongoing experience facilitating a team.	Comfortable and skilled working within a team, in inter-team situations, and organization-wide.
	Uses basic facilitator skills and methods in a group setting.	Comfortable working as a team member when not the facilitator.	Supports the work and development of other facilitators in the organization. Is an active team member in organization's facilitator support group, if any.

Areas of Competency and Experience	Level I Facilitator	Level II Facilitator	Level III Facilitator
Group Skills and Experience (*cont.*)	Demonstrates willingness and ability to learn and apply group facilitation skills and methods.	Applies basic understanding of group dynamics to work with the team.	Helps others understand and apply principles of group dynamics.
	Works well with a variety of people of different backgrounds, personalities, and interests.		
	Competent in organizing people (e.g., to plan an event, solve a problem, form a group).		
Listening	Listens without interrupting.	Role models good listening skills to the team.	Gives appropriately timed feedback to people at all levels in the organization on their listening skills.
	Willing to downplay own ego and agendas while listening to others. Can maintain neutrality.	Helps team members discover ways to improve listening habits.	Intervenes constructively to improve listening skills in the organization.
	Conveys understanding of others' points of view.	Intervenes to facilitate good listening among team members.	
	Demonstrates ability to accurately capture and record the key points of others in a meeting setting.	Designs and uses group processes that encourage good listening.	

Areas of Competency and Experience	Level I Facilitator	Level II Facilitator	Level III Facilitator
Participation Management and Methods	Models good facilitation skills one-on-one, as well as in group work.	Coaches team leader or managers present not to take over. Encourages manager to be informative, not controlling.	Applies facilitation techniques, even in settings in which involvement and openness may be resisted.
	Accurately captures and frames ideas presented by others.	Skilled and at ease using facilitation techniques.	Anticipates who will act in what ways and plans meeting accordingly.
	Uses facilitation techniques to draw out all group members.	Has developed own best systems for recording and preserving or documenting team data, perhaps even facilitated the team to do this work.	Able to unblock people's thoughts and feelings for the sake of organizational progress.
	Competent in taking notes on an easel or white board and summarizing information for the team.	Facilitates team to organize itself.	Influences organization in developing and implementing participation methods.
	Records group members' inputs briefly and accurately. Writes clearly on the flip chart or white board.	Successfully uses a variety of methods to bring the team to consensus.	Uses facilitation methods to help clients generate solutions to their own problems.

Areas of Competency and Experience	Level I Facilitator	Level II Facilitator	Level III Facilitator
Participation Management and Methods (*cont.*)	When using a recorder, coaches recorder so all ideas are captured as accurately as possible. Selects appropriate participation methods for the task at hand.	Records, organizes, and manipulates team data for ease of use by all.	
	Effectively explains the rationale of group methods (e.g., brain-storming, affinity diagramming).	Able to hear not only what is said but also the thoughts and feelings behind the words.	
	Addresses questions and resistance to the use of group methods.	Demonstrates ability to sense both verbal and nonverbal communication.	
	Effectively uses subgroups to facilitate the work of the larger group.	Encourages divergent viewpoints, increases team creativity, and guides team to more in-depth approaches.	
	Selects appropriate leaders or facilitators for subgroup work.		
	Gives clear, concise, verbal and/or written directions for group activities. Senses when directions are not clear.	Challenges a team to explore or question its own assumptions or conclusions.	

Areas of Competency and Experience	Level I Facilitator	Level II Facilitator	Level III Facilitator
Participation Management and Methods (*cont.*)	Demonstrates ability to "read" a group and make necessary adjustments to ensure group productivity.		
	Senses when to allow discussion and when to move a group toward consensus.		
Meeting Management	Is skilled and comfortable running meetings in either the presentation mode or the interaction mode.	Competent in working with the team leader to plan, facilitate, and follow up on meetings.	Skilled at managing cross-organization meeting logistics, facilitation, and follow-up.
	Starts and ends meetings on time or obtains consensus from the group to go overtime.	Develops team's ability to facilitate and manage its own meetings.	Ability to come into a group, department, or division as an outsider and facilitate meetings.
	Manages meeting time well.	Effectively coordinates pre- and post-meeting logistics; coaches team leader when necessary.	Adept at designing meetings and works collaboratively with clients to ensure their involvement in meeting planning.
	Senses the needs of group members and provides breaks and changes of pace as needed.	Manages the team's time well.	

Areas of Competency and Experience	Level I Facilitator	Level II Facilitator	Level III Facilitator
Meeting Management (*cont.*)	Helps group set norms for meeting behavior.	Reinforces the concept that everyone is responsible for effective meetings.	
		Facilitates team to create and revise its own norms for meeting behavior.	
		Maintains key balances in team meetings: between a tight and loose structure, fast and slow pace, process and results, concern for individuals and for the group, facilitator leading the team and the team leading itself, etc.	
Collaboration Skills	Explicitly articulates both sides of an issue.	Coaches team members in collaboration skills and in methods that lead to constructive and satisfying consensus.	Involves client in intervention activities and approaches.
	Acknowledges validity of viewpoints opposite one's own.	Collaborates with the team to design and facilitate team activities.	Facilitates client to interpret own data and to draw own conclusions. Offers ideas and possible solutions without expecting the client to agree.

Areas of Competency and Experience	Level I Facilitator	Level II Facilitator	Level III Facilitator
Collaboration Skills (*cont.*)	Seeks to reach consensus on goals and to facilitate creativity and adaptability in reaching those goals.		
	Helps group work to joint solutions that satisfy multiple needs.		
	Explains what consensus is and helps groups come to a decision that everyone can support 100 percent.		
Designing Meetings	Demonstrates ability to design short, simple meetings.	Competent in designing ongoing team meetings with the help of team members and the team leader.	Designs a successful meeting or intervention between individuals, within a team, or across the organization.
	Selects appropriate tools and processes for group work.	Selects appropriate meeting objectives and group processes.	Develops effective feedback systems.
	Bases the design on clearly stated, results-oriented meeting objectives.	Includes team-building activities in team meetings from time to time.	Competent in designing meetings for cross-functional groups and management and in meetings with representatives from outside the organization.

Areas of Competency and Experience	Level I Facilitator	Level II Facilitator	Level III Facilitator
Designing Meetings (*cont.*)	Includes a variety of activities when possible to keep up the interest and momentum of the group.	Involves team members in determining meeting objectives and agenda. Solicits ideas from team members about tools and processes to use.	Demonstrates ability to design a successful one-day or two-day meeting.
		Demonstrates flexibility and alters the design as needed.	Designs and facilitates learning activities that lead to organizational growth and change.
Coaching	Coaches individuals and groups to apply facilitation methods to be more productive.	Coaches the team in becoming an effective team.	Coaches team leaders and other facilitators across the organization as needed.
		Coaches the team to communicate both inside and outside the team.	
		Helps team understand the stages of team growth and development.	
		Helps team seek appropriate team training when needed.	
Understanding Group Dynamics	"Reads" group and improvises meeting processes when necessary.	Applies principles of group behavior to achieve effective group dynamics in the team setting.	Applies principles of group dynamics to inter-team and organization-wide situations.

Areas of Competency and Experience	Level I Facilitator	Level II Facilitator	Level III Facilitator
Understanding Group Dynamics (*cont.*)	Observes group interpersonal behaviors and forms conclusions of group effectiveness.	Helps the team avoid "group think" or hasty, ill-thought-out conclusions.	
	Coaches group to set its own norms and standards.	Facilitates team's own ability to maintain its sense of purpose.	
	Suggests helpful group norms (e.g., hearing one another out, attending all meetings).	Coaches team to assign team tasks based on strengths and preferences of individuals.	
		Facilitates team's periodic evaluation of itself.	
		Demonstrates ability to guide a team step by step from its inception through output and results.	

Areas of Competency and Experience	Level I Facilitator	Level II Facilitator	Level III Facilitator
Understanding Group Dynamics (*cont.*)		Demonstrates understanding of how teams develop over time. Understands the stages of team development. Supports the team from its inception to the development of the team as a cohesive work group; into an efficient, independent team; and into an effective interdependent organizational unit.	
Managing Conflict	Is not afraid of conflict. Recognizes conflict as natural and takes initiative to work through it.	Applies facilitation methods in dealing with conflict.	Facilitates inter-team or cross-functional resolution of conflict.
	Maintains a mature problem-solving attitude while dealing with interpersonal conflict, rejection, hostility, or time demands.	Keeps team focused on its goals during conflict situations.	Effectively mediates cross-organizational and inter-team conflict.
		Uses group processes that resolve or minimize conflict.	

Areas of Competency and Experience	Level I Facilitator	Level II Facilitator	Level III Facilitator
Managing Conflict (*cont.*)		Steers team members away from dysfunctional group behaviors.	
		Intervenes when group work becomes dysfunctional.	
Conceptual and Diagnostic Skills	States problems and objectives clearly.	Relates and explains information to a team in light of the bigger picture (organizational goals).	Designs simple models that relate and explain information in an understandable and motivating way.
	Probes to determine root of issues or problems.	Facilitates team to apply diagnostic methods when necessary.	Uses and explains the models of others.
	Organizes and presents data in a clear manner.	Explains the concepts of teamwork clearly to the team.	Has basic knowledge of how organization-wide team efforts progress over time.
	Able to summarize briefly from a large amount of data.	Understands the impact team efforts have on organizations and employees.	Obtains multiple perspectives on a problem or situation.
	Expresses own and others' thoughts and ideas clearly and concisely.	Accurately organizes and summarizes large amounts of information.	Delivers all relevant data, even if it was not part of the original assignment.

Areas of Competency and Experience	Level I Facilitator	Level II Facilitator	Level III Facilitator
Conceptual and Diagnostic Skills (*cont.*)	Helps client maintain logical steps in problem solving and decision making.		
Change Management	Accepts change; does not view change as threatening.	Influences team to take initiative, try new approaches, and explore different perspectives.	Understands the process of implementing change in organizations.
		Shows enthusiasm for team's efforts to reach beyond current limits and boundaries.	
	Shows willingness to learn from others about how to manage change.	Uses group processes that foster creativity and exploration.	Facilitates change and innovation.
		Role models an open-minded approach to change.	
	Takes initiative to try new things. Experiments with different perspectives and approaches.	Helps team understand the need for change.	Demonstrates ability to facilitate a project from inception to completion.
		Guides team in implementing change.	Modifies project design or activities to meet evolving needs.

Areas of Competency and Experience	Level I Facilitator	Level II Facilitator	Level III Facilitator
Feedback and Evaluation	Regularly solicits feedback from group members about how their meetings are going.	Facilitates the team's evaluation of its meetings and its progress.	Solicits formal (forms, questionnaires) and informal feedback from client.
	Asks whether feedback has been understood and makes necessary adaptations.	Is known to ask frequently for feedback on how the team meetings and processes are working.	Assists client in obtaining feedback on the progress and outcome of a project.
	Gives feedback to the group on its progress as a group.	Skilled at facilitating the team's evaluation of itself, its meetings, its work.	Helps client measure success based on stated objectives for the work.
	Assesses own contributions realistically.		Accepts or shares responsibility for success or failure, as appropriate. Avoids blaming others for failed or aborted efforts.
Building Client Relationships	Works collaboratively with the client when planning a meeting.	Considers the whole team to be the client and works collaboratively with the team to plan meetings and initiate improvements.	Develops clear, mutual agreements (the "contract") with client on a project.

Areas of Competency and Experience	Level I Facilitator	Level II Facilitator	Level III Facilitator
Building Client Relationships (*cont.*)	Clarifies the facilitator's role and the client's role in the meeting.	Ensures that the team "owns" its own work and encourages the team to copy and distribute meeting notes, decisions, action items, etc.	Knows when it is not wise to intervene in an organization.
	Communicates openly and promptly with client. Meets client commitments on time and as discussed.	Develops facilitation skills within the team so that eventually it will not need the facilitator.	Works with client to clarify own and client's role in the project.
	Returns phone calls and messages promptly.		Keeps client up to date and informed.
	Asks questions to clarify any confusion.		Works collaboratively with the client through all stages of a project.
	Speaks directly to the person with whom there is a concern or issue.		Works with client to clarify measurable outcomes for the project.
	Promises only what can be delivered.		Ensures client ownership of results and solutions by involving client in all decisions relating to the work.

Areas of Competency and Experience	Level I Facilitator	Level II Facilitator	Level III Facilitator
Building Client Relationships (*cont.*)	Explains the facilitation role and its rationale to client, if necessary.		Develops skill in determining who the various clients are on a project.
	Elicits client's expectations early in the project.		Makes an effort to understand the values and culture of the client.
	Maintains client confidentiality.		Accurately determines client's and organization's readiness for the project.
			Builds and maintains trust level with client.
	Successfully solicits the cooperation of client.		Revisits original agreement (contract) with client when necessary.
			Lets go when the work is finished.

CHAPTER 16

Facilitating Meetings

eetings are the fundamental way people get together as a group and the arena in which consensus decisions are often made. Traditionally, groups have engaged face-to-face to work through their issues, make plans, create solutions, share information, and decide upcoming actions. Facilitators apply most of their expertise during a group meeting.

Meetings have proliferated in recent years. People complain of spending their lives in meetings and never accomplishing any "real" work. One woman in one of my facilitation workshops had attended twenty-five meetings during the previous week! Although people have pointed out for years that there are too many unnecessary meetings and that not enough is accomplished in meetings, meetings are still as prevalent and seemingly as essential as ever.

What is happening here? Why are there so many meetings? Why are many of them still unproductive? Over the years, meetings have become an essential way for people to work together. Unfortunately, unless an organization has specifically targeted improving its meetings, poor meeting practices become a habit. Traditional meeting wisdom came out of an era in which meetings were used as one-way communication or at which a group of committee members met to tackle a task or project. Typically, people were not trained to facilitate meetings, but to present at them. Most managers and supervisors were not trained to facilitate lively discussions, manage group process, or help groups reach consensus. In addition, many managers and supervisors are reluctant to "lose control" by involving their groups in making decisions and plans.

During recent years, there has been a move to involve employees and organization members more in planning and decision making—not because this is a nice thing to do, but because it is the only way (or the most efficient way) to make something happen. Out of necessity, people come together in meetings. The more change there is in the world or in an organization, the more communication is needed and the more plans must be revised, revisited, and revamped. The more change there is, the more need there is for people to evaluate new processes, create new procedures, train in new systems, and react to new demands. The logical way to meet the demands of such change is to bring people together to discuss alternatives, decide the direction to take, and make plans to move forward.

The more change, the more meetings we seem to need! Even though we have phones and pagers and faxes and e-mail and the Internet, sometimes the best way to work things through is to bring everyone together in a room to meet. Meetings are like food: good or bad, but still necessary.

Facilitators are needed more than ever to help organizations improve attitudes toward meetings and to improve meeting productivity by coaching and influencing groups. Facilitators can help people decide why and whether to have a meeting and can then help streamline and focus the meeting so that group energy is tapped and synergy happens. Here are a few rules of thumb for keeping meetings productive:

- Meet only when it is essential;

- Focus the meeting on a reasonable end result;

- Give people assignments ahead of time, if necessary, to save time during the meeting;

- Take time to design a meeting that involves everyone, keeps people focused, and maximizes the synergy and creativity of the group;

- Make sure the right people are in attendance;

- Begin and end on time;

- Keep the group focused on the end result;

- Leave some time for diversions and light socializing to help build an atmosphere of openness and trust (not to waste time);

- Add some spice and variety with activities, visual aids, demonstrations, color, or a speaker;

- Do not plan too long a meeting, as people may have other obligations;

- If the meeting must be long, make sure people know its importance and make it worthwhile to attend; and

- If the group comes to a roadblock to achieving its goals, offer the group the option of disbanding the meeting.

As was discussed in Chapter 12, How to Design a Facilitation, much is involved in putting together a meeting at which people will be working together to achieve a goal. Facilitating a meeting requires more than simply leading a series of discussions. When you are asked to facilitate, work with the client to plan a meeting built around results-oriented objectives.

Facilitator's Role During the Meeting

Although planning and designing a meeting are important, what a facilitator does during the meeting is equally important. You play a key role in making meetings successful. After the meeting is underway, you will use many skills and techniques to keep the momentum going and to help the group overcome any roadblocks it encounters along the way. Explain the purpose and process of the meeting in a way that motivates each group member to engage fully in the tasks at hand. Also explain the role that you will take during the meeting and coach group members in the roles they must take to make the meeting successful. After the group is focused on the purpose and process of the meeting, continually monitor the process.

Managing the process is the facilitator's key focus. Stay relaxed, letting the meeting flow at a natural pace, while staying alert and observing how the process is working. If you are fidgety or too anxious for things to move along, the group will sense this and may feel overly controlled. Achieve a balance between providing structure for the group and giving it freedom as well—freedom to listen to one another, to explore ideas and issues, to think through a problem, to brainstorm, and to come to know and trust one another.

If necessary, intervene to change the design during the meeting. This may mean allowing more time than planned for an activity, dropping an activity, changing the process slightly, or even stopping an activity. Even though you always have the option to suggest a change in the process, do not be too quick to do so. Sometimes the design "drags" because the issue is a difficult one, not because the design is not working. Less experienced facilitators will benefit from spending effort on the design and then keeping to it. They evaluate how it went after the session and learn from the results. More experienced facilitators will know when the design needs to be changed and will sense how best to change it. This skill cannot easily be taught.

The main responsibilities of a facilitator during the meeting can be summarized as follows:

- Provide focus;

- Provide structure;

- Manage the meeting environment;

- Manage disruptions and difficulties; and

- Solicit feedback.

Providing Focus

Make sure that the objectives are results-oriented, that the group understands the objectives, and that they are written and posted in the room for everyone to see. Help the group leave the meeting with some tangible evidence of what it has accomplished: a decision made, plans developed, a list brainstormed, priorities set, or whatever the result.

Another way to provide focus is to record ideas throughout the meeting, providing a written "group memory" for accomplishing tasks. The effect of flip charts posted in the room motivates groups, as they can see their ideas, their work, and their progress.

Providing Structure

In addition to using results-oriented objectives and flip charts to focus a group, provide structure by organizing a group session so there is a beginning, a middle, and an end.

Design group sessions that meet predetermined objectives and maximize the interaction of group members. To do this, write brief, clear, and achievable objectives; plan an appropriate balance of presentation with group discussion and involvement; develop materials, if needed; judge the time needed for activities; anticipate the group's level of knowledge, skill, or awareness and design the session accordingly; and communicate clearly with participants about the planned structure of the session.

On the other hand, there cannot be too tight a structure, because facilitation is by its very nature informal, discovery oriented, and flexible. Plan a structure, but be willing to deviate from it when necessary.

The outline of the meeting, along with the confidence and positive attitude you display, have an effect on the mood, tone, and energy level of the session. A good meeting flow includes adequate time for people to become acquainted; allows sufficient time for brainstorming, discussion, and evaluation; and is punctuated with time for breaks, relaxation, and humor.

The goals or intended results of the session are the driving force behind the structure. The agenda and activities should be based on clear goals for the session, and these should be stated so that every participant is clear about what the purpose and intended results are. Goals can be published before the meeting, at the beginning of the meeting, during the meeting (when necessary), and at the end of the meeting to give the group a sense of direction and accomplishment. If the group does not achieve its goals, it should at least be given the opportunity to address why they were not met and whether new goals should be identified or more time set up to accomplish the original goals.

Facilitators are not responsible for identifying the objectives of a group meeting. However, do help the group and/or the group leader come up with realistic objectives for the session and to word those objectives so that they are clear and workable. Act as a coach to help the group be clear about what it needs to accomplish at the meeting (based on its larger aims and mission as a group).

Help the group understand that, even though it has clear overall goals and a mission, it needs a narrower focus at meetings. The group must identify the *results it intends to accomplish at each meeting.* Frequently, groups and group leaders are so concerned with what they are trying to achieve overall that it is difficult for them to narrow down the list to one or two things they can accomplish at a meeting. Help the group and/or group leader by asking questions such as:

- "What do you hope to accomplish at this meeting? How does this tie to your overall goals?"

- "When everyone leaves the meeting, what will be the evidence that something has been achieved? Will a plan be completed? A decision made? A problem identified? What will the group have to show for its efforts? (A document, a list, a decision?)"

- "If your group has identified its overall goals, what is the key thing it needs to do next?"

- "Is this a new group? If so, what key things can be accomplished at the first meeting?"

The facilitator's role is to provide a structure in which the group can accomplish its goals. Generally speaking, a facilitation has three parts, as described in the next few pages.

The Beginning

The beginning of a meeting is crucial to its success because this is when people's attention is caught and when you focus the group. Include the following at the beginning of a meeting:

- Welcome and introductions;

- Icebreaker to ease the tension;

- Goals and agenda announced and agreed on;

- Roles explained (facilitator, recorder, etc.); and

- Administrative information disseminated (time the session will be over, plans for breaks and lunch/dinner, location of phones and rest rooms, other announcements).

The first few moments of a group meeting set the tone for the work to come. The beginning of the meeting really starts before people arrive. Facilitators and group leaders can do several things to set a positive tone:

- Arrange the chairs so that people can see one another;

- Post a "Welcome to . . ." on a flip chart where people can see it as they arrive;

- Ascertain whether people already know one another;

- Adjust planned introductions accordingly;

- Greet people as they arrive;

- Offer refreshments, if they are available;

- Check to see whether everyone has arrived;

- Begin on time, checking to see whether everyone is ready to begin;

- Introduce yourself, explain your role (if necessary), and have others introduce themselves. Use an icebreaker, if one is planned;

- Confirm the purpose, objectives, timing, and administrative details of the meeting. Post the objectives and agenda. Check with the group to see if these are clear and appropriate;

- *(Optional)* Ask each person to share briefly what expectations he or she has for the meeting. (This is helpful for longer sessions, when people have not been together before, or when the meeting is designed to build team spirit or to launch a new effort.); and

- *(Optional)* Post a list of suggested ground rules and ask if everyone understood and can agree to them. Delete or add as necessary and then check for agreement. (This is particularly helpful when the participants are not accustomed to working together or when past meetings have not gone well because of behaviors such as interrupting, putting others' ideas down, not coming back on time from breaks, etc.).

If the opening activities take longer than an hour, which they may if the group is large or the session is long, give a short break after them. This gives people a chance to socialize, refill refreshments, and relax before the working session begins.

One of the challenges you will face is how to balance productivity with some informality and relaxation. If a session is too structured and tense, people will push through it, but not necessarily relax enough to think, ponder, discuss, and get to know one another. Another challenge is deciding whether to start right on time or not. Nine times out of ten, not everyone will be there when the meeting is scheduled to begin. Depending on the culture of the organization and/or the location and reason for the meeting, plan start times with some flexibility. Whether the meeting begins in the morning, midday, or evening, some people—for one reason or another—will be late. When planning a session, take logistics into account: Are people traveling to the site? Is the meeting in an unfamiliar place? How far is the meeting place from the work site? How were people notified of the session? Is something else going on that will affect attendance at this meeting?

The Middle

The middle portion of a facilitation is when the real work is accomplished. There is no set way to structure this portion of the meeting. It is usually a working session to accomplish goals and work through an agenda, which may include discussions, short presentations, small-group work, large-group work, summaries, and various activities to accomplish the goals, such as brainstorming, prioritizing, diagramming, listing, sorting, or evaluating. Because this is the longest portion of the meeting, it is helpful to provide breaks and a variety of activities.

When possible, design the flow of work ahead of time, selecting the processes you think will work best and allowing adequate time for discussion, breaks, and transitions from one activity to the next. Knowing how much time to estimate and knowing which processes will work comes with practice and experience. Some general guidelines for designing activities follow:

- *Allow time for discussion and transitions.* Do not try to cram too much into one session. People need time to think, discuss, be creative, and reach consensus.

- *Take frequent breaks.* People become tired after an hour or so of intense work or discussion.

- *Provide variety.* Vary the type of activities, break large groups into small groups, provide opportunity for people to stand up and move around, vary the pace, and vary the intensity.

- *Stay focused.* Keep people focused on where they are going, where they are, and where they have been. Refer back to goals and objectives, summarize before moving on to the next activity, and explain the purpose of each activity.

- *Be flexible.* If a particular process is not working, adapt it to meet the needs of the group. It may be necessary to give the group a break while revising the plans.

The End

The ending of a session is as important as the middle or the beginning. At the end of the session, decisions and actions are clarified and reviewed and the group feels a sense of completion and looks to the future. The end of a facilitation does not end the work of the group; it keeps the work going forward. The end of the meeting is really the beginning of the group's next task. The way a session ends may make the difference in whether anything is truly accomplished. Therefore, be clear about what needs to happen at the end of the session and plan enough time to end the meeting well.

Several things must occur near the end of the meeting. Group members should not leave until the following have been accomplished:

- All decisions recorded and agreed on by the group;

- All upcoming action items recorded and agreed on by the group, with dates and the name of the person responsible for each;

- The date, time, and place for the group's next meeting established, or someone appointed to schedule it;

- The meeting reviewed and evaluated with one or two areas for improvement targeted;

- Important agenda items for the next meeting listed;

- Expectations reviewed (if any were gathered at the beginning of the meeting); and

- Decisions made as to what to do with the flip charts (transcribe as minutes, transcribe only some, bring to next meeting, etc.).

Here is a brief agenda for the end of a meeting:

- Review what was accomplished at the session (decisions, action items, etc.);

- Decide agenda and date for next meeting; and

- Obtain feedback from participants on how the meeting went.

If this is the last meeting for the group, provide a chance for the group members to say good-bye to one another or to officially disband the group. Appropriate activities are needed to allow group members to share positive aspects of the group experience, to reflect on insights or what they have learned, and to determine ways to follow up with one another in the future. Depending on the group and the situation, these ending activities will vary in nature and in length. When a group has worked together for a substantial length of time or through a significant project or problem, the last meeting may be followed by a social event such as dinner, a picnic or barbecue, or an informal gathering. This eases the ending of a group or team experience and gives people a chance to solidify relationships before moving on.

Managing the Meeting Environment

The environment in which a group works can have a positive or negative impact on productivity. Room selection, surroundings, and room arrangement all make a difference. You may not always have a choice of room, but be aware of the qualities needed in a meeting place and try to influence room selection. At times it can be almost impossible to have an effective meeting because it is noisy, participants are cramped for space, the lighting is terrible, or it is too hot or cold. With some pre-meeting effort, even an inconvenient meeting space can become conducive to participation and productivity, but it is best to plan ahead. Some guidelines when selecting a site are given in the next few sections.

Appropriate Amount of Space

Provide a space large enough for people to move around comfortably, especially if they will be doing small-group work and/or writing on flip charts. Rooms that are too crowded do not allow people to relax, take notes, or stretch if necessary. Cramped space generally means there will not be enough room to work with the flip charts, move them around, or post pages. Usually when a group is crowded into a room, people want the meeting to end sooner. Sometimes they interact too much on the sidelines with one another and lose track of what is going on in the meeting.

On the other hand, do not meet in a space that is too large. A small group will "float" around and feel lost in an overly large room. If you must meet in a large space, define the group's space in some way. For example, move people into a corner and block off the extra space with partitions, easels, or a table to create a more intimate space. If possible, turn down the lighting in the unused portion of the room. Bring people together in a circle around tables where they will not see or be aware of the empty space.

Appropriate Type of Space

When people must work collaboratively with plenty of interaction and opportunity to focus on the issues at hand, they need a room that is conducive to productivity. A noisy room next to the cafeteria would be distracting. So might a hotel room overlooking the swimming pool. A room with no windows might be claustrophobic for a group that must work hard on a problem for one or two days in a row, while a room with too many windows might be too bright and discourage concentration. A room with no walls or space to hang charts will make it difficult for most facilitations. The ideal meeting room is located conveniently near rest rooms, away from distracting noise, pleasantly decorated, with windows, and an atmosphere in which people will want to work. When rooms are too dark and too plush, for example, it is harder to get people's energy levels up. A hot, stuffy room without adequate facilities may also keep people from doing their best work.

Appropriate Location

Several things must be considered when choosing the location of a room. Is it convenient? If not, will this hinder good attendance? Is it too close to where people work, thus tempting them to return to their work area during breaks and not coming back to the meeting on time—or at all? Is the room located too close to an area where "visitors" (bosses, colleagues, secretaries, those high up in the company) can easily interrupt the session? Some locations encourage hallway conversations that detract greatly from the meeting at hand. If the meeting is offsite, consider the distance and traffic patterns people must travel and find the most convenient location for everyone.

Appropriate Setup

Usually a meeting room is not set up for an interactive, facilitated session. The worst are auditoriums or classrooms in which some participants have their backs to others. The best setups for facilitation are those that allow maximum eye contact by everyone in the group, flexibility to move into smaller groups and/or breakout areas, and easy visibility of the flip charts. Seek rooms that can be arranged easily, as this allows for the most flexibility. Rooms with lightweight chairs and tables that can be moved around are the best. Arrange the tables and chairs so everyone can see everyone else, if possible. Tables arranged in a "U" shape are good for relatively small groups. (See Figure 16.1.) The facilitator can stand, sit, or move

Figure 16.1. Sample U-Shape Layout

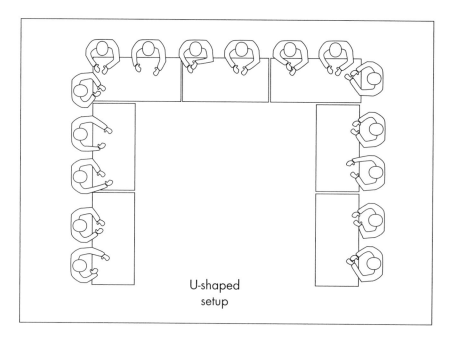

U-shaped
setup

around within the "U." Similar to the useful "U" shape is a "V" shape or a
semicircle. For breakout sessions, small groups can move chairs into a circle without a table, sit in "circles" at various sections of the "U"-shaped
setup, or move to another area furnished with round tables. Large groups
can be divided into smaller groups sitting at round tables, so that everyone
in the smaller groups can see everyone else.

If you are stuck with a big conference table that is not moveable, adapt
your facilitation style and the activities to allow as much interaction as
possible. Put people into small buzz groups and suggest that they move
their chairs away from the table. Set up flip charts so that everyone can see
them. Have people sit only on one side and end of the table, if possible.
Use your own verbal and nonverbal skills to draw everyone in and to help

them interact with one another. The big conference table setting is unfortunately a traditional power setting, with the "head" of the table generally reserved for a manager or high-level person and the rest of the table for subordinates. The size and weight of the table connote power, and people will naturally behave differently in this type of setting. It may help to let the group know at the start that you are concerned with the setting and encourage people to relax, interact, and pretend they are in a more informal setting. This is a particularly difficult setting in which to facilitate an intact work group, especially if the manager is present, and especially if he or she sits at the head of the table. Suggest a better setting while the meeting is being planned or suggest to the manager that he or she sit somewhere besides the head of the table—with the group, not in the back of the room.

Adequate Breakout Space

Some sessions require breakout rooms so that small groups have privacy and space to work. This is often difficult to obtain, as on-site meeting rooms are usually in demand and outside facilities cost extra. However, for some types of work, breakout rooms may be necessary. Take this into consideration when planning a session. For some breakout sessions, small groups can move to a cafeteria or a hotel lobby if there are not too many distractions. Sending groups out into hotel lobbies or poolside armadas can backfire, however. If the group is not wholly focused on the task at hand, participants can be distracted and have a leisurely conversation about something else.

A disadvantage to breakout rooms is that you are not as available to each group as when all groups remain in the main meeting room. When breakout areas are scattered, it is difficult to bring everyone back to the large group on time. In this situation, appoint a timekeeper for each small group and have that person report back at a given time. The timekeeper can let you know whether the group needs more time. An important advantage to breakout rooms or areas is that they give people a change of scenery and a chance to move around. When people have to sit in one spot too long, their bodies, as well as their minds, become numb.

Comfortable Temperature

Temperature is often difficult to control. Many hotels and buildings set all rooms at a uniform temperature (that is seldom uniform throughout a facility) so a maintenance person is required to change the controls. Another difficulty is that people prefer various temperatures. Some like it hot and some like it cold! To add to the problem, you are usually moving around a lot more than the participants and are thus usually warmer than the rest of the group. However, it is your role to seek the most comfortable temperature for the group or to appoint someone else to do so. If the room is too hot for too long, people become sleepy and find it hard to think. If the room is too cold, people lose their concentration while focusing on how to warm up.

In extreme cases, the group members will become so uncomfortable they will beg for another room, for more breaks, or even for an early end to the session. Although this is unfortunate, you may have to disband a meeting and acknowledge that the situation is counterproductive. I facilitated a training session at a hotel in a stuffy room that became warmer as the day wore on. When we found out the air conditioner was not working properly, we decided we could not finish the day in this room. We asked for another one in the hotel and were ushered back to another building to a cool, dark room. At first, we were all quite pleased. However, after about an hour, everyone was getting cold, wrapping up in a jacket or sweater, and even shivering! This took place in Phoenix, so we knew we were the victims of an overly aggressive air conditioner. We called a hotel representative to the room, but he could not change the central setting and told us that this room was always too cold. We ended up moving into the lobby area of the second building to finish off the day's program, but I never really regained the group's attention. Fortunately, there were two more days in the program, and the hotel found us a comfortable room for the last two days.

Make people as comfortable as possible, even if it means taking time out of the planned activities to address people's comfort.

Make sure your room setup is conducive to people interacting and working together. People should be able to see one another easily and should not be too far apart (as they are in large auditoriums) or sitting with their backs to others (as in classroom settings). There should be sufficient room for people to move about and working space and surfaces for individual and group work. If possible, select rooms with moveable tables and chairs and allow people to set up areas for working that are comfortable and support the task at hand.

Facility Checklist

Here is a list of questions for selecting and arranging a facility:

The Meeting Room

- How many people are expected?

- Is the room large enough, but not too large?

- Are the walls suitable for taping or hanging flip-chart paper?

- Will the facility be arranged for you or will you have to arrange the room?

- When can you arrive to set up the room?

- Are the tables and chairs moveable?

- Does the room have adequate lighting?

- Is it possible to control the heating/cooling? If not, who will be available to adjust the temperature if needed?

- What supplies or equipment will be furnished (easels, flip-chart pads, overhead projector, white board, marking pens, etc.)?

- What is the name and phone number of the person responsible for scheduling and/or setting up the room?

- Is another group using the room immediately prior to you? If so, when will they vacate the room?

- Is another group coming in the evening so that you cannot leave your supplies overnight?

Breakout Areas

- Will you need breakout rooms or areas for small groups to work? If so, what equipment and supplies will be needed in each area?

- Who will furnish equipment and supplies for breakout areas?

- Are the breakout areas clustered together or scattered? How will this affect your facilitation?

Location

- Is the facility far enough from work for people to concentrate fully on the meeting?

- Is the meeting room located near a noisy corridor or outside area?

- Is the facility a pleasant place to be (view, service people, cleanliness, decor, a businesslike atmosphere, etc.)?

- Are there rest rooms and telephones nearby?

- Are there vending machines, break areas, or a cafeteria nearby?

- Is the facility easy to find? Will people need a map or directions?

- If the meeting lasts two or more days, is the facility located in a desirable spot for pre- and post-meeting activities?

Room Setup

- What type of room setup is best (U shape, round tables, V shape)?

- Will this setup accommodate all participants and leave room for people to move around?

- Where will you place flip charts and other equipment?

- When will you set up the room?

- Where will you store extra materials and supplies during the session?

- Are you expected to return the room to its original arrangement when you leave?

Managing the environment begins with the selection of the facility and the meeting room(s), continues during the session, and ends when the room has been restored to order and the lights turned off. Even though there are many other important things on the mind of every facilitator (such as the flow of the session, interactions among participants, whether the group meets its goals, and accomplishing everything in the allotted time), the environment must be managed. Sometimes, this seems the least important concern, but paying attention to the environment from beginning to end can make a big difference in the way a group behaves and in whether quality work is done.

Managing Disruptions and Difficulties

Your role is to maintain equilibrium in the group and to deal with disruptions in a way that minimizes their negative impact on group productivity. You will have to deal with a variety of meeting disruptions and difficulties.

Meetings That Do Not Start on Time

Unfortunately, meetings typically do not start on time. Sometimes you can control this, but not always. Ask the client before a meeting if the meeting is likely to start on time, and discuss how to begin the meeting if everyone is not there. It is a good idea to design a meeting so that people have about fifteen minutes to arrive. State the beginning time as fifteen minutes earlier than you absolutely must begin. If everyone arrives at the stated start time, start "early." If not, make sure there is something for those who arrived on time to do, such as eat refreshments, read over material, start introducing themselves to one another, etc. This is an excellent time to introduce yourself to participants as they arrive and begin learning their names. Another alternative is to design an introductory exercise into which you can easily integrate latecomers.

Latecomers

Frequently, meetings must start even though one or two people haven't arrived. Find out how many people are expected and try to begin when 80 percent or more have arrived. Most facilitations will involve small groups (five to fifteen), so it is fairly easy to integrate one or two latecomers. Latecomers must be brought into the group, so the group will feel "complete" and the latecomer will feel a part of the group as soon as possible. Sometimes a latecomer has had a difficulty, an emergency, or a critical work issue to deal with and really wanted to be on time. It is important to bring these people in as soon as possible so they feel that they are part of the group. Assume the latecomer made every effort to be there and do not "punish" him or her in some way for arriving late. However, those who are habitually late should not be left with the impression that this is acceptable behavior. You or the group leader should talk privately with the person, find out the circumstances, explain why this makes a negative impact on the group, and obtain a commitment to be on time in the future.

The following are some general rules of thumb for bringing latecomers into the group:

*   *Do not interrupt anything in progress.* Wait for an appropriate break in the discussion. This gives the latecomer time to find a seat and settle in before being given attention.

*   *Do not wait too long.* Say something like, "Let me stop this discussion for a minute to welcome a newcomer to the group." Invite the newcomer to introduce himself or herself and briefly explain what is going on at the time. Then go right back into the process.

*   *Integrate latecomers without embarrassing them.* One way is to give them a few minutes to join the group, then welcome them and ask them to introduce themselves. If only one or two people are late, briefly bring

each person up to date after introductions have been made. For example, "Larry, we are glad you made it today. What we have done so far is go over our objectives and agenda for the day, and we have decided on these ground rules for our meeting." (Point out the posted flip charts with objectives, agenda, and ground rules.)

- *If necessary assign the person to a subgroup.* Introduce the newcomer to the subgroup members and explain the process. If any newcomers missed the introductory icebreaker, ask them to introduce themselves after a break, in the same manner others introduced themselves during the icebreaker. This is especially important if the icebreaker was designed for people to reveal interesting things about themselves. This ensures that the latecomers will be accepted as part of the group.

- *Do not neglect the group.* If someone comes really late, welcome the person and let him or her work into the meeting. Ask someone to bring the newcomer up to date at the next break. Your first priority is to the rest of the group, and most latecomers will catch up and work their way into the meeting.

- *Do not slow the group's progress.* If a latecomer insists on bringing up ideas or issues already discussed, gently tell him or her, "The group has already discussed that. We need to move on at this time. Please see me during the next break to get caught up on what has already been discussed."

Keeping Everybody There

Keeping people in the room for the entire meeting is one of the biggest challenges meeting leaders face. Because a great many meetings are long, boring, and unproductive, people cope by leaving the meeting to make phone calls or even to attend another meeting. Also, people often come back late from a break, and the flow of the meeting is disrupted.

You have a few options for dealing with this problem. One is to work diligently with the client to stress to the members the importance of the meeting and what will be accomplished. If the material is important to the members, and if the manager stresses the need for everyone's full attendance, people will be more likely to make arrangements ahead of time to be there for the whole meeting. State the goals of the meeting in the pre-meeting memo and mention why it is important that all members attend.

Another option is to stress the importance of full attendance at the beginning of the session. (This can be done in addition to having the client stress its importance.) A good time to do this is when stating and posting the guidelines for the meeting. One of the guidelines can be "Be here." Explain why everyone's full participation is valued and needed. Mention that you understand if someone has an emergency, but that you hope people will elect not to attend to other business during the meeting.

For long meetings, especially all-day meetings, it helps to build in designated break times for people to check their messages and make necessary phone calls. Allow fifteen or twenty minutes once or twice a day for checking in at work. When dismissing people for a break, state the exact time you would like people to return and be ready to continue the meeting.

When designing a meeting, be aware of the need and importance some groups have to socialize and build in time for this, either during icebreakers and activities or during lunch or breaks. Often, one of the goals of a facilitation is for people to become better acquainted and to learn more about one another's roles or jobs. If time is planned for this type of socializing, people are more apt to come back to the meeting on time and ready to continue.

The best approach is to design a meeting with goals and accomplishments that keep people motivated to participate, to keep the flow of activities meaningful and fast-paced, and to address the needs of the group as they arise.

Dealing with People Who Have to Leave

Despite precautions taken to ensure that people are present, there will be times when people must leave. Sometimes they will tell you or the group leader ahead of time. If someone must leave, speak with the person and suggest how to find out what happened after he or she leaves. It is a good idea to mention briefly to the group that someone will be leaving, so the group is not left wondering what happened to the person.

Interruptions

Interruptions are the norm in meetings. Beepers go off. People come in late. Someone makes an announcement that raises questions unrelated to the goals of the meeting. The room is too hot (or cold) and adjustments must be made to the thermostat. Supplies are needed or copies must be made. Lunch arrives early (or late). Someone wanders into the wrong room, joins the meeting, and then leaves embarrassed. Another group arrives, claiming that it has reserved the room! People are working on a construction project just outside the door, and so on.

Your role is to maintain equilibrium for the group and to deal with interruptions. Some interruptions are fine: they bring some levity or are necessary and expected. Others can be handled briefly with a few words from you or someone else in the room. Others can definitely hurt the progress of the group and must be dealt with differently. Sometimes you must ask the group for suggestions, and the whole group may have to come up with a way to deal with the interruption.

Soliciting Feedback

Skilled facilitators use a variety of ways to obtain feedback from participants during and after a meeting. Process can be checked during a meeting and a round of feedback conducted at the end. Allowing time for feedback helps group members learn ways to make their meetings more effective as well.

A process checkpoint conducted during a meeting gives group members a chance to think about how the meeting is going and to give you feedback. Process checks should be done quickly between activities, so progress and momentum will not be stopped. These give you a chance to alter the pace or flow of activities to benefit the group's work. Process checks should not be made too frequently—once during a short meeting, once or twice during a longer meeting. They can be used at these points:

- About midway through a meeting, to see how the group is doing and to make changes in process;

- At any point in the meeting when the progress bogs down or some people have shut down; or

- At a planned point in a meeting (or several points if the meeting is long) as part of the group's agenda.

A simple question or two will suffice. Ask the group one of the following sets of questions:

- "How is the meeting going so far? Are we accomplishing what we set out to do?"

- "Is this process working? Do we need to change how we are approaching this task?"

- "Let's stop briefly to check how our approach is working so far. Do we need to change anything?"

A short written survey can be conducted during a longer meeting, followed by a brief discussion of what changes need to be made in the process. Two or three questions suffice; a rating scale could be used as well. See the example in Figure 16.2.

Another method for evaluating meeting process is to use flash cards with words such as "yes," "no," "undecided," or "needs improvement" printed on them. When you ask a question to check process, each person responds by holding up the card that best describes his or her response.

Checkpoints are reserved for *process* observations and changes and are not intended to be used to evaluate how the content of the meeting is progressing. Make this clear by the way you ask the questions, word the sur-

Figure 16.2. Sample Process Survey

Directions: Rate how the meeting is going so far by using the following scale:

Yes = 3 points
Needs Improvement = 2 points
No = 1 point

_____ I am involved in a productive way.

_____ Other people are involved in a productive way.

_____ We are working collaboratively together.

_____ The timing and pace of the meeting are good.

_____ We are using appropriate methods and procedures.

_____ Our objectives are clear.

_____ We are focused on our objectives.

_____ We are making good progress.

vey, and draw out responses, coaching people to stick with process, not content, issues, and citing examples of each.

As the meeting progresses, ask for feedback from your client and from group participants. This can be done casually and without fanfare. Just ask, "How is the meeting going so far?" "How is this process working?" "Are we on track to meet our objectives for today?" Ask individuals at break or during a small-group exercise or ask the entire group just before it goes on a break or when it returns. It is not a good idea to overdo this; just once or twice during a meeting is enough.

When closing a meeting, it is important to receive feedback on how the meeting went for the group members. The feedback you receive at the end of a meeting is invaluable for further facilitations. It leaves the group members with a sense of being respected and valued for their opinions. The feedback from the group will contain information you could never have known, because you were not sitting in the group while you facilitated. I used to avoid this feedback, partly because my meetings always ran late and partly because I did not want to hear the negatives. Sometimes I was afraid I would be beaten to a pulp by the group and be left without a career! Usually I was just not being a good facilitator, because good facilitators learn to give and receive feedback with grace and aplomb. I can now say that I look forward to feedback sessions at the end of meetings.

Excellent facilitators want feedback! Over the months and years of facilitating, *listening to feedback from groups makes you a better facilitator, as you make changes in the way you design and facilitate.* Feedback can be the very thing that makes someone a good facilitator. Contrary to what you might think—that you are going to hear a lot of negatives—generally, the group is kind and may even tell you some things went well that you thought did not. I have been surprised at the good things that have come up, things I would not have known if I had skipped a feedback session.

Here is a format that usually works. Just before the last words you say to the group, ask them to give you some feedback about how the meeting went. Ask them first to mention what was helpful and valuable to them about the meeting. List these in front of the group to show that you are listening and have received the feedback correctly. Next, ask them to mention anything that could have made the meeting better ("something we could have left out or something that should have been added"). Now, here's the really important part: when members of the group are giving you feedback and you are writing it down, *do not defend, explain, or elaborate on the feedback.* Just listen, write it down, and make sure you heard it correctly. That's all. Remember the power in listening. Respond to the feedback alone later over a drink or a meal, but resist the temptation to say, "The reason we didn't do that was because. . . ." Defensiveness hurts the whole feedback process and makes you look less professional. Just listen, use good eye contact, write the response, nod your head, and do not look hurt or angry or embarrassed. A smile is a nice touch. As participants in my facilitator training class often say, "I remained neutral, but not without a bloody tongue." You may have to bite your tongue too for a few feedback sessions, but eventually you will relax and do just fine. This type of open listening is a powerful facilitator tool. Only when you listen in this manner will you hear the things that will help you learn and grow as a facilitator. Also, when you listen in this manner you will know what was helpful to the group and you can do those things with another group. When you hear over and over that something works well, you can be pretty certain it will work most of the time.

Handle feedback sessions at the end of a meeting in a variety of ways, especially if you facilitate the same group several times. Some ways to add variety to your feedback sessions are listed below:

- Go around the room and ask everyone to sum up the meeting in three words (or a single phrase). Write these down.

- Put everyone into buzz groups for three minutes and have each buzz group appoint a spokesperson to summarize what was valuable and what could have been improved about the meeting. This works well for larger groups.

- Go around the room and have everyone tell whether (and how) his or her initial expectations of the meeting were met.

- Hand out small pieces of paper or index cards and ask each person to write a sentence describing what it was like to be in the meeting and work with this group. Gather up the papers, shuffle them, and have each person draw one and read it aloud to the group.

- Go around the room once and ask each person to tell one thing that went well about the meeting. Then go around the room again and have each person tell one thing that could have been better. Ask one person to volunteer to sum up the session on a positive note.

Of course, you can always hand out written feedback questionnaires, but I avoid those for meetings because they are time-consuming to complete when people are ready to leave. Also, it is a good idea for group members to hear what others have said about the meeting; this gives them a broader perspective.

A note about feedback. Sometimes you will be surprised at the pettiness of people's observations. They may say the room was too hard to find or they wished lunch had been pizza instead of cold cuts or that the noise from the kitchen bothered them or that the breaks should have been longer. Remember to bite your tongue. Do not say things like, "You're lucky we even found a room" or "The other choice was next to the jackhammers!" or "We couldn't get everyone back from breaks as it was." Unless it is pretty obvious that someone is trying to make a joke, do not discount the feedback. If it is a joke, write it down along with all the other feedback because that lightens everyone's mood. What may seem petty to you may have been important to participants. Sometimes people just give petty feedback. They want fruit instead of popcorn for break and a room with windows facing east or they want the meeting to end at 4:30 instead of 5:00. That's OK. It is all just feedback at this point. Later, you can decide what feedback to take seriously and what to discard. Sometimes the feedback will not be very enlightening or people will ditto what has already been said because they all want to go home. That happens when the meeting goes too long or does not go very well. Sometimes you have insubstantial feedback, but most of the time you will receive a lot and be grateful. Consider feedback a gift; it will help make you an excellent facilitator.

Electronic Meetings

In today's world of sophisticated electronic communication, people can communicate via teleconferencing, videoconferencing, and what is likely to become more common—the computer meeting. Computer meetings can take place over the Internet via "chat rooms" or by using such applications as Lotus Notes®. New software will allow people to talk to one another by telephone while using the computer screen to record and share written material.

More and more people are telecommuting, and teams may be spread out in offices across the world. Many people travel so much for their jobs that they have only a "virtual office," the one they carry with them in the form of laptop computer, mobile phone, pager, and briefcase. Meeting electronically has become almost the only way for many people. Some teams now meet electronically most of the time, with a periodic face-to-face meeting.

Where does all this electronic capability and necessity leave the facilitator? Facilitation is needed during an electronic meeting just as much as during a face-to-face meeting. Ideas still must be recorded, people "introduced" to one another, and a structure and process followed to balance and encourage participation (perhaps even more so than during a face-to-face meeting). (See Chapter 18, Facilitating Virtual Teams, for more information.)

I recently facilitated a videoconference meeting of a team of people from the United States, China, Japan, Ireland, and Singapore. The team members were all from the same organization, all reported to a U.S.-based manager, and all had similar responsibilities. The client and I planned the meeting as we would plan a face-to-face meeting. We determined the goals of the meeting, how to introduce everyone, the timing and setup of the meeting, a process for balancing participation (with groups from different video sites), and how to structure the meeting to reach the goals. I wrote a meeting design, just as I would have done for a face-to-face meeting. We used a flip chart at the Phoenix site and set it up so that all locations could see it on their screens. The main difference between a face-to-face meeting and this electronic meeting was that we had to structure all the comments in round-robin fashion because it took a bit of time to bring in each location for comment. We varied the order in which we took comments, but once a location had commented on a certain issue, members there were not free to jump in with additional comments as they would have been during a face-to-face meeting. In a sense, this meeting was "face-to-face," as we were able to see one another when members were given the go-ahead to speak.

When facilitating an electronic meeting, apply what you know of good facilitation and make the necessary adaptations to accommodate the machinery and the distance.

In summary, because facilitators use most of their skills and knowledge during group meetings, it is important that they learn to manage meetings well by providing focus and structure, managing the meeting environment and equipment, managing disruptions, and soliciting feedback.

Facilitating Teams

A team facilitator not only facilitates team meetings but also guides and coaches the team to become more effective as a team. This requires knowledge of team development and the inclusion of team-building activities and team self-evaluations from time to time in the team's meetings. The facilitator must understand several important aspects of team facilitation and help the team to understand each one as well.

Role Clarification

Just what is the role of the team facilitator? Is there a team leader? If so, what is the leader's role? Is there someone higher up in the organization who is sponsoring the team, and what is that person's role? As a facilitator, it is wise to ask questions to help clarify the roles, and in some cases to coach the team as to an effective way to delineate them. A role matrix can be helpful and should be developed in collaboration with the team leader and client, if there is one, and shared with the team members. In the book *Teamwork from Start to Finish* (Rees, 1997), the roles of team leader, facilitator, sponsor, team member, and recorder are spelled out in detail on pages 75 through 83; these may be helpful to you for coaching teams.

Another role consideration is whether the team expects or needs a facilitator at every team meeting. If not, determine when you will be needed and how this will affect your work with the team.

Team Boundaries

Next, team boundaries need to be discussed and understood. The team leader should have (or should seek) a clear idea of the team's boundaries, that is, the decisions the team is free to make and implement and the decisions reserved for other teams or for management. As the team progresses, this discussion may need to be continued for the sake of clarity. When you sense confusion over team boundaries, call this to the teams and team leader's attention.

Developing Facilitation Skills in Teams

Determine, in collaboration with the team leader and the team members, whether facilitation skills are to be developed in the team so that, eventually, the team can facilitate itself. In this case, you will also take on the role of teaching the team about what is involved with facilitation. This can be done through modeling, coaching, or co-facilitating with team members and/or the team leader. In some teams, the role of facilitator is rotated on a regular basis so that no one is in the position of having to remain neutral all the time. Certain skills and effort are necessary to help a team become self-sufficient.

Internal Versus External Team Facilitator

There are three possible facilitation situations, each one with advantages and disadvantages. Consider these possibilities carefully before facilitating a team project.

Facilitator Is from Outside the Organization

The *advantages* to being an outside facilitator are that you are more likely to be objective and probably will have less trouble being neutral because you do not bring baggage or biases about the organization. The *disadvantages* are that you may not feel as much ownership for the success of the team, may not have a keen understanding of the cultural issues, and may not be around to see how the work of the team turns out.

Facilitator Is a Member of the Organization but Not Part of the Team

If you are an internal facilitator, the *advantages* are that you know the culture and understand better what the team is up against and you may have strong ownership in the success of the group. However, the *disadvantages* are that you may find it harder to be neutral on some issues and will have to work harder in your facilitator role and that your skills may be in great demand, causing your workload to be too heavy. Judge your time carefully when deciding whether to take on facilitation projects. In many organizations, facilitators have other jobs as well and are expected to facilitate only 20 or 30 percent of their time. As an internal facilitator, time and workload management will be key issues for you.

Facilitator Is an Active Member of the Team

If you are a member of the group you are facilitating, you face perhaps the most difficult role of all. Because you are part of the group and the organization, it is harder to remain neutral and gain the respect of your teammates. However, if you have had adequate training as a facilitator, possess the skills and tools to facilitate, and make it a priority to remain neutral, your team will undoubtedly accept you in the role over time. The *disadvantages* to facilitating your own team are that your ideas and opinions will not be put forth or considered and that you may not feel as much a part of the group as you would like. This role is a challenge but essential in many teams without other resources. If there are others on the team who have facilitation skills, rotating the facilitator role will ensure that everyone functions as a team member over time.

Providing a Team Road Map

Teams benefit greatly from road maps to follow in their work. Most teams know they must work together, meet occasionally, and parcel out tasks. They frequently do not know in what order to do things, where to begin, and how to stay focused, keep momentum, and achieve results. The ten steps outlined below (Rees, 1997) will assist you in guiding a team from its inception to the completion of its work and/or disbanding the team. The focus of these ten steps is twofold: (1) achieving results and (2) working well as a team.

There is a natural, healthy flow to teamwork and certain essential steps are necessary to start the team off well. Other steps refresh the team and help it evaluate and correct itself. All of these steps help move the team forward toward results, while creating team spirit and a sense of unity. Your role is to see that the team accomplishes each step, that team members know why each step is important, and that the team has the tools and capacity to continuously improve its functioning as a team. In summary, here are the ten steps:

1. *Focus the team.* Help the team clarify its purpose and write its charter.

2. *Assign roles.* Help the team assign roles: team leader, facilitator, recorder, sponsor (if any), and team members.

3. *Establish ground rules.* Assist the team in determining guidelines for working together.

4. *Plan the work.* Help the team lay out major goals and tasks, assign responsibilities, and determine deadlines.

5. *Do the work.* Help the team carry out the plan, meeting regularly to review progress and address problems.

6. *Review team performance.* Help the team periodically review its performance as a team and decide actions to take to become more effective.

7. *Complete the work.* Facilitate the team to complete the work and to document the results.

8. *Publish the results.* Help the team present the results to the appropriate people or groups.

9. *Reward the team.* Facilitate the team to celebrate its accomplishments and be recognized in the organization.

10. *Move on.* Help the team disband, restructure itself with a new focus, or renew itself by reviewing and revising its purpose.

Celebrating Team Milestones

Help the team recognize its successes and celebrate accomplishments along the way. When a team has completed an important step in its work (written its charter, finished its first project milestone, or published the results of its work, for example), it is a good idea to recognize the achievement by celebrating it in some way. A "celebration" can be anything from having a short meeting instead of a long one, serving pizza or refreshments at a meeting, or giving everyone a special prize or commemorative gift. Whatever form the celebration takes, mention why and what you are celebrating. Help the team members know that by achieving a certain step they have made important advances in their work and progress as a team.

Diversity and the Team Facilitator

One of your main responsibilities is to ensure full and balanced participation so that all ideas are fairly considered and each person is given a chance to be heard, and ultimately accepted, by the group. Be aware of and work through your own biases and beliefs about other people. Arming yourself with the skills and tools of facilitation is a good way to begin to help people in groups work through conflict, closed mindedness, and biases. However, excellent facilitators truly have open minds about other people; they do not make assumptions based on hairstyle, length of fingernails, shade of skin, style of clothes, or placement of earrings. Facilitators also do better if they can see beyond hierarchy, status, and position—even beyond wealth, beauty, and fame. Consider when you stand before a group with a marking pen in hand and a provocative open-ended question whether you are truly ready to listen (and model good listening) to everyone in the group. Will you record each person's idea with equal confidence and acceptance? Will you draw out divergent positions and opinions and encourage those with less-than-conventional ideas to speak out?

Whether they know it or not, facilitators' attitudes show—just as do the attitudes of those in a group. The more you can become aware of your own knee-jerk reactions to people, ingrained prejudices, and intolerance, the better you can overcome them. It is not wise to bury your biases or hide your intolerance from yourself. Explore them with the intent of working past them. Prove them invalid and begin gradually to forget them.

Facilitating is a wonderful way to work through incorrect assumptions about people. People in groups will surprise you over and over with their insights, creativity, hopes, fears, and desire to do a good job; there will be little time or room for old biases. New ones may crop up, however, and you will need to acknowledge, challenge, and work through them when they do.

It works this way: we let others know how we feel about them through our *behavior*. We behave a certain way toward others because of our *attitudes* (present thoughts and subconscious messages) about them. In turn, our attitudes are a product of our *beliefs*, which come from our own narrow range of *experiences*. These experiences include those in which we let ourselves be brainwashed by others, messages we have heard, and our inability to see our own experiences in perspective. This buildup of experiences and beliefs over time creates within each of us a set of *values*—those fundamental things we hold most dear and would pay a great price to have in our lives, such as freedom, peace, love, and shelter, or perhaps a strong sense of family, wealth, personal recognition, creativity, or beauty. These values are the very foundation of who we are, and they ultimately drive our attitudes about and behaviors toward other people.

To get along in this world, we become pretty good at camouflaging our true values and beliefs by adjusting our behavior to what is acceptable, especially if it means our own survival as an employable person or something essential like receiving love and affection from others. However, as facilitators and leaders and teachers and coaches—for anyone in influential positions—we must examine our behaviors, dig out our prejudices, and see them for what they truly are. We need to discover whether we are really the people we pretend to be. Facilitators hope the groups they lead will be open-minded and forthright, accept one another, and build trust. We must challenge ourselves to do the same in our roles as team facilitators.

Resolving Team Conflict

A common fear new facilitators have is dealing with conflict in groups. (See Chapter 11, "Facilitating Conflict Resolution.") Conflict in groups is natural. It can debilitate groups, but it can also be the fuel for creative problem solving.

Like the fear of speaking in front of groups, the fear of conflict in groups seems to be almost universal. The thought of conflict undoubtedly brings to mind memories of unpleasant confrontations, awkward silences, angry dialogue, embarrassments, and failures. The thought of standing before a group of people engaged in some unresolved conflict is enough to scare most facilitators away forever.

Many types of conflict exist in groups—some more serious than others, some easier to deal with than others. The fact is, conflict has received a pretty bad reputation over the years, and you must learn to deal with it realistically. Conflict in a team can be likened to a marital argument: nobody likes them, they make everyone nervous, and they end in a happy resolution of differences—or not. The "or not" scares most new facilitators. They worry about what would happen if everyone walked out angry and they were left standing there not knowing what to do. Or, a worse scenario, if everyone became hostile toward the innocent facilitator and assessed him or her as a failure.

No one wants to be caught up in a conflict that ends poorly. In fact, unresolved conflicts have a hard time dying out; they tend to live on in people's minds. Facilitators want their teams to be kind and happy and polite and productive. The reality is that people will not always be kind and happy or in agreement. People see things differently and, as a result, there will be conflict in groups (as in marriages). And, as in marriages, working through conflict may be the only way to help the team improve or keep it from disintegrating altogether.

Given that conflict is inevitable, how does a skilled facilitator deal with it? How can it be approached by facilitators, group members, teammates, and human beings in general so that it will be less painful and more apt to be resolved? The answer lies in the process used to resolve conflict. Here are a few choices:

1. Ignore the conflict and hope it will go away. In reality, what is ignored is not the conflict but dealing with the conflict. The conflict

festers into a bigger sore. Sometimes it goes away if other more important things take people's attention.

2. Confront people by being what is called "brutally honest." Usually this method hurts people's feelings and generates new conflict, rather than resolving anything.

3. Address the conflict by focusing on a constructive goal that benefits everyone, instead of destructive blaming or win-lose competitions. By focusing on a goal, the conflict can be resolved so that progress can be made and everyone wins something.

Resolving conflict does not have to mean that everyone agrees to agree wholeheartedly on every point forever. It means that everyone agrees enough on goals and methods to move forward. People sometimes agree to disagree, to focus on the end goal, and move on. Some groups realize, after bringing conflict into the open, that they did not disagree as much as they thought they did. The problem was a matter of misinterpretation or poor communication. Sometimes a group's best moments are those during which it deals openly with conflict and resolves it in some way.

Remember, and help your teams to remember, that conflict is normal. It is as natural as breathing and as inevitable as meetings not starting on time. Generally speaking, groups that appear to have no conflict are probably still at a polite—or even dysfunctional—stage. Healthy teams have conflict: people disagree and see things differently. Leaders sometimes fear conflict so they discourage it. Of course, teams should not be having knock-down, drag-out fights, but, if a team's work is important and meaningful to its members, there will be conflict, and this is good. And it is better when conflict is resolved.

Given that conflict in groups is inevitable, your role is to use processes that will either prevent it from becoming an issue or help resolve it as soon as it arises. Many of the processes and tools suggested in this book will help groups work through conflict. (See Chapter 11.) In fact, facilitation itself provides effective means of surfacing and working through conflict.

You can draw on many methods and tools to prevent and work through conflict. During discussion, draw out divergent opinions, encourage the group to discuss ideas and options, and help it reach a consensus. Tools are used to give groups time and a structured process to work through issues. Help the group define its goals early in the process and, when conflict arises, draw the group back to the goals by asking: "What method will most likely help us reach our goals?" Another important mediator of conflict is the group's own ground rules. You have helped the group set guidelines for how it will function. These guidelines are a standard against which the group plans to perform. When conflict arises because some group members, or the entire group, have violated the ground rules, point this out. Because the group members originally agreed to these standards, they are likely to readjust their behaviors accordingly and thus alleviate the conflict. You or group members can also suggest that the group add to its ground rules to help resolve conflict in the future.

Act when conflict arises. When something is wrong, you will sense it. The group's productivity and cohesiveness will be affected. When this happens, try first to identify the behavior that is causing problems. Perhaps group members are increasingly late to meetings or people are not following up with one another between meetings. Perhaps consensus has not actually been reached and some members are still reluctant to support the decision. Perhaps open disagreements and hostility are halting the group's progress.

If the conflict seems minor at this point, simply bring up your concerns about it, saying something like: "I am feeling uncomfortable about the lack of communication between meetings. Let's talk about what is going on." Or, to someone who does not seem to go along with a group decision: "Bruce, I sense some reluctance from you to support this decision. Do you have some reservations?" Make sure that, as a facilitator, you give the group or group member plenty of time to think about a response and to respond fully. Listen carefully and do not interrupt. Ask other group members to respond as well.

If the conflict is more substantial or if a lot of confusion and anger surfaces in the group, stop the proceedings and acknowledge the conflict: "Whoa . . . there seems to be some conflict here that we need to work through. Let's take a break and come back to deal with it." During the break is a good time to determine a technique or process that will help the group resolve the issues. One way to deal with several issues that may have surfaced at once is first to categorize and list the issues. Then help the group prioritize them and decide which to focus on first. Remember to coach the group to focus on those issues that directly or indirectly hinder it from reaching the goals. Ask the group if there are any issues that can be deleted and forgotten because they are not key to the group's progress.

Hidden agendas, those beliefs and wishes group members do not want to talk about in front of the group, also create conflict. Hidden agendas take the form of unexpressed fears, hostility toward other group members, desires for position and influence within the group, set ideas about how the group should proceed, minds made up about solutions, and the desire to have a certain role or set of responsibilities in the group. A hidden agenda stems from someone's mind being already made up about something the group should decide. These "personal goals" can obstruct group progress and cause conflict. One way to deal with hidden agendas is to try to bring them out in the open, and, if appropriate, ask the group to decide if meeting these personal goals will help or hinder the achievement of the group's goals. Ask, "What are some of your personal hopes and fears in regard to this project?" "What are some of your own goals in relation to the project?" "How do you see these personal goals helping or hindering the progress of the group?" This discussion should occur when the project goals are being defined.

Another technique you can use to manage conflict is to educate group members about their own role in resolving conflict. When group members understand that each of them plays an important role in reaching a mutually agreeable solution, they will begin to develop skills to deal constructively with conflict. Techniques for you to use are summarized in Figure 17.1. You may also want to post or hand out a list of behaviors and techniques such as the one in Figure 17.2 to remind group members of their own role in resolving conflict.

Figure 17.1. What Facilitators Can Do to Help Groups Resolve Conflict

- Provide guidance and clear direction during the goal-setting process;

- Make sure the group develops guidelines for how it will function as a group;

- Use proven team processes, tools, and techniques for brainstorming, problem solving, decision making, and analysis to help groups address conflict naturally, as part of the process;

- Make sure that people understand the various group roles (facilitator, leader, member) and that these roles are carried out;

- Help the group determine whether a disagreement is central and important to its progress, or peripheral and not important to its progress;

- Keep the group focused on its goal and when conflict arises, ask, "Does this need to be resolved for us to reach our goal?";

- When group members are buried in conflict, refocus them on the end result by asking, "What do we want the end result to be? What is it we are trying to achieve?"; and

- Help group members deal with hidden agendas. Make it acceptable to acknowledge personal goals and desires and even try to meet them, but make it unacceptable for personal agendas to stop the progress of the group or keep the group from being as effective as it could be.

Figure 17.2. What Group Members Can Do to Help Resolve Conflict

- Keep the end goal in mind. Help others do the same;

- Consider other views by:
  - Listening actively
  - Finding merit in others' views
  - Understanding the other person's main points

- Restate the other person's viewpoint to show understanding;

- Restate if you did not understand the first time or two;

- Avoid defending your own views until you have fully understood the other person;

- Do not hold back when you disagree or have another idea;

- State your own view clearly, firmly, and without excessive emotion;

- When interrupted, ask people politely to let you finish;

- Avoid harping on your own position, but rather let your idea stand on its own merit;

- Try not to become personally attached to or invested in your own position, keep the end goal in mind, and do not take it personally if the team decides to take another approach;

- Offer suggestions or alternatives, rather than simply disagreeing with another approach; and

- View group conflict as natural, and help your group work toward a mutually agreeable solution that will satisfy as many of everyone's needs as possible.

Evaluating Team Performance

A healthy team takes ownership for its ongoing growth and improvement and learns to evaluate itself periodically and make corrections. One of the critical roles of a facilitator is to provide guidance to a group so that it can evaluate its own progress.

Successful teams make it a habit to regularly review ground rules, meeting behaviors, work habits, and cohesiveness. It makes sense not to stop a team's positive momentum for evaluation or to evaluate too frequently. However, when a team's momentum has slowed down, when it faces obstacles that do not seem to be going away, or when members are complaining about how the team is functioning—these are signs that it is time to do a self-evaluation.

One of the easiest ways to get a group into the habit of evaluating itself is to stop work periodically and ask a few questions: "Let's take a break in our work for a minute and look at how we're progressing. How is the team working so far? Are there suggestions for how we might improve the way we work?" To check on how the group is working against its own standards, ask, "How are we doing against the norms we set for ourselves?" Another way to encourage the group to evaluate itself is to obtain feedback about how the meetings are going (see the section on Soliciting Feedback in Chapter 16, pages 307 through 312).

Continually look for activities and tools that will help teams evaluate themselves. These activities do not have to be elaborate. They can be brief, fun, and nonthreatening. Sometimes, they must be more thorough and serious, but the key is for teams to be accustomed to doing this kind of assessment.

How to Facilitate Team Self-Evaluation

It is important to find instruments, activities, and questions that will help the team improve its performance. The Team Evaluation Form on pages

332–334 (from my book *Teamwork from Start to Finish*) is suitable for this purpose. An effective team self-evaluation is designed to do all of the following:

- Assess all important areas of teamwork;

- Look at the team as a whole;

- Avoid embarrassing team members;

- Not grade, rank, rate, or single out team members;

- Help all team members take ownership for the team's performance as well as its improvement;

- Foster discussion among members, rather than focus on numerical results;

- Acknowledge the team's strengths, as well as areas needing improvement;

- Make teams aware of the characteristics of an effective team;

- Leave the team energized with one or two areas to focus on for improvement; and

- Let the team decide what to work on and how to work on it. The Team Evaluation Form reflects characteristics and practices of a high performing, successful team. Although this is not an exhaustive list, it represents key characteristics and covers the major areas of teamwork: goals, consensus, team leadership, roles, resources, support, membership, and habits and behaviors that make teams productive and cohesive.

If the team you work with has standards that are not represented here, add them to the questionnaire. If some of the standards are not important for your team, delete them, or reword them to fit your team's needs.

Some teams and organizations prefer not to use a numerical scale such as the 1 to 6 scale used here. In organizations in which rating and ranking have been abused or made people uncomfortable, teams may choose to drop the numerical scale and use an agreed-on verbal scale, such as "No, Sometimes, Always" or "Needs Improvement, Satisfactory, Outstanding."

The objective for doing a team self-evaluation should be *to identify an area or two in which the team can improve its performance as a team and decide how to do it.*

Here is a suggested process for using the Team Evaluation Form:

1. Hand out a copy to each team member.

2. Explain that the form will help the team identify areas needing improvement and that the team may want to alter it for later use.

3. Give team members quiet time to complete the form or have them complete it prior to the next meeting.

4. Make sure everyone knows which "team" is being evaluated.

5. Have someone tally the results of the evaluation. Usually someone on a team is skilled at tallying, averaging, and displaying scores so team members can see an accurate picture of the overall team responses. Show the average response for each item and, if you wish, the range of responses. For example, item number 1 may have an average score of 3.8 with a range of responses from 2 to 6. Post the results for everyone to see.

6. Ask team members to read through the results and then jot down any surprises, questions, or ideas that come to mind. After a few minutes, ask people to share their observations. Encourage everyone to comment and probe so that people are open and thoughtful in their responses.

7. Ask team members what they see as the key strengths or assets of their team. List these and post them for everyone to see. Next, ask team members to look at the items that were scored lowest and to discuss them. Allow plenty of time for discussion and the voicing

of opinions on each one. Ask team members to share voluntarily why they rated a particular item as they did. Ask, "Why should our team improve in this area?" List and post responses along with the list of strengths.

8. Next, have the team members come to agreement on what one or two areas they want to work on first. Decide what actions the team will take to make improvements in these selected areas. Record the actions and people responsible (it may be everyone). Make these action items part of the agenda for the next team meeting. Document them in the minutes. Continue to make them part of the agenda in future meetings, if necessary.

9. At a later meeting, ask the team members if they think the team made sufficient progress on the selected areas and check to see how each person would rank those areas now. If they have improved, ask how they will maintain good performance in these areas in the future. At this time, the team may want to return to the list of improvements needed and select another one or two areas to work on.

Do not hesitate to use the Team Evaluation Form again and again to check what progress the team has made.

Team Evaluation Form

The word "team" in this survey refers to _____ (write in the name of the group you are evaluating).

Directions: For each statement below, consider how strongly you agree or disagree and mark your response by circling one number. For example, if you mildly disagree with a statement, circle the number 4.

Example:	**Strongly Disagree**					**Strongly Agree**
The team has full responsibility for a well-defined segment of work.	1	2	3	(4)	5	6

Evaluation Scale
(Circle one number)

	Strongly Disagree					**Strongly Agree**
1. The team's mission and goals are written, clear, reasonable, and motivating.	1	2	3	4	5	6
2. Members aim for the same goals and are highly committed to the team's mission.	1	2	3	4	5	6
3. Consensus is reached without sacrificing quality.	1	2	3	4	5	6
4. The team's work is planned, organized, and carried out in an effective way.	1	2	3	4	5	6
5. Team meetings are timely and productive.	1	2	3	4	5	6
6. The team is kept well-informed about events, changes, or data that affect it.	1	2	3	4	5	6

Source: *Teamwork from Start to Finish* by Fran Rees (San Francisco Pfeiffer, 1997).
The Facilitator Excellence Handbook, Second Edition. Copyright © 2005 by John Wiley & Sons, Inc.

	Strongly Disagree				Strongly Agree	
7. Members are clear about their individual roles on the team.	1	2	3	4	5	6
8. The team has full responsibility for a well-defined segment of work.	1	2	3	4	5	6
9. The team has decision authority over how its work is done.	1	2	3	4	5	6
10. New members are accepted, supported, and well integrated into the team.	1	2	3	4	5	6
11. Team members have adequate equipment, resources, and skills to accomplish team goals.	1	2	3	4	5	6
12. The team's leadership is clear, effective, and supportive.	1	2	3	4	5	6
13. The team's tasks are reasonable in light of members' workloads.	1	2	3	4	5	6
14. Members know one another and work closely together.	1	2	3	4	5	6
15. Members trust one another; communication is open and unguarded.	1	2	3	4	5	6
16. Members feel a strong sense of responsibility to help the team be successful.	1	2	3	4	5	6
17. I feel that I am fully accepted as a member of the team.	1	2	3	4	5	6

	Strongly Disagree					Strongly Agree
18. Team members actively listen to one another and strive to fully understand one another's views.	1	2	3	4	5	6
19. Our team capitalizes on one another's differences, strengths, and unique capabilities.	1	2	3	4	5	6
20. Team members give feedback and receive feedback from one another in a caring and constructive way.	1	2	3	4	5	6
21. Working on this team is an enjoyable and satisfying experience.	1	2	3	4	5	6
22. Team goals are linked to goals of the larger organization.	1	2	3	4	5	6
23. The team and its members communicate and collaborate with other groups in the organization.	1	2	3	4	5	6
24. The team is effective in presenting its recommendations and decisions to others in the organization.	1	2	3	4	5	6
25. The team's recommendations and ideas are given open-minded and fair consideration by people higher in the organization.	1	2	3	4	5	6
26. The team periodically reviews its progress toward goals.	1	2	3	4	5	6

	Strongly Disagree				Strongly Agree	
27. The team periodically reviews how well it is working together as a team.	1	2	3	4	5	6
28. The team celebrates and recognizes significant team milestones and accomplishments.	1	2	3	4	5	6
29. The team encourages and recognizes individual, as well as team, performance.	1	2	3	4	5	6
30. The team receives encouragement and recognition from people higher in the organization.	1	2	3	4	5	6
31. Team members share successes and problems with one another.	1	2	3	4	5	6
32. Team members learn from one another.	1	2	3	4	5	6

Tips for Conducting a Team Self-Evaluation

Keep in mind the following general principles when you are facilitating a team self-evaluation:

- Only the members of your team should be present for the discussion, with the team leader participating as a team member, with equal (not weighted) input;

- Set aside plenty of time for discussion and minimize outside distractions;

- Allow team members several minutes of quiet time in the meeting to complete the form and later to study the results;

- As team members read through the results, have them write down their main reactions (surprise, questions, areas for improvements, strengths, etc.);

- Appoint a facilitator who will remain neutral during the discussion to move the discussion along and record team agreement on key points;

- Discuss team member reactions to the results by encouraging team members to share different perspectives, but making it voluntary to divulge scores;

- Record the team's ideas for improvement on a flip chart for all to see;

- Review and prioritize the list of ideas for team improvements;

- Arrange to have the list of ideas typed and distributed to the team; and

- Decide what follow-up is necessary (e.g., a meeting to define actions and responsibilities, a time to review the team's progress).

To summarize, a team facilitator must attend to a variety of aspects of teamwork, not only the team's meetings. Team facilitators are not just meeting facilitators, but coaches, mentors, and teachers as well. To the extent that a team facilitator understands how teams work and develop, he or she will be able to help the team achieve results and become a unified team.

Facilitating Virtual Teams

orkplace environments are changing and will continue to change. What was once thought of as a workplace—a geographical location where people were physically present, with defined hours, and where teams were able to meet face-to-face on a regular basis—is becoming rare. Increasingly, the "workplace" of today is geographically dispersed and relies heavily on electronic communication, long-distance travel, working across multiple time zones, and adapting to multicultural and personal requirements and challenges.

People work flexible schedules, they work from home or on the road, they work "a job," not a place or a time schedule. And that job is more of a project that will probably evolve into another job fairly quickly (if they are lucky!). Cell phones and computers make communication not only possible but also required from morning into evening hours. Some people define their job as "24/7," because work they are involved with proceeds twenty-four hours a day, seven days a week. Their cell phones go with them to restaurants, on personal errands, to family gatherings, and (alas!) even on vacation.

Incidentally, most of us know that working this way is verging on insanity, but so far it seems as though nothing will stem the tide of this trend. The way of the work world today in the year 2005 is global, fast, and ever-changing. Speed, commercial results, timeliness, competition, price-cutting, and "lean and mean" workforces dominate our workplaces, and even our lives. The world of work has virtually become the world!

What Is a Virtual Team?

It is more and more common for teams to be geographically dispersed, even though they must still operate as a functioning team. In recent years, these teams have come to be called virtual teams. The term *virtual* is defined as "being such in force or *effect*, though not actually or expressly such" (*The Random House Dictionary of the English Language*). In *Virtual Teams That Work*, editors Christina Gibson and Susan Cohen (2003) provide us with a framework to understand virtual teams. A virtual team has the following three attributes: (1) It is a functioning team, a collection of individuals who are interdependent in their tasks and share responsibility for outcomes, (2) the members of the team are geographically dispersed, and (3) the team relies more heavily on technology-mediated communications than on face-to-face interaction to accomplish its tasks.

Facilitation in Virtual Teams

Virtual teams are faced with the same challenges and dilemmas that face-to-face teams face, but with the *added dimension* of distance. "As teams become more virtual, they confront greater uncertainty and complexity, increasing the difficulty of the information processing and sense-making tasks that they do. Virtual teams face an upward climb, needing to overcome powerful barriers to effectiveness" (Gibson & Cohen, 2003, p. 7). Facilitation of team communication and "meetings" has become more complex, as well. Facilitators (who are often team leaders) are faced with the challenge of adapting facilitation skills, which have become successful in face-to-face meetings, to environments where electronically mediated communication is the norm. The question, of course, becomes: Is this possible?

The role of the facilitator does not change. There is still the need to have someone design and lead processes that give teams and work groups the ability to work together creatively and productively. Because individual team members are busy with jobs that make high demands on them, it is generally not possible for them to oversee the larger arena of team communication and collaboration. Someone else (the team leader or a facilitator) must do this. Without face-to-face meetings, however, the question remains: What are the best methods for facilitating virtual teams? How can a spirit of teamwork, cohesion, open communication, and adequate information sharing be fostered when team members are scattered geographically? How can problems be addressed creatively? How can detailed planning take place? How can timely decisions be made and conflict resolved?

These are crucial questions that facilitators are just beginning to deal with and those who develop, guide, and coach teams must wrestle with. Virtual teams themselves will identify what resources and help they need to function well as a team. Much thought and dialogue need to occur over the next few years. It is likely that facilitation skills themselves will require substantial augmentation.

Despite these challenges, the basic rationale for using facilitation skills in team and group work remains strong. Groups need processes and neutral facilitation to help them work through the many issues they face. Neutral and skilled facilitation (whether it comes from outside facilitators, the team leader, or a team member whose role is to facilitate) will still be necessary. The basic tenets of effective and high-performing teams remain the same. A successful team must have clear and realistic goals, resources to support achieving those goals, adequate and appropriate team member skills and expertise to achieve the goals, time, open communication, an atmosphere of trust, and a team environment that allows for individual expression and resolution of conflict. A virtual team needs all of the above, *plus* successful mechanisms for working and communicating electronically.

Strategies for Facilitators

Given the challenges of facilitating in virtual team environments, facilitators must work with their teams and team leaders to strategize how to work collaboratively as a virtual team. First, it is important to acknowledge to the team that being a virtual team creates certain challenges. Some of these challenges should be listed and discussed at the initial team meeting(s) and in the early correspondence. All team members should be invited to make suggestions for team processes and communication. One of the team's goals could be to identify effective ways to work together as a virtual team.

The following questions should be kept in mind as the team's work proceeds:

- How can *team identity* be established and maintained?

- What particular skills and knowledge does the *team leader* need to lead this virtual team? What are the main challenges, and how will they be addressed?

- What *cross-cultural issues* need to be addressed for the team to function well?

- How can *communication* be enhanced? What modes of communication work best and in what instances?

- Where are the opportunities for team members to *work together* on tasks and how should communication and task ownership be managed?

- What particular challenges do *team member locations* place on the team and how can these challenges be met?

- What needs to be accomplished at *face-to-face meetings*? When and how often should these be scheduled?

- What are the *"red flags"* that will alert the team to problems early on?

Facilitators should work with team leaders and team members (during face-to-face meetings and via e-mail and telephone) to come up with strategies for the above areas. Simply acknowledging these as areas needing attention may help team members come up with suggestions and solutions. Letting team members know up front that everyone will be working to establish "teamship" from a distance will help establish a common goal for the team.

For example, working with the team to establish *team identity* as soon as possible lays the foundation for team members' sense of connection to the team. Maintaining team identity is an ongoing process. Some *team identity strategies* are

- Facilitate an initial face-to-face meeting to acquaint team members with one another.

- Solidify overall team goals, norms, and key initial tasks as soon as possible, preferably at the initial face-to-face meeting.

- Involve team members early on in discussions about how to keep connected and build cohesion as a team.

- Create a name and a slogan for the team; refer to the name and slogan often.

- When appropriate, build a cross-cultural component into some of the team's face-to-face meetings. This is especially important when team members from different cultures need cross-cultural understanding and awareness to do their job well and to build a team rapport. Generally, the more cross-cultural understanding there is, the greater the chances that team members will be motivated to work effectively together.

- Help the team assign roles and responsibilities for tasks and make these clear to all team members simultaneously.

- Identify tasks that can and should be worked on in subgroups or pairs.

- Consider forming a subgroup to work regularly on the issue of team communication and cohesion; rotate subgroup members in and out so that all team members eventually have a chance to work on these issues. Ask the subgroup to create workable strategies and revise them, if necessary, so that they become guidelines for the team.

- Encourage the team leader and team members to think of ways to reinforce the concept of "team" in their correspondence, their presentations, and their references. (For example, team e-mail correspondence could include the name of the team, along with the names of *all* team members.)

Facilitating Across Distance

Those who facilitate virtual teams should keep in mind two important concepts: (1) A virtual team is still a team and requires all the basics of a regular team to function, and (2) many facilitation concepts and techniques work long distance if team members can connect easily electronically and by telephone. For example, facilitators should not forfeit the ongoing involvement of team members in formulating goals and norms or in problem solving. Instead, facilitators of virtual teams must find ways for team members to give input, see one another's ideas, respond to teammates' ideas, and brainstorm effective solutions. In addition, periodic face-to-face meetings should not be abandoned but be carefully planned to take advantage of team members' being together in one location.

A great disadvantage, of course, to virtual teams is that team members will not see or hear one another's ideas on a regular basis. Instead, comments, suggestions, and plans will have to be written and transmitted via e-mail or by telephone. This can prove problematic for those working in other than their native language, and teammates will need to be sensitive to this. Although the telephone is convenient for some types of communication, the use of e-mail simulates a facilitated meeting, since the ideas are written down, summarized, and published for all to see. E-mail discussions also help those with language barriers, since it is generally easier to read a foreign language than to hear it spoken.

When facilitating discussions and decisions via e-mail, the facilitator must describe each round of the process, set time limits, and let team members know what is expected each step along the way. This will have to be done online and should be clear and brief. It will undoubtedly take practice for facilitators to do this well. I hope that the example below will give some initial guidelines to facilitators working online. This example illustrates how to facilitate the surfacing and resolution of an issue with team members via e-mail.

Raise an Issue. Someone poses a question or raises an issue and invites others to discuss it. The facilitator agrees to monitor the dialogue process and announces this to the team via e-mail.

State the Topic for Discussion and Agree on Objectives for the Dialogue. The facilitator asks the contributor(s) to state an objective for the discussion up front. The suggested objective is transmitted to team members with the question: Is everyone in agreement on the objective for this discussion? Once the objective is agreed on—or amended so that it is agreed on—the dialogue begins.

Dialogue on the Issue. Team members each present their response, opinions, and ideas via e-mail and read all inputs. The facilitator uses traditional facilitator techniques such as probing, summarizing, and setting time limits. Members continue dialoguing for a specified period. Because members may be working in different time zones, the facilitator sets realistic time frames for each "round" of the work. It might be helpful to label each round of the process (for example, Round #1 Dialogue, Round #2 Dialogue) so team members are clear about what process they are working on.

Clarify Ideas. Continuing to work via e-mail, the facilitator directs team members to ask questions of any ideas they don't understand. All questions and answers are presented via e-mail to all team members, the team leader, and the facilitator.

Identify the Strongest Ideas. Next, the facilitator asks team members to select what they think are the most viable options and explain their reasons briefly to the team. After all team members have contributed, or after a predecided time limit is up, the facilitator compiles the results and summarizes them for everyone. The facilitator suggests what the next process will be, such as further prioritization of the items or subgroup work to gather more information. Along the way, the facilitator checks with team members before moving on, just as he or she would do if facilitating a face-to-face meeting.

Decide How to Best Meet the Stated Objective(s). The facilitator reviews the initial objective with the team and calls for the decision by asking each team member to declare one or more (preferably more than one) decision he or she can support 100 percent. As in a face-to-face meeting, the facilitator briefly reviews what was suggested or decided and checks for common understanding and interpretation along the way. Based on this input, the facilitator, team leader, and team come to agreement as to how to proceed. If no clear decision emerges, the team leader may pose a solution and ask whether everyone can support it.

Ask for Feedback from Team Members. Before closing the dialogue and decision process, the facilitator asks for feedback on the process from team members. Each person is invited to name one or two things that went well and should be done in subsequent dialogues, and one or two things that did not work well or could have been done differently. All team members read the feedback. The facilitator announces the end of this process.

Involving team members in this way is the same process a facilitator would use in a face-to-face meeting. Working through issues in this manner will take more time, since people need to be given opportunity and time to respond and read others' responses. However, if the issue is urgent it can be marked so, and all team members can make an effort to respond in a timely fashion. Due to differences in time zones, there will be a lag in the responses. With experience, facilitators will learn how to monitor the time issue in distance facilitation, perhaps suggesting at the beginning of a dialogue or problem-solving session what the time frame will be. For example, one week might be sufficient to dialogue among team members and to come up with the initial list of top priority items. Another week might be needed to decide which items should be acted on, and a third week might be needed to plan how to parcel out the tasks to implement the decision. If team members are kept posted as to the process and the time frames, they will be more likely to contribute. If decisions made this way are actually implemented, it will no doubt encourage further participation of team members.

Involving Team Members in Creating Successful Processes

Since the actuality of virtual teams is still relatively new, facilitators and team leaders will benefit greatly by involving team members all along the way in suggesting and experimenting with various communication and decision-making processes that work. The overall goals should be to keep the team working well together, achieving the team goals, and building strength and cohesion as a group. As in regular teams, the goal should not be to force teamwork where it is not needed but to work *interdependently because the work demands it*. When the work demands it, team members of virtual teams will succeed because they develop effective means of working together across distance.

Some questions facilitators and team leaders can ask the team are

1. What is working well in our team communication? What is not working?

2. What suggestions do you have for better communication and team efforts?

3. Can you describe a specific part of the team's work or communication that needs improvement? How would it function if it were working better?

4. What skills and knowledge do you need?

5. What makes you feel a part of the team? What causes you to feel isolated, or disconnected, from the team?

To keep team members involved in coming up with effective methods, questions such as these can be posed on a regular basis and answers collected from team members. The questions and answers can be posted for all to see on a common e-mail communication or electronic message board, if one is used. Responses to these questions become material for further consideration in subsequent meetings.

Improving Distance Facilitation Skills

In addition to experience and careful listening to members of virtual teams, facilitators should make an effort to network, dialogue, and learn from other facilitators and team leaders about effective methods for facilitating virtual team challenges. An efficient avenue for sharing information and knowledge about virtual team facilitation is critical if today's facilitators are going to get up to speed quickly. Also, keeping an open mind about facilitation in general—what it is, how it can be applied in global environments, and what adaptations have to be made—will increase a facilitator's chance for success.

For example, knowing how to balance face-to-face with electronic meetings will be an important skill of today's facilitator. There will also need to be new ways to monitor the "health" of a team, since the facilitator will not be privileged to seeing the group in action. Software might be needed to make distance communication among team members more efficient and speedier. Checklists, forms, ranking and rating input capabilities, and other tools might also be helpful.

Summary

Facilitators should keep in mind the following as they adapt their skills and methods to a global environment:

- Teamwork across cultures and distance is a fact of life in global work environments.

- Distance facilitation is relatively new. Much remains to be discovered about what works well and what doesn't.

- Facilitation remains important to teams regardless of where the team members are located. If the work is interdependent, facilitation methods and practices are critical to the team's success.

- The goals and purposes of facilitation may have to be redefined in global environments.

- Networking with other facilitators, media experts, and experienced team leaders is important.

- Members of virtual teams themselves are key to discovering what facilitation and communication methods work best.

- Many facilitation methods and goals can be adapted to electronic communication.

- As with regular teams, facilitators need ongoing feedback from team members so they can customize their facilitation processes to fit the needs of a particular team.

- Facilitators will have to work via electronic communication. In today's global environment, it may be difficult to get all team members together frequently enough to rely on face-to-face meetings to resolve critical issues. Face-to-face meetings will call for careful planning and skilled facilitation, since there will be fewer of them and much will need to be accomplished.

CHAPTER **19**

Facilitating Organization-Wide Projects

As you become skilled and experienced at facilitating meetings and teams, you may be asked to facilitate meetings and projects that affect and involve people across the organization. In this role, you will act both as a consultant and as a facilitator. This type of assignment requires an additional bank of skills, which could be called consulting skills. Such a project may involve working with leaders in one or more departments or divisions to improve processes, communication, or company practices or to implement company-wide systems or policies.

The Consulting Role

Some facilitators who work at this level have only one job: to consult as needed to the organization. They are full-time facilitators or consultants on organization-wide projects or team/departmental issues that require special facilitation skills. Others work on these assignments in addition to their regular jobs. Some examples of assignments that may require consulting skills are:

349

- Facilitating a task force to examine company diversity practices;

- Facilitating a cross-functional project to implement a new computer system or formulate new employee practices;

- Facilitating management and executive meetings and strategic planning sessions;

- Intervening in a department or division to help a client group identify and solve problems;

- Facilitating conflict resolution within or among groups;

- Initiating and facilitating a departmental or organization-wide effort; or

- Facilitating difficult team projects, especially those that require working across the organization.

This level of facilitation may require inter-team work or working with several levels of management, including top management. These cross-company projects and concerns may be sensitive in nature and difficult to facilitate. A high level of skill is generally required to design and carry out the sessions that may be involved. It may require laying out a series of interviews and/or talk sessions with employees, compiling and diagnosing data, and presenting findings to management and employees. This role implies that the facilitator will help the client diagnose the situation, decide which approach to take, and collaborate on how to implement the process. It may involve overseeing communication, follow-up, and evaluation of the project as well.

Skills Required

Ideally, all facilitators would have some knowledge of the consulting process, because even designing a simple meeting requires planning and diagnosis and may require some consulting skills as well. There are, however, many opportunities to facilitate meetings and work with teams that do not require the same level of consulting skills as those discussed in this chapter. Organizations need plenty of people with basic facilitation and team facilitation skills and usually not as many with consulting skills.

Distinguishing between facilitating and consulting helps facilitators assess what is required and helps them develop confidence and skill in intervening at various levels of the organization. It would not be fair to expect a new facilitator to take on a full-blown consulting project without considerable experience as a meeting and/or team facilitator. It is not enough simply to gain experience and then move on into a consulting/facilitating role. The consulting role requires a more advanced skill level. Those filling this role often find themselves training and coaching teams and individuals in facilitation, communication, and teamwork skills.

The skills needed in a consulting role can be organized into four major categories: *technical, self-management, interpersonal,* and *consulting*. Consulting skills can further be categorized into six skill areas: *role shaping, contracting, diagnosing, problem solving and decision making, implementing, and evaluating*.[1] Here are some examples of skills in each category:

Technical Skills

- Possesses sufficient technical training and experience in an area of specialty, such as human resources, finance, project management, management, or computer science;

- Keeps up-to-date in area of specialty; and

- Effectively explains and applies own technology or expertise to client issues and problems.

---

[1] A more detailed list of these skills can be found in the Consulting Skills Inventory by Fran Rees, published in *The 1998 Annual: Volume 1, Training* by Pfeiffer.

Self-Management Skills

- Is aware of own strengths and weaknesses;

- Seeks help, opinions, and advice from another professional when needed; and

- Determines and maintains client confidentiality.

Interpersonal Skills

- Encourages participation and involvement from all concerned;

- Works effectively with a variety of people;

- Successfully solicits the cooperation and commitment of others; and

- Facilitates clients to generate solutions for their own problems.

Consulting Skills

- Works with clients to clarify measurable outcomes for projects;

- Makes an effort to understand clients' business goals and culture;

- Helps clients consider different strategies and alternatives before making a decision; and

- Solicits periodic feedback from clients and others involved.

Intervention Defined

A facilitator *intervention* is the process of entering into a group or system for the purpose of helping those in the system (Argyris, 1970). The facilitator who works across the organization will, over time, help a variety of clients and conduct a variety of interventions. Because each intervention is a separate case, facilitators must guide the client through the steps necessary to diagnose, plan, and implement the intervention. To be successful, an organizational facilitator must collaborate and partner closely with the client through all phases of an intervention. Generally speaking, the client knows help is needed and calls on the facilitator/consultant to help design the approach and facilitate the process. Sometimes, the client has a preconceived notion about how to proceed, but you must work with him or her to determine whether this is indeed the best approach.

Clients will approach you with varying degrees of certainty about the problem and its potential solution. When first working with a client, you will do best not to assume that the client has accurately diagnosed the situation and not to assume that the client has misdiagnosed the situation. The best approach to take is to ask questions to gather enough information to know how to proceed.

Types of Clients

To work at the organizational level, you must learn to distinguish between the various "clients" you will work with during an intervention.

Primary Clients

In his book *The Skilled Facilitator*, Roger M. Schwarz (1994, p. 48) explains critical differences between clients. He defines the *primary client* as "the group that has accepted responsibility for the problem—the group with which the facilitator will ultimately work." However, to carry out an intervention, you will frequently come in contact with other types of clients who may or may not be members of the primary client group. Schwarz makes a clear distinction among the types of client.

Initial Clients

Initial clients are the people who make the initial contact with the facilitator. They may be staff members, managers, or secretaries. They may or may not be part of the primary client group.

Intermediate Clients

Intermediate clients are people involved in the early stages of diagnosing and/or planning the intervention. You may work with clients such as group or human resource managers or even customers of the primary client group while diagnosing or planning the intervention.

Ultimate Clients

Ultimate clients are people whose interests should be protected, even though they may not come in direct contact with you or others involved in the intervention. According to Schwarz (p. 48), "The ultimate clients include the organization as a whole, the customers who use the services of the organization or buy its products, and the larger community or society."

Your goal as a facilitator is, through discussions with the various clients, to determine who the primary client is and to plan an intervention that will address the needs and goals of that person or group. Sometimes this involves interviews with primary client members. Often you will work with one or a few members of the primary client group but seek the support and buy-in of the entire primary client group before proceeding with the intervention. Buy-in can be sought at the first meeting of the group when suggested goals and processes are presented to the group.

Steps in Working with Clients

In your consulting role you will benefit greatly from understanding the phases of consulting and what the important steps are when working with clients. In the book *The Consulting Process in Action*, Lippitt and Lippitt (1986, pp. 11–35) outlined six major steps each consultant should take to ensure a successful process. This book, along with Peter Block's ground-breaking 1981 book for internal consultants, *Flawless Consulting* (updated 1999), are key resources for you in consulting roles.

The six steps to working with clients outlined by the Lippitts include:

1. Engaging in initial contact and entry;

2. Formulating a contract and establishing a helping relationship;

3. Identifying problems through diagnostic analysis;

4. Setting goals and planning for action;

5. Taking action and cycling feedback; and

6. Completing the contract (continuity, support, and termination).

Engaging in Initial Contact and Entry

The first step begins when the client calls on you for help and ends when you and the client have adequately explored the potential for working together. The entry phase is a critical point in the consulting process because during this time the tone and expectations for how you will work together are set. Block (1999) convincingly illustrates how important it is that the client and facilitator (or internal consultant) work collaboratively and that collaboration be established in the early phases of the project.

Formulating a Contract and Establishing a Helping Relationship

The second step, formulating a contract and establishing a helping relationship, ends when an agreement has been reached as to how you and the client will proceed with the intervention. This agreement is also referred to as the "contract," which Block (1999) calls "an explicit agreement of what the consultant and client expect from each other and how they are going to work together. . . . It is designed not so much for enforcement, but for clear communication about what is going to happen on a project." Although usually verbal, this agreement, or contract, is sometimes put in writing.

As the consulting facilitator, you face three difficulties in these early stages of the process: (1) determining who the real client is; (2) deciding whether an intervention is appropriate and what the focus of the intervention should be; and (3) establishing a healthy, collaborative relationship with the client. During these stages you have the option not to intervene but should carefully explain the rationale of this decision to the client.

Identifying Problems Through Diagnostic Analysis

The third step, identifying problems through diagnostic analysis, gives you and the client data needed to proceed with the project. This may be as simple as posing a set of questions to a select group of people or it might be as complex as an organization-wide survey.

Setting Goals and Planning for Action

Step four, setting goals and planning for action, requires you to determine each goal and the steps that will be taken to achieve it. During this phase it is highly important to identify a single person who is responsible for each action step, even though several people may be involved. One person needs to have bottom-line responsibility for completing each step. This is also a good time to identify important milestones, especially if the project requires a long time to complete, so that those implementing the project have points in time at which to stop and celebrate progress. After these milestones are clear, the group can brainstorm ways to celebrate or receive recognition as milestones are completed.

Taking Action and Cycling Feedback

During step five, taking action and cycling feedback, you help the client group to be successful by doing some or all of the following:

- Facilitating meetings to review progress and establish new action steps;

- Facilitating resolution of problems and concerns;

- Facilitating the group's evaluation of its efforts and taking corrective action;

- Helping the group find resources or obtain necessary skills to increase its chances of success;

- Suggesting ways the group can receive feedback from those outside the group about its progress and efforts;

- Keeping the group focused on goals; and

- Helping the group become less dependent on you—in other words, teaching the group to facilitate itself.

Completing the Contract

Step six, completing the contract (continuity, support, and termination), means that you will stay with the project long enough to ensure that it has a good chance of succeeding. Work with the client group to ensure that the good efforts or improvements are continued after the project has been implemented. Frequently, facilitators may be needed for support but leave a group before it has encountered any of the difficulties that occur after initial implementation. Of course, at some point the work of the facilitator is (or should be) complete and the client group left to carry on by itself. Ideally, the group would have identified this point during the planning stages and taken appropriate steps to ensure a smooth continuation of the project or work after you are gone. Most consultants and facilitators consider it their responsibility to make themselves unnecessary at some point and plan accordingly. It may be helpful to the client group if you gradually decrease your involvement over time, but are available periodically to help the group review its progress and needs. Again, this option should be decided collaboratively with the client group.

In this chapter, only a small portion of what it means to be an organizational facilitator has been covered. At this level of facilitating, you are likely to work on projects that are more sensitive or complex in nature and will benefit greatly from being trained and/or mentored in consulting skills.

Facilitator Excellence

Good facilitation is not simply a matter of applying appropriate skills and tools at the right time. There is no formula for good facilitation. Facilitating is an art, an improvisation, and an act of thinking on your feet. It takes continual and dedicated practice to learn and apply skills and methods. For facilitators to grow and develop, they need to understand this art and must take care of themselves, the artists. Chapter 20 covers how to manage oneself, Chapter 21 describes some of the artistry of facilitation, and Chapter 22 addresses what makes a "great" facilitator.

Managing Yourself

Most of us know, intellectually at least, that to do good work we must take care of ourselves. Those in professions that require a good deal of taking care of others are frequently the first to forget about the importance of taking care of oneself. Facilitators are no exception.

You must have a clear perspective on the role and issues of being a facilitator, grow and develop as a facilitator, and take care of personal needs in the process. An important element in managing yourself as a facilitator is to remain centered and grounded or else be tossed about by the issues, concerns, and wanderings of the group being facilitated. You must have a sense of your own power, understand power (its use and abuse), and know how others react to power issues in a group. You must learn to navigate your own development and growth as a facilitator, largely without mentoring or formal training.

Ego, Power, and the Facilitator

Facilitators do not control or dominate. They provide opportunities. To be effective, you have to let go of the need for power: the ability to control, direct, impress, inspire, command, and influence the core actions of others. Instead, you must work alongside others in a less directive way to guide them. You are a "servant" to the group, one who inspires in others the power to act and make decisions. You must understand your own beliefs and attitudes toward power and be aware of your personal susceptibility to it.

When you come into a group, it is best to leave ego outside, although this is difficult to do. Ego makes you aware of your own behavior and importance, to the detriment of group progress. Ego is a strong and focused attention on "me, myself, and I." When you are bound up in ego, your attention is turned inward, not outward to the group. When you expect to raise your status or gain recognition from facilitation, you may not be very effective in the role.

When your ego is strongly present, the whole process will suffer. Facilitation is not about you; it is about the group. Facilitation is not about elevating you to a position of power, or even recognition, although it is fine if the group recognizes that you played a part in its success. Facilitation is about seeing what the group needs to move forward and then providing guidance. In order to see this, to pay full attention to the group, you cannot be overly concerned with status or position or reputation in the organization. Showing off as a facilitator can backfire. The group really wants a facilitator, not a leader or manager or trainer or preacher or teacher or parent. The facilitator role is a humbling one because credit goes to the group, while you remain in the background, hauling the charts around, asking questions, listening, giving feedback, and finding marking pens. Sometimes you may feel superfluous. This is probably just good facilitation. As long as the group is productive, you are doing your job. Your power and credit must come from the group's success, not your own. This is a difficult attitude for many professionals, especially if they have been used to taking charge, presenting and defending their own opinions, and taking risks to lead others. Facilitation involves taking risks too, but by listening, questioning, and helping.

You must be there fully, whether the group is aware of this or not. You must let the group struggle through its own problems and find its own answers, even if you know the answer. Your position of power comes from influencing the process, and even this cannot happen without the consent, whether verbal or tacit, of the group. You are always in the position of suggesting and negotiating with the group. Your power comes from how skillful you are in empowering the group. Power comes from unleashing the group's power, so that together group members experience the collective power of synergy.

An image that will help you move into this role is one of an infinite pie. Each piece of pie represents a slice of power, but the pie never diminishes. There is always enough power to go around. A slice here, a slice there, and yet another slice! And yet each slice is critical to the whole pie. Everyone has a piece of power, and all of the power is needed. You have a slice of the pie, so does the group leader, and so do the group members. Everyone shares power, and there is always plenty of power to go around because there is so much to be done.

Good facilitators have a keen awareness of power and power issues in a group. After you have a sure sense of your own power and are content to use it only for the sake of group progress, observe the goings-on within the group. Inevitably you must guide the group beyond its own "power outages," those times when individual power issues blind the group to its own potential. If certain members of the group are overly conscious of the power of one or more individuals, this will hinder progress of the group. On the other hand, members who see power as evil or out of place may hold back valuable contributions rather than assert themselves; this is also detrimental to the group's progress.

You will use processes and tools to help the group forget power inequities (at least temporarily) and move forward as if each individual had equal power to influence the work of the group. This is one of your most important tasks as a facilitator: to neutralize the effect misdirected or misunderstood power has on the group by ensuring that everyone takes the risk to contribute substantially so that power is channeled for the overall progress of the group. Avoid giving added power to "power figures" in the room or hindering less assertive people from trying to influence. Instead, by the processes and behaviors you use, nurture group members to tap their own resources and speak up. Make it safe, and not shocking, to do so.

Because of the fact that well-facilitated groups generally produce much more than groups that lack adequate facilitation, your role is truly a powerful one. Facilitation can be the force that turns the tide of group work. Good facilitators are not weak, self-effacing figures. They are people with tremendous catalytic power, with the ability to infuse groups with constructive energy and creativity to minimize the ill effects of misused power.

Being Centered and Authentic

I once knew a therapist-turned-organization-consultant who said, "Work from your center." Although I was not sure what working from my center was, I noticed her ability to remain calm during crises, while continuing to work steadily and with strength on the issue at hand. Somehow she managed to stay thoroughly involved in what was going on without becoming angry, withdrawing, or resorting to sneaky tactics to accomplish things. Yet she had courage to let others know how she was feeling and how their behaviors had an impact on her.

Being "self-centered" is not a very desirable trait, as it often gets in the way of relating well to people. It especially gets in the way of good facilitation. But being "centered" is different. Being centered means being comfortable with yourself, being strong enough to hold to your values around other people, and respecting the fact that others will not always think and act as you do. Being centered means you are comfortable learning and growing, not because something is wrong with you but because you are fundamentally okay with yourself. It means you are busy being yourself, not trying to be better than others. When people are centered they accept themselves and allow others to do the same. Being centered does not come easily or automatically, and it usually signals someone with a certain level of maturity. Age is irrelevant, for being older does not mean that you have a greater capacity for remaining centered.

Facilitators must remain centered because if they are not comfortable continuing to learn about and accept themselves, it will be harder for them to accept group members. When you are not centered, the group members sense an incongruence between your surface behavior and your underlying messages. Group members sense when you are covering up; this causes them, whether consciously or subconsciously, to cover up as well.

Being centered means keeping your balance even if things are busy and chaotic around you. If you are centered, you have something to fall back on when things become frantic or confused. You know who you are and where you come from and are not thrown off balance when you discover something new or surprising about yourself. You will be able to see yourself, acknowledge who you are, and work with it.

In *The Art of Facilitation*, Hunter, Bailey, and Taylor (1995a, p. 10) discuss the importance of facilitators empowering themselves. Centering and self-empowerment go hand in hand. "Empowerment is *coming into your own unique place of power where you are most truly your own self.* . . . It does not always mean being strong and confident—you may be most *in your power* when you are feeling very vulnerable. It is more to do with being truly authentic and present." Empowering yourself and remaining centered both require you to be authentic, which means not covering up genuine feelings or vulnerabilities. It means accepting strengths as well as weaknesses, and using them both in constructive ways.

Improving Performance as a Facilitator

You have wonderful opportunities to learn as a facilitator. You have the chance to see people interacting and working together in many different situations. You interact continually with individuals and groups. Facilitating provides many opportunities to learn about others, yourself, group dynamics, and the relationship of people and groups to larger organizations. Sometimes there is so much to learn that it is difficult to know where to begin.

After receiving some basic training, facilitators are usually tossed out into the world of facilitation without a lot of coaching and feedback. In some organizations there are only a few people with facilitation skills, most of whom are so busy they have little time to mentor one another. The best way for you to grow is to devise a simple system for your own learning and development. The best teacher, of course, is experience and practice. Feedback is critical, and so is seeing other facilitators work. There are also numerous resources on the market that you can use.

Perhaps the most important factor in facilitator growth and development is attitude. You must have a balanced attitude—one that says, "I am doing my best as a facilitator and am providing valuable assistance to the groups I facilitate. I am continuously learning how to improve and welcome feedback about my facilitation skills. I have the ability to give myself constructive feedback as well. As I incorporate this feedback into future facilitations, I will continue to learn and improve." This attitude comes from knowing you are providing a valuable service to the groups you facilitate, while continually finding ways to do better.

Avoiding Burnout

Facilitators, by the nature of their role, may have heavy demands placed on them. If they also have a strong dedication to helping their clients and organization make improvements and maintain high levels of productivity, they may overextend themselves. Facilitators can be candidates for burnout. To avoid burnout, familiarize yourself with the symptoms and causes, in order to recognize it both in yourself and in those with whom you are working. Perhaps even more importantly, study and practice ways to avoid personal burnout and then encourage client groups and organizations with whom you work to incorporate some of these methods into their own systems.

A person can be said to be in "burnout" when his or her usual energy and optimism are depleted and personal effectiveness diminished. Burnout is both hard to recognize and difficult to cope with. Symptoms of burnout are frequently evident to others while the person himself or herself remains unaware of the condition until obvious difficulties arise and performance is consistently affected.

All human beings can potentially reach a state of burnout in their personal and/or professional lives. Students and children face possible burnout. Those in the "helping professions," however, have even greater opportunity for burnout because of heavy demands made on them by others, long work hours, high visibility, and the pressure for results. Easy-going, complacent workers are not at such a high risk for burnout. Those who are energetic, impatient, insistent on high standards, idealistic, and overly critical of themselves are more likely candidates. They are more apt to work harder and harder when things are difficult and less apt to decrease their efforts or take a much-needed break. Whether it is self-imposed or system-generated, burnout is the end product of stress that has not been dealt with effectively.

Burnout occurs when, over a period of time, more energy is expended than is replaced. This energy may be mental or physical or emotional—or all three. Here are some of the telltale signs of burnout:

- Frequent fatigue;

- Work increasingly seems boring and unrewarding;

- Irritability and anger;

- Loss of concern for others;

- Hostile, cynical, or apathetic attitude toward work, life, and others in general;

- Desire to withdraw from others and from new involvements or amusements;

- Difficulty thinking clearly or making even a simple decision;

- Lowered efficiency;

- Feelings of resignation and futility;

- Exhaustion, even when receiving enough sleep;

- Feeling that there is not enough time to do all the work;

- Forgetfulness excused by saying, "There is just too much on my plate!";

- Worry about little things and anxiety about bigger things; and

- Increased headaches, backaches, colds, sore throats, etc.

Some more severe symptoms of burnout may include:

- Chronic or serious illness (diabetes, ulcers, high blood pressure, migraines, etc.);

- Sloppy, ungroomed appearance;

- Emotional outbursts (temper tantrums, crying spells, hysterics);

- No motivation or enthusiasm for work;

- Vices such as overeating, gambling, drinking, or compulsive shopping;

- Procrastination, even on important tasks; and

- Alienation from the people in one's life.

Everyone has a bad day, or even a bad week, now and then. With burnout, however, the symptoms continue over a much longer period of time. If left unattended, they can lead to serious work, physical, and personal disorders.

Each of us deals with stress and pressure differently, and each person must learn to recognize his or her own burnout signals. Read over the previous lists, check those that are your warning signs, and add any you can think of. Place a copy of this list in your daily planner or calendar and look at it now and then. When you experience any of these symptoms, try to rebalance your life so that you will not become a candidate for burnout. Remember, burnout is the end result of stress that is not dealt with.

The best way is, of course, to avoid burnout in the first place, which also makes one's life a good deal more pleasant. Three main areas must be attended to: our work, ourselves, and our relationships.

Tips on Dealing with Work

1. *Learn to say no.* Keep your commitments and your schedule as realistic as possible. Learn to leave open time for the unexpected.

2. *Slow down.* Do not try to do everything quickly or to do several things at once. Learn the power of calm focus on one task at a time.

3. *Make realistic time estimates.* Be aware of how long it actually takes to do certain tasks and types of projects and make realistic estimates of how long it will take to accomplish things. Always plan for 20 percent more time than you think it will take.

4. *Keep your career goals in mind and make plans to attain them.* At the same time, do not be too rigid or inflexible. Life has a way of dumping unplanned opportunities in your path.

5. *Learn to stop and celebrate your achievements.* Reward yourself when you have finished a difficult job.

6. *Remember your basic facilitation skills.* When you communicate and work with people, listen for understanding, ask questions, keep communication open and honest, admit your vulnerabilities as well as your strengths, probe for more information, let others know you understand what they are saying, and clarify action items and commitments that were made. This will make your relationships with others more fulfilling and successful.

7. *Regularly do things to replenish your energy.* If you do not know what builds your personal energy, experiment and find out.

8. *Avoid falling into bad habits.* Escapism or bad habits such as overeating, drinking, procrastinating, etc., will make things worse.

9. *Try to change only what is possible.* Realize what you cannot change and avoid wasting energy by complaining, worrying, discussing, or resisting.

10. *Have some fun.* Find many things in life you enjoy and make sure plenty of them are not connected with work. Be sure some of them are simple and easy to incorporate into your daily life. Make it a habit to enjoy them!

11. *Put work in perspective.* Remember the "big picture" of your profession, your company, your career, and your life. Most worries become trivial when placed against the truly important things in life.

12. *Value your work.* The job each person does is valuable in the context of the whole. There is a reason to do even the smallest and most tedious tasks. Take pride in what you do and focus on doing the best job you can, and the process of the work itself will lift your spirits. Do not fall into the trap of thinking you will be doing this forever; instead, know that you will have many jobs in your lifetime and that each one will build on the next.

13. *Consider a change.* If necessary, reevaluate your job situation and plan to make a change.

14. *Practice good time management and organization.* Sometimes stress and eventually burnout are exacerbated by disorganization and lack of attention to detail.

15. *Beware of "temporary" overload.* Avoid accepting a work overload situation that is liable to become permanent. If your temporary overload lingers on, negotiate with your boss to hand off or eliminate certain tasks before you become burned out and ineffective.

Tips on Dealing with Yourself

1. *Have faith in yourself.* Know deep inside that you can do good work, be an admirable human being, and have a rich and productive life.

2. *Dwell on possibilities and options rather than limitations.* Look for the opportunity in adversity and find ways to be creative.

3. *Let perfectionism go.* Few of us will ever be perfect in what we do, and perfectionism is the enemy of productivity. Allow yourself to make mistakes; aim for doing a fine job (not a perfect one).

4. *Set yourself up for success.* Take realistic challenges that will stretch you a bit but will not undo you.

5. *Know yourself.* Learn as much as you can about yourself: what you love, what your skills and abilities are, what you value in life, how you want to live your life, what satisfies you, what frightens and challenges you, and what support you need.

6. *Keep in touch with yourself.* Knowing yourself is a lifetime job. Realize that you will change over time; your tastes, attitudes, and needs will vary. Stop from time to time to take stock of who you are, where you are going, what is missing in your life, and what is truly important to you.

7. *Simplify your life.* Most of us want to accomplish quite a bit in life, but it is unreasonable to think that we will have it all, all of the

time. If you feel overwhelmed and confused, allow time to move at a pleasant pace and learn to prioritize for each period of your life.

8. *Learn to relax and do nothing.* This can be very difficult for people who have too much to do.

9. *Try to become more patient.* Place value on the quality of a task as well as the quantity or speed with which it is done. Recognize that there are always unforeseen things that can hold you up: traffic, illness, a change in plans, forgetfulness, a catastrophe, the weather, a person in need, a sick child, a company reorganization. Think of life more as a flowing river than as something you control through planning and manipulation. Make your plans and act, but readjust when necessary.

10. *Stop being in a hurry.* Know that living takes time and there are many things that simply will not be rushed.

11. *Lower your expectations.* When you feel pressured and unable to cope, lower some of the expectations you have of yourself, skip something, take a break, and regroup. Learn to schedule solitary time to muse, putter, read, or enjoy a hobby.

Tips on Dealing with Others

1. *Be realistic.* Remind yourself that you are a *helper* to others, not a cure-all for their problems. You do not need to rescue the groups you facilitate or the people you spend time with. You can be there to listen and to help, but they are responsible for their own work.

2. *Think of others.* Focus fully on others and their lives, as well as your own. Being overly concerned with your own issues can isolate you from others.

3. *Learn to ask for help and support.* Your co-workers, boss, family, and friends can all be there for you, just as you are there for them. You do not have to take charge all of the time.

4. *Take pride in others' accomplishments.* Be pleased for others as well as for yourself. Giving others credit allows you to take a broader perspective on life—plus it opens your eyes to all sorts of interesting information.

5. *Do not take yourself too seriously.* Think of the millions of human beings on the earth and all that goes on to keep the earth humming. Imagine all the mistakes and accidents that happen every day. Imagine how much each person's life is sacred to him or her, and yet how little ultimate control anyone has. Do not try too hard to be thought of in a certain way. Bring yourself to each moment with anticipation and awareness, but realize yours is only one of many egos!

6. *Do not promise what you cannot (or will not) deliver.* Over-promising and not delivering causes stress for yourself and lowers others' trust in you.

7. *Improve your skills.* Continually improve your communication skills to increase real understanding of others and to provide an opportunity for you to express yourself.

8. *Look for compatibility.* Find places to work and people to associate with that allow you to be comfortable being who you are. Trying to be someone you are not is stressful and depletes your energy, enthusiasm, and output.

9. *See others for who they are.* Even if others are complex, remember that people cannot be reduced to simple formulas or types. People are complicated, multi-dimensional, and ever-changing.

10. *Do not see others as a means to an end.* Avoid viewing others as a means to what you want. This constant "networking" style of relating to others puts you and them in a favor-giving mode and hinders the development of genuine friendship or mutual trust. Lack of trust and friendship makes stress and burnout more likely. This does not mean that people should not do things for one another,

but that the first and foremost reason for relating to others is genuine interest, not finding ways to use one another. People usually know when you are genuinely interested in them and when you are trying to garner a favor. Networking should be a natural outgrowth of previously established, healthy friendships and good working relationships. First, show interest and respect for others. Later they may be there to help you.

To do good work, you must first take care of yourself. Learn to recognize the symptoms of stress before you reach burnout. Stress is a reality in any profession and facilitators will face their share. Learn to deal with stress on an ongoing basis and practice being kind and considerate to yourself.

In summary, a facilitator spends a lot of energy helping others in significant ways. At the same time, he or she must take care of himself or herself in a variety of ways. This includes not letting ego get in the way of facilitating, learning to remain centered and authentic, striving to improve performance as a facilitator, avoiding burnout, pacing oneself, and learning to decrease stress.

The Art of Facilitating

Facilitators can learn skills and tools fairly quickly. It is the art of knowing when and how to apply those skills and tools—and when to do something else—that comes more slowly. The art of facilitation arises from the facilitator's powers of observation and keen sense of the group. It is a product of intuition, experience with groups, attention, and something deeply human within. To become an excellent facilitator, you must possess a genuine, grounded reverence for individuals within a group context and a respect for how much has to happen in a group before trust is built or progress made.

Just as any interaction or human relationship is complex and ever-changing, so is the relationship between you and the group. It is this dynamic relationship that you will seek to harness for the sake of synergy. The art of facilitation is born from your dedication to the fact that when you and the group work at your best toward a purpose, amazing things can happen.

Group work is ticklish business, to be approached both with caution and confidence. The study and understanding of group behavior is a lifelong learning process fraught with enigmas and surprises not unlike what is encountered when trying to understand human nature.

Excellence Versus Perfection

No facilitator will ever be perfect because no facilitation is truly perfect. A facilitation does not need to be perfect to be excellent. The same is true for your work as a facilitator. The art of facilitation lies in knowing that one must strive for excellence without ever achieving perfection. Group work is messy. There is always something left undone, unsaid, or set aside. But if the group achieves its main purpose, all those involved have achieved a certain degree of excellence.

If and when excellence happens, it is certainly not a solo act, but a fine collaboration of group members, group leader, and the facilitator. In reality, other factors, too, contribute toward excellence: the environment, the tone or mood of the organization, and the task or topic at hand.

To be an excellent facilitator, you must pursue it as an art, with dedication both to the results and the human element. Neither should be sacrificed for the sake of the other, for there is little true satisfaction in results without the mutual respect of group members for one another, and there is little benefit to an organization's promoting a close-knit but nonproductive group.

In the performing arts, a distinction is made between those who are technically proficient and those who are true artists. When I studied piano as a young girl, my teacher made sure I spent a good deal of time on scales and arpegios and practiced sonatinas to develop the facility to get from note to note on the piano. But technique was only the foundation. Next came the ability *to really play the music.* She coached me to refine the phrasing, to add expressiveness and feeling, and to use tempo and dynamics to add beauty and vitality to the music. Good musicians play from the mind, the body, and the soul. They use the notes as a vehicle for creating a work of art.

You can become proficient at the technique of facilitating by using the basic skills and tools, but playing the music comes with a more intimate and dedicated understanding of group process. This dedication comes from continual observation, questioning, feedback, and experimentation.

An excellent facilitator senses the right time to remain silent, the best time to intervene, how to switch processes or bridge to deeper levels of openness and understanding in a group. The artistic facilitator listens to hear more than the words and asks questions to seek more than answers. Everything that happens in a group is relevant to the process; each group has its own personality, its own style, and even its own soul. Although you may consciously not influence the content or outcome of a facilitation, your very presence, style, and quality of work influence the performance of the group.

Despite your catalytic role in a group's performance and development, the credit goes not to you, but to the entire group. Be comfortable as a part of a process larger than yourself, and, although you play an important role, know where the power lies—not in an individual but in the truth that groups, when given proper guidelines and processes, produce more than what all their members could produce separately. A design is only a framework, and a natural flow to the activities arises when group members become fully and enthusiastically engaged in the work at hand. Improvise the design if necessary, the way a group of jamming musicians takes liberties with the melodies and rhythms, never losing the overall recognizable quality or shape of the piece of music.

The Natural Flow

The art of facilitation is not artificial, but natural. It occurs when the act of guiding the group is not forced but flows from the needs of the group. The outcome of natural facilitation is that members are caught up in the group's progress and its forward movement; the process is both logical and iterative, but not strained. Ideally, you will accompany, rather than direct, the group, and become an on-the-spot resource for the group's evolving needs. Know when to *ask* the group and when to *tell* it what to do. Know or sense what difficulties lie at the heart of the group, pick up on the hopes, fears, and expectations of group members in relation to their assignment, and use this knowledge to assist the group in meeting its goals. Learn the difference between an *efficient* and an *effective* group. An efficient group accomplishes a lot; an effective group does the most important work in a way that solidifies the group and moves it forward in its development as a team.

The art of facilitating is not something you set out to do, as in "Today I am going to pursue facilitation as an art." This approach would probably not work. The art of facilitating comes naturally out of the needs of the group and your awareness of and attention to those needs. You may or may not be aware at the moment that it is "art" that you are making. It simply seems best and most natural at the time. You may apply traditional skills and tools, but do so with timing or an approach that makes it "art." A strong foundation in skills and tools, coupled with experience, is essential. Just as a musician needs training to read and play the notes, you need training in the basic skills and tools. After that, it is sensing, observing, applying, and adapting—taking risks and "playing the music."

Love the Questions

The art of asking questions is perhaps the most important ability a facilitator possesses. Questions are at the heart of good facilitation. A question inspires a response. A well-placed question provokes problem solving, creativity, and action. When you use questions, the group will seek its own advice and not waste time rejecting your advice. When it seems there are no answers, when groups are struggling or lost, you will need the effectiveness of questions to bring the group back. It is frequently the well-placed question that unblocks the group and gives it impetus to move ahead.

When you seek the questions, not the answers, you empower the group to find its own answers. Often when you do not know the answer, someone in the group does. When answers come from the group, there is more ownership and buy-in. Questions keep you from falling into the trap of giving advice. Facilitation is not about giving advice, but about suggesting, pointing out what is going on, and asking questions to open up the eyes of the group.

Know finally and faithfully that you do not have all the answers. Not knowing is wiser than striving always to know. Let your wisdom come from your questions.

What Makes a Great Facilitator?

hat makes a great facilitator? Is it skills, techniques, accomplishments, smoothly flowing meetings, challenging organization projects, high levels of responsibility, or a reputation among certain circles as being "great"? Is it the accumulation of positive changes that occur as a result of our facilitation? Undoubtedly, all of these contribute to what makes us good facilitators, but is there something more?

Thinking about this question, I have reached the following conclusion: there is a deep and more prevailing force that makes one a great facilitator. I call this force *a core purpose,* a central belief, that motivates and drives what we do as facilitators. We must, of course, have knowledge, skills, and techniques to facilitate. But equally important is to have a keen sense of *why* we facilitate, an underlying belief—or set of beliefs—that provide foundational reasons for facilitating. Greatness is fueled by both *how* we facilitate and *why.* When we are clear about *why* we facilitate, we actively seek the techniques and skills we need rather than simply learning them by rote. We continually search for ways to bring into being what we value.

When we tap into something we value deeply, we are more apt to *add value* to the work we do.

Finding Your Core Purpose

I suspect that because you are reading this book, you have some core values and beliefs that lead you to seek out facilitation as a way of integrating those values into your work. To determine your core purpose as a facilitator, examine what you value at the deepest level in relation to this role. What led you to learn more about facilitation? What motivates you to work at becoming a good facilitator? What is it that you believe about people and organizations that propels you to become a catalyst for collaboration and synergy?

Once you have uncovered these values, ask yourself, What is my core purpose for being a facilitator? If, for example, you discover that you value people working together as a team because you have seen how working in isolation causes problems, your core purpose may have something to do with promoting teamwork and a sense of belonging in organizations. If you find that you value group creativity and synergy and what that brings to the workplace, your core purpose might be to promote creativity and synergy through facilitation.

I define my core purpose as follows: to attend diligently to building and fostering workplaces where the human spirit flourishes. I value the results that are achieved when people are engaged and involved in their work. I value environments where people are encouraged to bring their best selves to their work and the best of humanity to the workplace. I also value and believe in the inherent ability of people to work hard to solve the problems they face at work. I value allowing people to have a say in their work and in the decisions that affect their daily lives. These are some of the values that contribute to what I define as my core purpose for facilitating.

Once you are clear about your values and core purpose in relation to being a facilitator, you can explore the best avenues for carrying out that purpose. There are many arenas in which you can apply facilitation: as a team leader, a team facilitator, a team member, a human resource specialist, a manager, a counselor, a leader, a teacher, a trainer, and many more. Early on in my exposure to facilitation, I felt led to influence organization leaders by teaching and demonstrating the value of facilitation skills to motivate, involve, and tap into the power of people's knowledge and experience. In addition to becoming a practicing facilitator, I chose to carry out my core purpose through the avenue of writing and workshops.

Facilitation is broad and important enough to encompass many different values, beliefs, and purposes. It is important that you develop your own core purpose, and even revise it if needed, rather than adopt someone else's core purpose.

I hope I haven't left the impression that I think I am a "great" facilitator. I am still a learner and a practitioner. However, I do think I have a laudable, and even "great" core purpose. The title for this book was chosen because I think we can, and should, all *aspire* to excellence as facilitators. Whether we reach it or not isn't for us to decide. The aspiration becomes the inspiration and the motivation. It is important not to become overly concerned about whether you are a great facilitator. Focusing too much on being "great" will probably place a large roadblock in your path!

Summary

Throughout this book we have looked at both the *science* and the *art* of facilitating. The methodologies and skills are a kind of "science," things most people can learn: guiding participation, using the flip charts, and applying specific tools. The "art" of applying those skills requires a sense of when, how much, and how often to use them. It calls for sensitivity to people, groups, and the environment that practicing facilitators develop over time.

We have discussed how facilitation is a form of *leadership*. The facilitator becomes, for a time, the leader from the side: nudging, probing, suggesting, waiting, listening, asking questions, providing structure, giving feedback. The skilled facilitator becomes a wise leader who helps build an environment in which people with a variety of abilities, knowledge, and experience collaborate creatively to meet present challenges. This kind of leadership is not often taught in courses on management and leadership. Although some leaders have these skills intuitively, others must work to develop and hone them and seek mentors and role models to encourage them in the process.

We have thought about what it means to be a *great* facilitator and how important it is for facilitators to possess a deep, underlying sense of purpose about their work. Having a *core purpose* gives facilitators momentum to continually seek new arenas for contribution and develop new methods for achieving their purpose.

We have touched on the idea that facilitators play a key role in fostering workplaces that are *humanizing*, rather than dehumanizing. Facilitators help organizations become "people-sustaining" places to work, workplaces where people are not pushed into burnout but are allowed to thrive as individuals, not just organization units. Facilitators help build more humane workplaces by marshalling people to bring their best selves to the work.

We have examined the *role* of the facilitator. The facilitator is a catalyst with an exciting role: to help people and organizations accomplish goals and create positive work environments. Facilitators provide energy, spark, confidence, and structure to a group. Without a facilitator, a group often loses its sense of direction and process. Facilitators are both leaders and servants: they lead the groups they serve from the side by supplying processes and structure so that goals are accomplished; they lead the organizations they serve by modeling a method of leadership that gives people an opportunity to thrive in the workplace.

This book was written to help people learn and apply facilitation skills to their job. In actuality, there are only a few people who have the title of "facilitator" at work. Instead, there are numerous situations that call for someone to take on the role of facilitator, whether to lead a team, conduct a meeting, resolve cross-functional conflict, manage a project, or other such function. There are those who may be given the title of "facilitator" for a short time, and there are people who spend important time at work facilitating, despite what their actual title is.

In reality, there are many roles that require facilitation skills for the job to be done: team leader, manager, trainer, customer service representative, educator, counselor, salesperson, meeting leader, and so on. Those who develop facilitation skills and become experienced at facilitating will find many situations where these skills are valuable: at home, in the community, with friends and family, at work, and in virtually all professional and leadership positions.

Argyris, C. (1970). *Intervention theory and method: A behavioral science view.* Reading, MA: Addison-Wesley.

Bianchi, S., Butler, J., & Richey, D. (1990). *Warmups for meeting leaders.* San Francisco: Pfeiffer.

Block, P. (1999). *Flawless consulting* (2nd ed). San Francisco: Pfeiffer.

Brandt, R. C. (1986). *Flip charts: How to draw them and how to use them.* Richmond, VA: Brandt Management Group.

Burn, B. E. (1996). *Flip chart power: Secrets of the masters.* San Francisco: Pfeiffer.

Daniels, W. R. (1986). *Group power: A manager's guide to using meetings.* San Francisco: Pfeiffer.

Fisher, K., Rayner, S., Belgard, W., & the Belgard, Fisher, Rayner Team. (1995). *Tips for teams.* New York: McGraw-Hill.

Forbess-Greene, S. (1983). *The encyclopedia of icebreakers: Structured activities that warm-up, motivate, challenge, acquaint, and energize.* San Francisco: Pfeiffer.

Gibson, C., & Cohen, S. (2003). *Virtual teams that work: Creating conditions for virtual team effectiveness.* San Francisco: Jossey-Bass.

Glassman, E. (1991). *The creativity factor: Unlocking the potential of your team.* San Francisco: Pfeiffer.

Harrington-Mackin, D. (1996). *Keeping the team going.* New York: American Management Association.

Heider, J. (1985). *The Tao of leadership: Leadership strategies for a new age.* 1482 Mecaslin St., NW, Atlanta, GA 30357-0400: Humanics New Age.

Howell, J. L. (1995). *Tools for facilitating team meetings.* Seattle: Integrity Publishing.

Hunter, D., Bailey, A., & Taylor, B. (1995a). *The art of facilitation: How to create group synergy.* Tucson, AZ: Fisher Books.

Hunter, D., Bailey, A., & Taylor, B. (1995b). *The Zen of groups: The handbook for people meeting with a purpose.* Tucson, AZ: Fisher Books.

Kaner, S. (1996). *Facilitator's guide to participatory decision-making.* Gabriola Island, British Columbia, Canada: New Society Publishers.

Kearny, L. (1995). *The facilitator's toolkit: Tools and techniques for generating ideas and making decisions in groups.* Amherst, MA: HRD Press.

Leonard, D., & Swap, W. (1999). *When sparks fly: Igniting creativity in groups.* Boston: Harvard Business School Press.

Levine, S. (1998). *Getting to resolution: Turning conflict into collaboration.* San Francisco: Berrett-Koehler.

Lippitt, G., & Lippitt, R. (1986). *The consulting process in action* (2nd ed.). San Francisco: Pfeiffer.

McLaughlin, M., & Peyser, S. (2004). *The new encyclopedia of icebreakers.* San Francisco: Pfeiffer.

Parker, G. (2003). *Cross-functional teams: Working with allies, enemies, and other strangers.* San Francisco: Jossey-Bass.

Pfeiffer, J. W. (Ed.). (1986). *The encyclopedia of group activities: 150 practical designs for successful facilitating.* San Francisco: Pfeiffer.

Phillips, S. L., & Elledge, R. L. (1989). *The team-building source book.* San Francisco: Pfeiffer.

Quinlivan-Hall, D., & Renner, P. (1990). *In search of solutions.* Vancouver, British Columbia, Canada: PFR Training Associates.

Rees, F. (1993). *25 activities for teams.* San Francisco: Pfeiffer.

Rees, F. (1997). *Teamwork from start to finish: 10 steps to results!* San Francisco: Pfeiffer.

Rees, F. (1998). Consulting skills inventory. In *The 1998 Annual: Volume 1, Training.* San Francisco: Pfeiffer.

Rees, F. (2001). *How to lead work teams: Facilitation skills* (2nd ed.). San Francisco: Pfeiffer.

Saint, S., & Lawson, J. R. (1994). *Rules for reaching consensus.* San Francisco: Pfeiffer.

Schindler-Rainman, E., & Lippitt, R. (1988). *Taking your meetings out of the doldrums.* (Rev. ed.). San Francisco: Pfeiffer.

Scholtes, P. R. (1988). *The team handbook.* Madison, WI: Joiner.

Schwarz, R. M. (1994). *The skilled facilitator: Practical wisdom for developing effective groups.* San Francisco: Jossey-Bass.

Tagliere, D. A. (1993). *How to meet, think, and work to consensus.* San Francisco: Pfeiffer.

Tague, N. R. (1995). *The quality toolbox.* Milwaukee, WI: ASQC Quality Press.

Thomas, K. (1976). "Conflict and Conflict Management." In *The Handbook of Industrial and Organization Psychology,* ed. M. Dunnette. Chicago: Rand McNally.

Energy group dynamic level, 108

Enthusiasm, 71–72

Environment: defining, 187; facilitating difficult situations in, 187–188; facilitating and managing meeting, 295–303; group dynamics affected by, 104. *See also* Workplace

Evaluation: competency in, 281; of team performance, 328–335

Experience: competency in, 269–270; designing facilitation using past, 234

Eye contact, 64–66

F

Facial expressions, 67

Facilitate, 2

Facilitation: applied to situations, roles, and outcomes, 17, 18*t*; benefits of, 13–15; defining, 2; designing a, 213–234; goals of effective, 15–17; leadership and role of, 17, 19; levels of, 4–5; organizational vision for using, 20–21; as science and art, 3–6, 375–379, 383–385

Facilitator Competency Matrix: on building client relationships, 281–283; on business knowledge, 266; on change management, 280; on coaching, 276; on collaboration skills, 274–275; on conceptual and diagnostic skills, 279–280; on credibility, 264; defining levels of facilitator competency, 263; on designing meetings, 275–276; development of, 261–262; facilitator development using, 262; on feedback and evaluation, 381; on group skills and experience, 269–270; on human relations, 265; on judgment, 264; on learning orientation, 266; on listening, 270; on managing conflict, 278–279; on meeting management, 273–274; organization facilitator training using, 262; on participation management and methods, 271–273; on presentation skills, 268; on risk taking, 265; on role understanding and application, 268–269; on self-management, 266–267; on understanding group dynamics, 276–278; on workload management, 267

Facilitator intervention, 352–353

Facilitator roles: as continuously evolving, 25–26; description of, 6, 17, 18*t*, 29–30, 384–385; humanizing the workplace, 27–29, 28*e*; manager of group process, 23–24; responsibilities of, 16–17, 24–25

Facilitators: appropriate dress for, 72–74; characteristics of great, 381–383; defining, 2; identifying group dynamic levels, 106–110; leaders as, 17, 19; levels of competency of, 261–283; modeling positive conflict resolution behaviors, 200; role/responsibilities during meetings, 287–289; self-management of, 266–267, 352, 361–374; skills required of, 251–252

Facility checklist, 301–303

Feedback: competency in giving, 281; conflict resolution, 206; designing facilitation using, 234; soliciting meeting, 307–312, 309*fig*; virtual team, 344–345; working with clients and cycling, 356–357. *See also* Communication

Fishbone diagram: advantages of using, 133–134; beginning, 135*fig*; how to use, 135–136; illustration of, 134*fig*; overview of, 133; sample categories for, 136*fig*; variations of, 136–137

Flawless Consulting (Block), 354

Flip Chart Power: Secrets of the Masters (Burn), 85

Flip charts: additional uses for, 85–87; art of charting, 90–91; cautions against rewording comments for, 79; dealing with problems, 94*fig*; easels used with, 88, 92; equipment and supplies for using, 91–93, 95; knowing how to write ideas on, 77; organization and handling of, 84, 87–89; "ownership" of, 83–84; using recorder vs. self for recording on, 81–82*fig*; summarizing tips on using, 95; value of using, 80–81. *See also* Recording discussions

Flow charts: advantages of/when to use, 139–140; defining, 139; how to use, 144, 146; types of, 140–141*fig*, 142*fig*–143*fig*, 145*fig*; variations of, 147

Focus on message, 56

Focusing on speaker, 57–62

Force-field analysis: advantages of/when to use, 163–164; defining, 163; how to use, 164–165, 168; sample diagram of, 166*fig*–167*fig*

G

Getting to Resolution: Turning Conflict into Collaboration (Levine), 209

Gibson, C., 209, 338

Goals: brainstorming conflict resolution, 206–207; of effective facilitation, 15–17; establishing developmental, 17; facilitating meetings using, 185, 290–291; using flip charts to stay focused on, 86; generating consensus flow and stating, 113; identifying win-win

F ran Rees is an experienced manager, consultant, and trainer in both the public and private sectors, and the owner and principal consultant of Rees & Associates, a Phoenix-based training and consulting firm, which marked its eighteenth year in business in 2004.

Fran has designed and led workshops in management development, teamwork, facilitation, presentation, workforce diversity, and internal consulting. She has consulted to a variety of industries and organizations, including computer manufacturing, health care, city and state governments, biomedical technology, utilities, and food production. Much of her work has focused on team development, team leadership, and team facilitation.

Fran's L.E.A.D. model of leadership, her books, and workshops are used in a variety of organizations to develop facilitative leaders, guide self-managed teams, and train meeting leaders to design and facilitate productive meetings.

She is the author of five books: a publisher's bestseller *How to Lead Work Teams: Facilitation Skills* (Second Edition, Pfeiffer, 2001), *Teamwork from Start to Finish* (Pfeiffer, 1997), *The Facilitator Excellence Handbook* (Pfeiffer, 1998), *The Facilitator Excellence Instructor Guide* (Pfeiffer, 1998), and *25*

Activities for Developing Team Leaders (Pfeiffer, 2004). She authored the chapter introductions for the book *25 Activities for Teams* (Pfeiffer, 1993), a book based on her L.E.A.D. model of leadership. *How to Lead Work Teams* has been published in Spanish and Polish, and the first edition of *The Facilitator Excellence Handbook* has been published in Japanese.

HOW TO USE THE CD-ROM

System Requirements

PC with Microsoft Windows 98SE or later

Mac with Apple OS version 8.6 or later

Using the CD With Windows

To view the items located on the CD, follow these steps:

1. Insert the CD into your computer's CD-ROM drive.

2. A window appears with the following options:

   Contents: Allows you to view the files included on the CD-ROM.

   Software: Allows you to install useful software from the CD-ROM.

   Links: Displays a hyperlinked page of websites.

   Author: Displays a page with information about the author(s).

   Contact Us: Displays a page with information on contacting the publisher or author.

   Help: Displays a page with information on using the CD.

   Exit: Closes the interface window.

If you do not have autorun enabled, or if the autorun window does not appear, follow these steps to access the CD:

1. Click Start -> Run.

2. In the dialog box that appears, type d:‹<\\><\\>›start.exe, where d is the letter of your CD-ROM drive. This brings up the autorun window described in the preceding set of steps.

3. Choose the desired option from the menu. (See Step 2 in the preceding list for a description of these options.)

In Case of Trouble

If you experience difficulty using the CD-ROM, please follow these steps:

1. Make sure your hardware and systems configurations conform to the systems requirements noted under "System Requirements" above.

2. Review the installation procedure for your type of hardware and operating system. It is possible to reinstall the software if necessary.

To speak with someone in Product Technical Support, call 800-762-2974 or 317-572-3994 Monday through Friday from 8:30 a.m. to 5:00 p.m. EST. You can also contact Product Technical Support and get support information through our website at www.wiley.com/techsupport.

Before calling or writing, please have the following information available:

• Type of computer and operating system.

• Any error messages displayed.

• Complete description of the problem.

It is best if you are sitting at your computer when making the call.

Pfeiffer Publications Guide

This guide is designed to familiarize you with the various types of Pfeiffer publications. The formats section describes the various types of products that we publish; the methodologies section describes the many different ways that content might be provided within a product. We also provide a list of the topic areas in which we publish.

FORMATS

In addition to its extensive book-publishing program, Pfeiffer offers content in an array of formats, from fieldbooks for the practitioner to complete, ready-to-use training packages that support group learning.

FIELDBOOK Designed to provide information and guidance to practitioners in the midst of action. Most fieldbooks are companions to another, sometimes earlier, work, from which its ideas are derived; the fieldbook makes practical what was theoretical in the original text. Fieldbooks can certainly be read from cover to cover. More likely, though, you'll find yourself bouncing around following a particular theme, or dipping in as the mood, and the situation, dictate.

HANDBOOK A contributed volume of work on a single topic, comprising an eclectic mix of ideas, case studies, and best practices sourced by practitioners and experts in the field.

An editor or team of editors usually is appointed to seek out contributors and to evaluate content for relevance to the topic. Think of a handbook not as a ready-to-eat meal, but as a cookbook of ingredients that enables you to create the most fitting experience for the occasion.

RESOURCE Materials designed to support group learning. They come in many forms: a complete, ready-to-use exercise (such as a game); a comprehensive resource on one topic (such as conflict management) containing a variety of methods and approaches; or a collection of like-minded activities (such as icebreakers) on multiple subjects and situations.

TRAINING PACKAGE An entire, ready-to-use learning program that focuses on a particular topic or skill. All packages comprise a guide for the facilitator/trainer and a workbook for the participants. Some packages are supported with additional media—such as video—or learning aids, instruments, or other devices to help participants understand concepts or practice and develop skills.

- *Facilitator/trainer's guide* Contains an introduction to the program, advice on how to organize and facilitate the learning event, and step-by-step instructor notes. The guide also contains copies of presentation materials—handouts, presentations, and overhead designs, for example—used in the program.

- *Participant's workbook* Contains exercises and reading materials that support the learning goal and serves as a valuable reference and support guide for participants in the weeks and months that follow the learning event. Typically, each participant will require his or her own workbook.

ELECTRONIC CD-ROMs and web-based products transform static Pfeiffer content into dynamic, interactive experiences. Designed to take advantage of the searchability, automation, and ease-of-use that technology provides, our e-products bring convenience and immediate accessibility to your workspace.

METHODOLOGIES

CASE STUDY A presentation, in narrative form, of an actual event that has occurred inside an organization. Case studies are not prescriptive, nor are they used to prove a point; they are designed to develop critical analysis and decision-making skills. A case study has a specific time frame, specifies a sequence of events, is narrative in structure, and contains a plot structure—an issue (what should be/have been done?). Use case studies when the goal is to enable participants to apply previously learned theories to the circumstances in the case, decide what is pertinent, identify the real issues, decide what should have been done, and develop a plan of action.

ENERGIZER A short activity that develops readiness for the next session or learning event. Energizers are most commonly used after a break or lunch to stimulate or refocus the group. Many involve some form of physical activity, so they are a useful way to counter post-lunch lethargy. Other uses include transitioning from one topic to another, where "mental" distancing is important.

EXPERIENTIAL LEARNING ACTIVITY (ELA) A facilitator-led intervention that moves participants through the learning cycle from experience to application (also known as a Structured Experience). ELAs are carefully thought-out designs in which there is a definite learning purpose and intended outcome. Each step—everything that participants do during the activity—facilitates the accomplishment of the stated goal. Each ELA includes complete instructions for facilitating the intervention and a clear statement of goals, suggested group size and timing, materials required, an explanation of the process, and, where appropriate, possible variations to the activity. (For more detail on Experiential Learning Activities, see the Introduction to the *Reference Guide to Handbooks and Annuals*, 1999 edition, Pfeiffer, San Francisco.)

GAME A group activity that has the purpose of fostering team spirit and togetherness in addition to the achievement of a pre-stated goal. Usually contrived—undertaking a desert expedition, for example—this type of learning method offers an engaging means for participants to demonstrate and practice business and interpersonal skills. Games are effective for team building and personal development mainly because the goal is subordinate to the process—the means through which participants reach decisions, collaborate, communicate, and generate trust and understanding. Games often engage teams in "friendly" competition.

ICEBREAKER A (usually) short activity designed to help participants overcome initial anxiety in a training session and/or to acquaint the participants with one another. An icebreaker can be a fun activity or can be tied to specific topics or training goals. While a useful tool in itself, the icebreaker comes into its own in situations where tension or resistance exists within a group.

INSTRUMENT A device used to assess, appraise, evaluate, describe, classify, and summarize various aspects of human behavior. The term used to describe an instrument depends primarily on its format and purpose. These terms include survey, questionnaire, inventory, diagnostic, survey, and poll. Some uses of instruments include providing instrumental feedback to group members, studying here-and-now processes or functioning within a group, manipulating group composition, and evaluating outcomes of training and other interventions.

Instruments are popular in the training and HR field because, in general, more growth can occur if an individual is provided with a method for focusing specifically on his or her own behavior. Instruments also are used to obtain information that will serve as a basis for change and to assist in workforce planning efforts.

Paper-and-pencil tests still dominate the instrument landscape with a typical package comprising a facilitator's guide, which offers advice on administering the instrument and interpreting the collected data, and an initial set of instruments. Additional instruments are available separately. Pfeiffer, though, is investing heavily in e-instruments. Electronic instrumentation provides effortless distribution and, for larger groups particularly, offers advantages over paper-and-pencil tests in the time it takes to analyze data and provide feedback.

LECTURETTE A short talk that provides an explanation of a principle, model, or process that is pertinent to the participants' current learning needs. A lecturette is intended to establish a common language bond between the trainer and the participants by providing a mutual frame of reference. Use a lecturette as an introduction to a group activity or event, as an interjection during an event, or as a handout.

MODEL A graphic depiction of a system or process and the relationship among its elements. Models provide a frame of reference and something more tangible, and more easily remembered, than a verbal explanation. They also give participants something to "go on," enabling them to track their own progress as they experience the dynamics, processes, and relationships being depicted in the model.

ROLE PLAY A technique in which people assume a role in a situation/scenario: a customer service rep in an angry-customer exchange, for example. The way in which the role is approached is then discussed and feedback is offered. The role play is often repeated using a different approach and/or incorporating changes made based on feedback received. In other words, role playing is a spontaneous interaction involving realistic behavior under artificial (and safe) conditions.

SIMULATION A methodology for understanding the interrelationships among components of a system or process. Simulations differ from games in that they test or use a model that depicts or mirrors some aspect of reality in form, if not necessarily in content. Learning occurs by studying the effects of change on one or more factors of the model. Simulations are commonly used to test hypotheses about what happens in a system—often referred to as "what if?" analysis—or to examine best-case/worst-case scenarios.

THEORY A presentation of an idea from a conjectural perspective. Theories are useful because they encourage us to examine behavior and phenomena through a different lens.

TOPICS

The twin goals of providing effective and practical solutions for workforce training and organization development and meeting the educational needs of training and human resource professionals shape Pfeiffer's publishing program. Core topics include the following:

Leadership & Management

Communication & Presentation

Coaching & Mentoring

Training & Development

E-Learning

Teams & Collaboration

OD & Strategic Planning

Human Resources

Consulting